F
by

THE HILLS OF NORTHERN ENGLAND
AND THE ISLE OF MAN

Advice to Readers

This guidebook has been carefully researched and prepared. However, whilst it is, to the best of the author's knowledge, accurate at the time of writing, paths, rights of way and access agreements are liable to change. Readers are advised to check locally before walking if in doubt. Neither the author nor publishers accept any liability for any disputes, accidents or damages arising from following any of the routes described in this book.

Come heart, where hill is heaped upon hill:
For there the mystical brotherhood
Of sun and moon and hollow and wood
And river and stream work out their will.

From W.B. Yeats, 'Into the Twilight'

Contents

Acknowledgements

Whilst writing this book, I have received help and support from many people to whom I am indebted. I must thank Colin Dibb and Amelia Withers for their company whilst walking and checking the routes in all weathers, as well as investigating alternatives through rough and tough terrain. I must also thank Colin Dibb for generously giving many hours of his time to read through the typescript, leading to many helpful and useful suggestions that have all been very much appreciated.

Without doubt, writing this book would have been much more difficult if a published list of the relevant hills had not been available. Therefore, I would like to thank Alan Dawson, who wrote the original list, and all the others who have made suggestions that have prompted amendments to it. My thanks are also due Dr C.M. Huntley, Clerk of the List of Munroists for the Scottish Mountaineering Club, for providing me with up-to-date statistics on the number of Munroists.

I would like once again to thank Mary Philip for her advice regarding lead smelting whilst writing *England's Highest Peaks*. That material has now been incorporated into this book as well, as part of Section 2. I must also thank all those at Cumbria County Council who have given me valuable up-to-the-minute advice regarding the reopening of footpaths during the foot-and-mouth crisis. On the same note, I must express my thanks to Terry Hooper for generously allowing me to cross his land by means of an officially closed footpath towards the end of the foot-and-mouth outbreak. Last, but by no means least, I would like to thank Sarah Archer, Emma Baker, Jane Byrne, Mrs Firth, Chris Green, Hannah Khan, Alan Kydd, Anne-Marie Martin, Cathy May, Judith Price, Steve Rayner, Lesley Ridgway, Simon Thompson, Jeff Trim, Julie Usher, Grisella Vignalli, Debbie Rocky, Hazel Mackintosh, Catherine Stevenson, Amelia Withers, Susan Antal and anyone else who I have unintentionally overlooked for their useful pieces of advice and encouragement.

It only then leaves me to wish all of my readers the same enjoyment that

I had in the pleasure of experiencing some of Britain's most beautiful and 'forgotten' hills.

Alasdair Dibb
Tilehurst, Spring 2002

Introduction

Scafell Pike is England's highest mountain. Rising to 3,210ft (978m), its rocky summit plateau, girdled by crags, sees countless visitors every year, drawn by the lure of its altitude and the pleasure to be gained in reaching its summit. Meanwhile, Mellbreak is one of the Lake District's most distinctive summits. It stands at a mere 1,680ft (512m) but dominates the scene around Crummock Water and Loweswater. Encircled by fearsome precipices and long scree fans, tumbling to the lakeshore, its summit sees far fewer visitors each year.

The Lake District is one of Britain's finest landscapes. Nowhere else is there that special combination of rock, woodland and lake. In autumn, the russet-coloured trees stand beside the deep-blue curving lakes, below the black crags of the hills, whilst wisps of cloud curl around the hillsides and lie in the lee of the treetops. This is not, however, the landscape of the high mountains. These are the lower hills. How many fine mountaineers started their climbing on the lowly heights of Hallin Fell? How many experienced walkers have got lost among the countless hidden valleys on Loughrigg Fell? How many people have gazed in awe at the dripping crags and the wild tumble of scree above Wastwater on the slopes of Illgill Head?

Why toil in all weathers to cross that seemingly magic 2,000ft (610m) contour when there are such great hills at a lower height? There is no answer other than blind determination, ignorance or, perhaps, that condition for which mountaineers are best known – madness! For whatever reason, it is these lower hills that have retained their appeal – the absence, in general, of wide paths, hordes of walkers and, sadly, the blight of badly restored paths on which it is difficult to walk.

I hope that this book will begin to spread the load – to help walkers appreciate, in greater numbers, the enjoyment to be gained from climbing the lower summits and foothills. The hills of Northumberland, the dramatic landscape of the Isle of Man and the hills of the Pennines share one thing in common – their incredible beauty. And the lower hills are not the easy option either. Many are quite wild and a few are very remote.

Sighty Crag is almost sufficiently rough and remote enough to put it on a par with some of the prized Scottish peaks.

So, what makes a hill, or even a mountain? It may sound like a simple question but it is one that has perplexed many climbers for at least a hundred years. In 1891, Sir Hugh Munro published the first 'list' of hills, including all summits in Scotland above 3,000ft (914m), which he considered to be separate, and, today, the majority of British hills and mountains have been included in some list or another. The publication of Alan Dawson's list of his so-called 'Marilyns' in 1992 meant that all the summits which rise more than 492ft (150m) from their surrounding landscape have been listed, although all the individual lists are remarkably different.

The way in which the lists differ is in their definition of what makes any given summit separate from another. Sir Hugh Munro made a personal decision, but since then the majority of authors have come up with at least one criterion to define the summits on their list. John Rooke Corbett was the first to do this when compiling his list of the Scottish mountains between 2,500ft (762m) and 3,000ft (914m) in altitude. He said that each summit on his list must have a drop of at least 500ft (152m) on all sides to detach it from a neighbouring peak. Later lists also adopted this criterion, including Fiona Graham's list of the Scottish summits between 2,000ft (610m) and 2,500ft (762m) in height and Alan Dawson's list of the 'relative hills' of Britain.

When studying the hills below 2,000ft (610m) in altitude, it is Dawson's concept of relative height that is most appropriate to define a hill. This is because it is the height of the hill *relative to its surrounding landscape* that is important. Hills of quite lowly altitudes can be very high *relative* to their surroundings. We could compare Mont Blanc, the highest summit of the Alps at a height of 15,771ft (4,807m) above sea level, with Mount Everest at 29,028ft (8,848m), but this would make little sense because, as anyone who has visited the town of Chamonix knows, Mont Blanc is massive. It towers high above the town and to describe it as a low and incidental summit is ridiculous. But, compared to Everest, Mont Blanc is low and incidental.

The fault is in the comparison between two summits, whose altitude differs by a factor of two. The fundamental flaw here is the concept of absolute height; we should, instead, talk in terms of relative height. If the concept of relative height is taken to define a hill, there is one remaining question – what quantity of relative height is most appropriate? The figure of 500ft (152m) is most traditionally used and with good cause too. When studying two neighbouring summits from a nearby peak, a drop of 500ft (152m) is, in my opinion, about the correct height to define them as truly separate. It is generally agreed that a mountain is a summit above 2,000ft (610m). Thus, a hill is defined as a summit between 492ft (150m) – to follow the metric measures now used on maps – and 2,000ft (610m) in altitude, provided it is separated from any higher summit by a descent of at least 492ft (150m).

This is the concept that Alan Dawson used to write his list of 'Marilyns' in 1992. Dawson's extensive table covers the whole of Britain, giving a total of 1,552 summits. Of these, 179 are in England (49 in Northern England) and 5 on the Isle of Man. A total of 51 in England and 1 on the Isle of Man exceed the height of 2,000ft (610m). Dawson's tables are published in his book *The Relative Hills of Britain* (see Further Reading).

As shown on the map in figure 1, the hills of England can be split into three convenient sections. This book, the final one in a series of three, details the 54 separate hills that lie between 492ft (150m) and 2,000ft (610m) in altitude in northern England and the Isle of Man. In total, the other two books and *England's Highest Peaks* cover all the separate hills and mountains of England, as defined by a descent of 492ft (150m) on all sides.

The Hills of England

Vol 1: Southern England includes the Cornish Hills, Exmoor, Quantocks, Mendips, Blackdown Hills, Wessex Downs, Isle of Wight, North and South Downs, Weald, Chilterns and Cotswolds (37 hills).

Vol 2: The Midlands and South Pennines includes the Forest of Dean, Welsh Marches, Shropshire Hills, Clent Hills, Charnwood Forest, Lincolnshire Wolds, Derbyshire Dales & Peak District, Peckforton Hills, South Pennines and Forest of Bowland (42 hills).

The Hills of England

Scotland

Vol 3: Northern England and the Isle of Man

Vol 2: The Midlands and South Pennines

Wales

Vol 1: Southern England

Figure 1: **The division of the books in the *Hills of England* series.**

Vol 3: Northern England and the Isle of Man includes the Yorkshire Wolds, North York Moors, Yorkshire Dales, North Pennines, Kielder Forest, Simonside Hills, Cheviots, Lakeland and the Isle of Man (54 hills).

The Mountains of England

England's Highest Peaks details all the 2,000ft (610m) summits of England, including Dartmoor, Black Mountains, Peak District, Yorkshire Dales, North Pennines, Cheviots, Lakeland and the Isle of Man. It is written and presented in the same style as *The Hills of England* series (52 mountains).

Notes: 1. Potts Moor is included in *The Hills of England; Vol 3*, as well as *England's Highest Peaks*, as there is doubt as to whether its summit is above or below 2,000ft (610m). This explains why the hills would appear to total in all four books to 185 instead of 184.

Some beautiful summits have been excluded from the selection described in this book, but, in the vast majority of cases, those omitted are simply tops or shoulders of higher ground. By keeping to the strict criterion of a 492ft (150m) descent outlined above, this book has the advantage that every hill described really is worth climbing. All the summits are pronounced and distinct, both on the ground and in the view from the surrounding valleys and hills. In many cases, the views from their summits are absolutely superb and, although they may seem widely spaced in places, it is rare that another separate summit is not visible, at least on a clear day.

Although the higher summits are seen as a more fulfilling challenge by many ardent hillwalkers, the lower hills should not be dismissed or postponed as they are equally as rewarding in terms of natural beauty. The Scottish Munros, with summits above 3,000ft (914m), get many more visitors than the Corbetts, Scottish summits between 2,500ft (762m) and 3,000ft (914m). However, although the Corbetts are not as high as the Munros, the views they have of their higher neighbours are spectacular and reveal hidden corners and corries that the dogged Munro bagger would not even know existed.

The same is certainly true of the hills in much of the area covered by this book, particularly the Lake District, and it is this that, at least in part, gives them their special charm. However, many of these hills *are* the highest summits in their locality. They are the 'Munros' of their area, commanding views that are just as far-reaching as the views from the summits of Scottish mountains. As such, it seems remarkable that so few people have climbed to all the summits in this book. It is even stranger that fewer hillwalkers still have climbed to the summits of all the separate hills and mountains of England. Whilst the Munroists are in their thousands (2,530 by June 2001), the number of summiteers of the separate English summits are only just creeping into double figures.

There are certainly some summits that are best left to those committed walkers who intend to do them all. In this book, Housedon Hill (Section 3) does not have a public right of way to its summit, as is the case on Swinside (Section 6), and these hills are probably best left to those who intend to do them all. These summits, together with, for example, Sheepcote Hill, Carnmenellis and Hensbarrow Beacon (Volumes 1 and 2), are collector's pieces, not Sunday afternoon strolls.

Perhaps the forthcoming 'right to roam' legislation will help improve access to some summits. In other cases, where this book is concerned, the new legislation will make little difference to the currently agreed voluntary access. The 'right to roam' does not apply to agricultural land and would, therefore, make no difference to the access problems on Housedon Hill (Section 3), for example.

All the summits included in this volume are, without fail, interesting and dominating, but there were some unfortunate casualties as a result of applying the 492ft (150m) descent rule. It is a well-known fact in Scotland that the Ordnance Survey can magically declare that a mountain has gained or lost many feet or metres of altitude between editions of maps. However, in England, especially southern England, this is less of a problem and one can be fairly certain that the summit heights and col heights are fairly accurate. However, there are a few summits that fall just short of inclusion and these are listed below.

SUMMIT	HEIGHT	GRID REFERENCE	SECTION	NEAREST 'SEPARATE' SUMMIT
The Chevin	282m/ 925ft	SE 199441	02	Ilkley Moor
Green Crag	489m/1604ft	SD 200982	04	Harter Fell[1]
Lowscales Hill	189m/ 620ft	SD 153819	04	Black Combe
Hen Comb[2]	509m/1670ft	NY 132181	06	Blake Fell
Knock Murton	447m/1467ft	NY 094190	06	Blake Fell
Beacon Hill	286m/ 938ft	NY 521313	06	Great Mell Fell
North Barrule	565m/1854ft	SC 442909	07	Snaefell[3]

Notes: 1. Harter Fell is over 2,000ft (610m) in altitude and is described in *England's Highest Peaks.* 2. Hen Comb could easily be included in the walk on Blake Fell (Section 6) by extending the route further to the east. 3. Snaefell, the highest point of the Isle of Man, is over 2,000ft (610m) in altitude and is described in *England's Highest Peaks.*

Defining Separateness Precisely

This seemingly pointless definition has taken on some significance over the course of this series; it is important which landscape features can be used to mark a summit and/or make up the 492ft (150m) descent required to define a hill as separate. For the purposes of this book, summits have been taken as the highest point that looks – or at least appears to be – natural. This includes grassed-over ancient burial mounds but not china clay spoil heaps, for example. The tops of towers, masts and other such paraphernalia are excluded from the process of defining a summit.

In defining the col height between two summits, the height of the lowest point on the ridge that the walker must theoretically cross *on the ground* is used. Thus, railway cuttings are included but bridges over railway cuttings are not. These are not simply pedantic meanderings: several summits in Volumes 1 and 2 are only included or excluded because of these facts. Meanwhile, Wansfell, or Baystones, as the summit is known, was included only after the Ordnance Survey resurveyed it and found the final few precious feet of separateness.

For most walkers, however, these details make very little difference because, to be honest, a summit is just as worth climbing whether it is surrounded by a 489ft (149m) descent or one of 492ft (150m)! However, for the purposes of writing this book, an exact definition was required.

The Routes

Due to the decline in public transport, particularly in rural areas, many walkers will use cars to reach the hills that they wish to climb. As a result, the routes in this book all start and finish at the same point, where car-parking space is available. However, in some places, space may be limited and this is mentioned in the text where appropriate.

With this in mind, most walks are circular although, sadly, this is not always possible due to access restrictions and, in such cases, an up-and-back route has been described instead. Each route climbs the hill in the most interesting way, although this may not necessarily be the quickest, shortest or easiest approach.

As most of the hills lie in popular tourist areas, there is usually no shortage of accommodation of any kind. However, this may not be the case in the North Pennines (part of Section 2) and it may be particularly advisable to make arrangements in advance. The Lake District is becoming increasingly busier during the summer months. With this in mind, it is now difficult to find accommodation close to the hills unless it is pre-booked.

As already mentioned, the walks are mostly circular and, as all routes from a hilltop involve a descent, all the walks involve some degree of climbing. In fact, most routes begin, or at least reach the local valley level at some point, if for no other reason than to give a circle of meaningful length and interest. However, the climb to the summit also ties in with the idea of quality being the determining factor. It is generally much more satisfying to have climbed to a given summit from a natural valley level, or the closest practicable point to it, than it is to ascend from a higher-level starting point. Of course, if you wish to park closer to the summit, then you will probably have to accept that a circular walk is not possible and a short stroll is the only option.

In the most popular areas, there is no shortage of public rights of way. These were originally designed to allow local people to reach church from outlying farms and habitations. As such, they were not originally intended for the heavy usage that many of them receive today and, thus, courtesy and respect should be shown at all times for the landowner's land and property. After the hillwalker's code (below) the mutual rights of walkers and landowners are outlined. Not all paths are visible on the ground, however. Across large grass fields, the route may be far from clear if not waymarked and compass bearings are, therefore, occasionally given in the text. In such cases, it would be advisable to carry a compass and know how to use it. Also, some of the footpaths and routes described may not be public rights of way, especially on open moorland where access is not a problem. However, care should be taken not to abuse this trust. It is important to remember that the hills are part of estates and farms and the following code is recommended to minimise conflicts between walkers and landowners or farmers.

A Hillwalker's Code (based on the Countryside Code)

1. Avoid damage to fences, gates and walls. When fences and walls must be crossed, use stiles and gates where possible.
2. Boundaries have an important function, to keep livestock either in or out. Leave closed gates closed. Conversely, gates may have been left deliberately open to make larger fields, so leave them as you find them. However, in cases where there is a specific instruction to shut the gate, this should be followed regardless.
3. Keep to footpaths and other rights of way where this is possible. Do not damage crops.
4. Respect other people's belongings; leave farm machinery alone.
5. Keep dogs under control. Always have your dog on a lead, especially on the open hill or in fields containing livestock. Dogs pose a threat not only to livestock but also to wild animals. Remember, they live there throughout the year and it is their home – do not disturb them. Also remember that it is within a farmer's legal rights to shoot a dog found worrying his sheep.
6. Do not leave litter. Dispose of organic debris such as tea bags discreetly under stones or better still take them home. Take special care with cigarettes, matches and anything else that could cause a fire. Dry moorland and the underlying peat can burn very easily and quickly get out of control.
7. Keep to the right and in single file when walking on country roads – 'face oncoming traffic'. It is particularly important to employ common sense when walking along roads. Although you should generally keep on the right-hand side, you should cross to the left-hand side before walking around sharp right-hand bends to make yourself visible. Not all drivers drive at a speed at which they can stop quickly.
8. Do not pick wild flowers – it may be illegal and they can be enjoyed by all if they are left where they are.

9. Tread carefully on eroded paths. Do not create erosion scars by short-cutting hairpin bends or widening wet or muddy footpaths. If a footpath is too wet or boggy to walk on, do not walk on the edge, which will cause erosion, but on vegetated ground a few yards away on either side.

10. Do not build extra cairns in upland areas – too many can be a hindrance rather than a help. However, conversely, do not demolish any existing ones; someone else may be relying on them. Cairns on summits, however, are different as they are an indication of the highest point and a measure of achievement.

11. Make no unnecessary noise – it only serves to disturb the scene and other people's enjoyment. As well as disturbing local wildlife, the owners of isolated country houses may be trying to enjoy a peaceful afternoon in their gardens.

12. Try to keep streams and rivers clean. They are often used as the basis for the drinking water supply to isolated villages and farms.

13. Heather moors are often used for grouse shooting, which begins on 12 August and continues into the winter. Do not disturb a shoot or get shot! Heather moors are often carefully managed for grouse so do not damage them (see 6).

Adhere to this code – other people's livelihood, enjoyment and welfare depend on your doing so.

Potential Dangers

1. Attacks by cattle upon humans are becoming increasingly common. Whilst it is illegal to keep a dairy bull in a field with a public right of way running through it, it is perfectly legal to keep a beef bull with a herd of cows in a field to which the public have access. When they are with cows, bulls are normally not interested in passers-by, but it is still wise to check for a bull, avoid it and keep an eye on it at all times. Young bullocks and heifers may express an interest in walkers but usually this is nothing more than curiosity. Cows with calves pose a more serious problem. A cow will attack any person or animal (particularly dogs) that she sees as a potential threat to either her or her calf. The vast majority of recent attacks, most of which have led to either serious injury or in some cases death, are due to dog owners being attacked as they try to help their dog.

    Cattle are frequently to be found in the pastures of this area. If you must walk your dog through a field with cattle then keep your dog on a lead and as far away from the herd as is possible. Keep an eye on the cattle and keep close to a boundary that you can cross if necessary. If your dog is attacked by cattle then leave the dog and get away as quickly as possible – dogs are smaller and more agile and certainly much less likely to come to harm than you are. The important thing to remember is that well-behaved dogs on leads can provoke cattle, as well as those that are unleashed.

Public Rights of Way: Your Rights and the Landowner's

The landowner's rights and responsibilities
1. A farmer may shoot a dog found worrying his sheep. However, as dogs should be on a lead, as mentioned below, this conflict should not arise.
2. A farmer may not plough or otherwise disturb a right of way running around the *edge* of a field.
3. A farmer may plough or disturb a footpath or bridleway crossing the field (i.e. not running around the edge) for agricultural purposes, although its surface *must*, by law, be restored within two weeks.
4. The landowner must not block the right of way by erecting a fence, wall or hedge without providing some reasonable means of crossing it. Take care with electric fences, on which crossing points are often provided by means of detaching the fence by unclipping it using an insulated grip. If no such crossing point is provided then the fence is an illegal obstruction. However, as they are normally low they can be crossed by pulling the top strand of wire down using some sort of insulating material, e.g. jumper, handkerchief etc. They are generally very low current but they may nevertheless give you a very nasty shock. This affects some people more than others.

Your rights and responsibilities
1. You can use a public right of way, provided you are legally entitled, as detailed below. You can do so without intimidation.
2. You can stop by the right of way, although you should *never* block it.
3. Provided your dog is under control and *on a lead*, you are legally allowed to take it with you.

4. At the edge of the field, you are allowed to walk the following widths:
    footpaths: 4½ft (1½m)
    bridleways: 10ft (3m)
    byways: 16ft (5m)
5. Across fields, you are allowed to walk the following widths:
    footpaths: 3ft (1m)
    bridleways: 6½ft (2m)
    byways: 10ft (3m)
    Any person or notice advising you otherwise is incorrect.
6. If a crop has been planted across a right of way, you are still allowed to walk its route, provided that you only damage any crops within the widths above. Outside these, you are liable to be prosecuted for criminal damage. No person may intimidate you from walking along a right of way; farmyard dogs do not qualify in this respect, provided they are not causing an 'obstruction'. If, however, they attack you, you have a claim against the landowner.
7. If the path is obstructed then you are entitled to travel the shortest and least-damaging route around it. This includes both natural and artificial obstructions.
8. You must follow all legal footpath diversions, as authorised by the highways department of the local council.

Rights of Way definitions
A *footpath* is a right of way that only walkers are allowed to use. Cyclists, walkers and horseriders may use a *bridleway*. All traffic, including off-road vehicles, may use a *byway*. It should, however, be noted that landowners may, of course, use the tracks as they wish. Thus, although a footpath should, in theory, be reserved for foot traffic, the farmer may, and is entitled to, use it as a farm road.

At least, in theory, these rights and rules work well to the advantage of both parties. Unfortunately, there are those on both sides who fail to respect them. This is no reason to avoid following the right of way, although you should show care and extra consideration towards the farmer or occupier if they have shown to be unwilling to provide access, perhaps by ploughing up paths etc. However, before entering into a dispute with a farmer or occupier, remember that you are not allowed to use physical force to exercise your rights. You may also like to consider that guns are often kept on isolated farms. An unfriendly landowner may, in their blinkered vision, see you as a trespasser.

Technical Difficulty

I have tried to resist the temptation to include scrambling in the routes. Occasionally, very short and simple scrambles have been included where they improve the climb or make it more interesting. However, inexperienced walkers may well take their hands out of their pockets (in theory making it scrambling) on other routes as some are steep and arduous – not simple country strolls. Most of the simple scrambling can be avoided by longer and generally less interesting alternatives.

Scrambling is (at its highest level) one of the most dangerous of mountaineering pastimes as it is largely done over difficult terrain unroped. Even on very simple scrambles, such as the ascent of Mellbreak or Barf (Section 6), the consequences of a slip would be severe and these routes are best done in good, dry conditions, except by the experienced.

At-a-glance Grids and the Grading System

A grid accompanies each route, showing the difficulty of terrain, difficulty of navigation and quality. The name, metric and imperial heights, OS grid reference, OS Landranger Sheet number, distance, time and starting point are also shown.

The timings are calculated by assuming that for every 1,000ft (305m) of ascent undertaken, an average walker could cover 2 miles (3km) on the level. An average walking pace over the whole route of 1½ miles per hour is then used to work out the given time. Obviously, this speed will differ from walker to walker and a small difference is given on either side of the calculated time to allow for this. However, on the short routes, which are designed to be completed in an afternoon, the time allowed for lunch is minimal, whereas, on the routes of middle length, if you plan to complete them on a long summer's afternoon, you may wish to take off 20 minutes to half an hour to compensate for the lunch break, which, presumably, would not be taken. However, if you make a long stop for a cream tea, drink at a pub or pub lunch on the walk then you will probably have to add on this time.

The gradings below are used throughout the series and are similar to those used in *England's Highest Peaks*.

(i) Terrain gradings

All the routes in the series are walks or simple scrambles so there is, therefore, little difference in technical difficulty. However, terrain does differ considerably and the grading is based upon the table below. It is fair to comment that Grade 1 routes are suitable for all the family in good weather and/or underfoot conditions, Grades 2 and 3 are more serious walking and Grades 4 and 5 are simple scrambles.

1. Easy terrain
2. Steep and/or arduous over short distances
3. Appreciable sections of rough, difficult ground
4. Some handwork may be required in places
5. Longer unavoidable sections of simple scrambling

(ii) Navigation gradings

It is assumed that other than for odd occasions where a compass bearing is given in the text, there will be no problem with navigation in clear weather. The gradings listed below are the worst possible, i.e. in misty conditions. Under a covering of snow, Grades 1 to 3 become 4 and Grade 4 becomes 5.

1. Clear paths; easy to follow in mist
2. A few pathless sections but a compass is unlikely to be required
3. Some pathless sections on which a compass may be needed
4. Long pathless sections over which a map and compass are necessary
5. Featureless – a high standard of navigation required in bad weather

(iii) Quality gradings

Quality is very subjective so there will be many different opinions. With these gradings, I have tried to keep my personal interests and experiences out of my mind when assessing each route.

1. Generally dull and uninteresting
2. Some interesting parts
3. Interesting
4. Fine views and good scenery or consistently interesting
5. Excellent, a wide variety of scenery and views

However, as the quality gradings are based on a wide range of factors, some readers may wish to see the hills indexed by subjects of interest and this is shown below.

(Numbers in brackets are section numbers)

Archaeology: Urra Moor route (1), Thorpe Fell Top (2), Ros Hill (3), Hard Knott (5), South Barrule (7), Mull Hill (7).

Caves and Potholes: Hoove (2), Loughrigg Fell (6).

Cliffs: Urra Moor route (1), Hoove (2), Kisdon (2), Ilkley Moor (2), Tosson Hill (3), Long Crag (3), Hutton Roof Crags (4), Whitbarrow (4), Illgill Head (5), Black Combe (5), Hard Knott (5), Lingmoor Fell (5), Holm Fell (5), Lord's Seat (6), Mellbreak (6), High Rigg (6), Bradda Hill (7), Mull Hill (7).

Coastlines: Bradda Hill (7), Mull Hill (7).

Geological Interest: Urra Moor route (1), Bishop Wilton Wold (1), Hoove (2), Kisdon (2), Dufton Pike (2), Shillhope Law (3), Long Crag (3), Wansfell (4), Hallin Fell (4), Hutton Roof Crags (4), Grayrigg Forest (4), Whitfell (5), Mellbreak (6), Lord's Seat (6), Slieau Freoaghane (7), Mull Hill (7).

Gorges: Whitfell (5).

Impressive Scenery: All routes awarded a grade 4 or 5 for quality.

Mining and Quarrying: Hove Fell (2), Lambrigg (4), Kirkby Moor (5), Holm Fell (5), Loughrigg Fell (6).

Railways: Peel Fell (3).

Scrambling: Kisdon (2), Hutton Roof Crags (4), Lingmoor Fell (5), Lord's Seat (6), Mellbreak (6).

Waterfalls: Kisdon (2), Whitfell (5), Hard Knott (5).

A question I am frequently asked is what would I consider to be the finest hill of those in this region. I find this a very difficult question to answer as the quality of any hill depends upon the route taken. However, I have listed below, in order, the summits that I consider to be the ten finest in the book:

1. Mellbreak (6)   (Loweswater Fells)
2. Bradda Hill (7)   (Isle of Man)
3. Holm Fell (5)   (Coniston Fells)
4. Hutton Roof Crags (4)   (Kendal)
5. Long Crag (3)   (Simonside Hills)
6. Blake Fell (6)   (Loweswater Fells)
7. Illgill Head (5)   (Western Lakeland)
8. Lord's Seat (6)   (Northwestern Lakeland)
9. Claife Heights (4)   (Southern Lakeland)
10. Sighty Crag (3)   (Kielder Forest)

Directions

Points of the compass and compass bearings are often given to indicate direction. Compass bearings begin at north (0º) and run through east (90º), south (180º) and west (270º). Any directions such as left and right refer to the direction of travel and walkers following the routes in reverse may have considerable difficulty in following the description. In reference to the banks of rivers and streams, the phrases 'true left' and 'true right' are not used and 'left bank' refers to the left-hand bank and 'right bank' the right-hand bank, both in the direction of travel and not necessarily the direction in which the water is flowing.

How to Use This Book

Each area is given an introduction in which accommodation and geology are discussed. A map of the region showing the hills, towns and important roads is included to give an understanding of the geography of the region. Each route is given a description and a map to give the reader an idea of the route whilst reading the text.

Those not experienced in walking in this area may like to read the pages on **General Advice** that follow and those readers with little or no geological knowledge may find the geological descriptions of each section a little more meaningful after reading the **Geological Introduction**. Any terms that may be unfamiliar are explained in the **Glossary** at the back of the book. The **Useful Telephone Numbers** section lists the telephone numbers of all places mentioned in the text and Tourist Information/ National Park Centres. Also, there is a **Reader's Personal Log** for your own records and a section on **Hill Names and their Meanings** for those interested in their derivations.

The words path and track have been used in the text with very specific meanings that are intended to help readers identify the correct route on the ground. I have defined them as follows:

Path – A strip of ground eroded by the passage of feet, along which it is too narrow to drive an all-terrain vehicle.

Track – A strip of ground eroded by either feet or vehicles so that it is wide enough to drive an all-terrain vehicle along (although this may not be practically possible due to rocks or other obstructions).

Walking Routes in Reverse

There are very few routes that can be reversed without some loss of quality. The routes are planned so as to keep the most impressive views of the scenery ahead rather than behind. Also, use is made of simple, less steep descents at the end of long days. Indeed, many of the descriptions will be difficult, if not impossible, to use in reverse, as what may appear very obvious in one direction may be far from obvious in the other, particularly when walking unwaymarked paths across a complex maze of fields. Therefore, the walking of routes in reverse is not recommended.

The Descriptions

Too often, in my opinion, guidebooks tell you little more than that which can be seen from a 1:25,000 scale map. 'Follow the south ridge from the car park to the summit' is not an adequate description unless the route is very obvious indeed. I have tried to give clear and detailed descriptions to help those using the book. Some authors claim that if the descriptions are too detailed, some walkers will feel that they have lost the sense of adventure but, personally, I see the purpose of a guidebook as being to guide.

The Maps

The route maps are drawn approximately to a 1:50,000 scale (2cm = 1km; 1½ inches = 1 mile) and show only important information, to avoid clutter. They are provided to give an idea of the route, not specifically for navigation on the ground in bad weather, as they are not as accurate as an Ordnance Survey map. The section maps are drawn approximately to a 1:625,000 scale (4cm = 25km; 1 inch = 10 miles), except where otherwise noted. Again, unimportant information is excluded to avoid clutter. All the maps have north at the top. A list of symbols is provided overleaf. There are some minor variations in the scale of the maps so that they can conveniently be fitted onto a page. However, these variations are small and unlikely to cause any problems.

KEY TO SECTION MAPS:

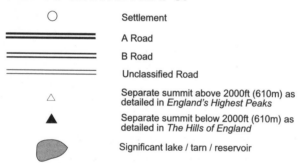

○	Settlement
═══	A Road
═══	B Road
───	Unclassified Road
△	Separate summit above 2000ft (610m) as detailed in *England's Highest Peaks*
▲	Separate summit below 2000ft (610m) as detailed in *The Hills of England*
⬭	Significant lake / tarn / reservoir

KEY TO ROUTE MAPS:

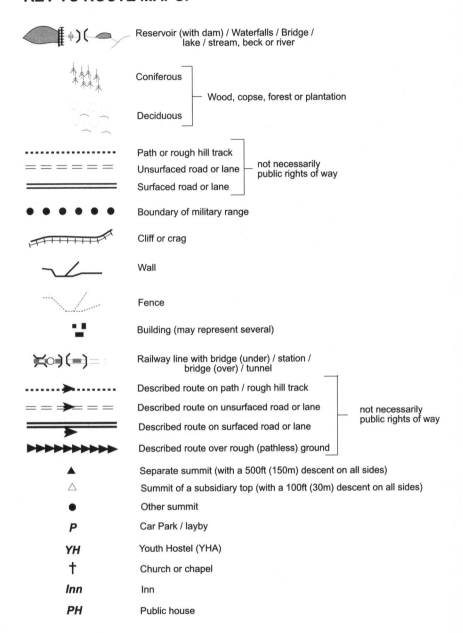

Reservoir (with dam) / Waterfalls / Bridge / lake / stream, beck or river

Coniferous

Deciduous

Wood, copse, forest or plantation

Path or rough hill track

Unsurfaced road or lane

Surfaced road or lane

not necessarily public rights of way

Boundary of military range

Cliff or crag

Wall

Fence

Building (may represent several)

Railway line with bridge (under) / station / bridge (over) / tunnel

Described route on path / rough hill track

Described route on unsurfaced road or lane

Described route on surfaced road or lane

Described route over rough (pathless) ground

not necessarily public rights of way

▲ Separate summit (with a 500ft (150m) descent on all sides)

△ Summit of a subsidiary top (with a 100ft (30m) descent on all sides)

● Other summit

P Car Park / layby

YH Youth Hostel (YHA)

† Church or chapel

Inn Inn

PH Public house

Accompanying Maps

The use of accompanying maps is somewhat dependent on the route. Many of the hills have weather conditions associated with mountainous terrain. As such, a map is required because the weather can change very quickly and the route may be lost in bad weather. In any case, a map is useful to identify features in the view. The hills upon which a map is not required are listed below:

Section 1: Bishop Wilton Wold.
Section 2: Ilkley Moor and Sharp Haw.
Section 3: Ros Hill.
Section 4: Gummer's How, Claife Heights and Whitbarrow.
Section 6: Watch Hill and Swinside.
Section 7: South Barrule, Bradda Hill and Mull Hill.

For the other hills, an Ordnance Survey 1:50,000 scale Landranger map of the areas involved will suffice but alternatively all these hills are covered by the Ordnance Survey's Explorer and Outdoor Leisure Series at a 1:25,000 scale, with the exception of the Isle of Man. Therefore, the following Landranger sheets will be required: 75, 79, 80, 81, 89, 90, 91, 92, 93, 94, 95, 96, 97, 98, 100, 103 and 104; they could be replaced with the following Explorer sheets: 287, 332 and 339, together with Outdoor Leisure sheets 2, 4, 5, 6, 7, 16, 19, 26, 30 and 42. However, as the Isle of Man is not covered by the 1:25,000 mapping, Landranger 95 will still be required.

The hills listed above, with the exception of Bishop Wilton Wold, are also covered by the Landranger sheets listed above. Bishop Wilton Wold is covered by Landranger Sheet 106. If an Explorer map were desired in preference to the Landranger sheets on the listed hills then Explorer sheets 294, 297 and 340 would be required.

General Advice

Walking in the hills and mountains is a very different experience from walking in more lowland and 'tame' areas. Most mountaineering accidents are caused by walkers and climbers who stray onto the hills without adequate preparation or tackle routes which are beyond their technical ability. I would, therefore, urge novice walkers to take careful note of this section before undertaking the routes that follow, especially those on the higher hills of the Lake District (Sections 4, 5 and 6) and Yorkshire Dales (Section 2).

Winter walking is once again completely different from walking in the same place in summer. Not only do the very low temperatures lead to a greater energy expenditure but also snow and ice bring their own inherent dangers and navigational problems.

Weather Conditions

Upland areas often have their own microclimates, which are generally of a wet and windy nature! Whilst some of the lowland hills described in this book have relatively tame climates, the higher peaks should not be underestimated, especially in winter.

As regards the weather in the uplands, nothing can be taken for granted and a weather forecast should always be consulted before departure. Most national television, radio and newspaper forecasts are unreliable above valley level although ITV Teletext does have a climbing forecast. A detailed climbing forecast should always be sought locally before departure. These are available at youth hostels and most National Park Information Centres or by recorded telephone answering services in the more popular areas. Even a good weather forecast cannot be relied on as moorlands often produce and attract showers whilst everywhere else is dry and sunny. Some form of waterproof clothing should be carried at all times.

Lightning is again much more dangerous on hilltops than elsewhere; it usually strikes the highest point around and if you are standing on a mountain top, that's you! Keep your feet close together and do not lie down, only crouch. The greater the distance between your extremities, the higher the potential voltage and, therefore, the possible danger. Get rid of metal equipment (including frame rucksacks) and crouch on your rucksack to help insulate you. Seek low ground and depressions (not those containing water). Do not stand under lone trees or on or near summits, rock peaks or pinnacles. Move immediately if you hear any kind of static crackling (as in touching a television screen) or feel your hair stand on end. Keep a check on thunderstorms. Time the difference in seconds between the lightning flash and hearing the thunder. The bigger the gap then the further away the strike is; if there is no difference then the storm is overhead (very dangerous).

Winter weather in England is not as bad as is often thought, especially given the recent trend for milder winters with little snow. If you can choose to go when the weather is good, you can enjoy the charm of the popular areas when they are almost deserted. Remember, though, that winter and summer walking are completely different. Showers often fall as snow, sleet or hail and things can quickly turn into a 'white-out'. Knowledge of compass use is essential in these circumstances given that only a few centimetres of snow can quickly obliterate landmarks and turn fell tops into arctic landscapes. If there is a signficant amount of lying snow, take an ice axe and if there is hard snow, take a pair of crampons and know how to use them – snow is very slippery, a slide can be very difficult to stop with bare hands and can prove fatal. Carry gloves, scarves, bobble hats, spare jumpers and a polybag (insulated 'sleeping bag'), which is a good idea in case of injury.

In the lowlands, however, the weather is generally more settled and in summer it can get very hot. With the recent trend for summers with temperatures exceeding 25 degrees Centigrade on many days, the heat can pose its own problems and it is very easy to get dehydrated or get some other serious condition like heatstroke.

Boots

A good pair of boots is a precondition to successful walking. Shoes and trainers do not have the necessary grip, are not strong enough and not waterproof when it comes to crossing streams or bogs. Wellington boots do not have a good enough grip either. A pair of flexible, broken-in, well-fitting leather boots is essential. Buy a pair with some bend in them, but not too bendy, so that a pair of flexible crampons can be fitted if required. Fabric boots are rarely as waterproof or sturdy as leather boots. Make sure your boots are well dubbed (carry a spare tin of dubbing) and, most importantly of all, make sure they fit and are broken in! All too often a pair of badly fitted boots can ruin a walking holiday when they cause blisters. However, that said, carrying plasters and a blister kit is always a good idea since, however well your boots may fit, there is always a first time.

Underfoot Conditions

Many of the lower hills of the Lake District can be just as rough as the higher mountains. Summits, such as Illgill Head and Mellbreak, are fairly high and share far more in common with their neighbouring mountains than the other hills in this book. Thus, the routes on these higher summits are generally quite tough, steep and difficult. Meanwhile, many of the Pennine summits have the potential to be quite wet, boggy, rough and pathless, so few of the hills in this book should be treated lightly. The fact that a number of the hills in this book are very infrequently visited makes them demanding expeditions that are, in many cases, at least as difficult as the higher mountains.

Rucksacks

Almost as important as boots is a rucksack, which is an essential walker's tool. It keeps equipment dry and provides a safe and comfortable way of carrying it. I would not recommend frame rucksacks, as they are big, heavy and bulky and become easily wedged in tight, difficult situations. A mesh next to the back is a good idea, as this allows air to circulate and helps stop your back from becoming too hot and sweaty – a particular problem on the lower hills. Chest and waist straps are also important to look out for. Although most rucksacks now have waist straps, they do not all have chest straps, which are very helpful in distributing weight and load. Outside pockets are another consideration. A good selection of easily accessible pockets and hoops is very important, as it is very awkward to store small things that are in frequent use in the main compartment where they fall to the bottom and become lost amongst larger, bulkier items.

Perhaps the best piece of advice is to buy what feels comfortable in the shop. If possible put some weight in it and walk around. If it is not comfortable in the shop, it certainly will not improve at 1,000ft. As for size, many walkers find 35 litres more than adequate for day expeditions. However, in winter, I usually take a 65-litre rucksack as I find it difficult to fit large bulky jackets and waterproofs into the smaller sizes along with my other equipment.

Whatever it may say on the label, very few rucksacks are actually waterproof and, although sandwich bags will suffice for the outside pockets, a rucksack liner is a good investment for the main compartment since it saves wrapping items up individually.

Clothing

Clothing is certainly very much dependent on the time of year. Mountain clothing consists of three layers:

(i) Next to skin layer

This is very important and possibly the most critical of the three layers. Except in very cold weather, climbers will sweat quite a lot. The layer next to the skin must 'wick' this sweat away from the skin and also off itself and onto another outer layer. If a cotton garment is worn next to the skin, it will become waterlogged and damp, leaving your back cold and clammy. Cotton is sometimes called 'death cloth' because of its notorious reputation of causing hypothermia.

The best clothing to wear in this layer consists of 100 per cent polyester. Clothing such as this is quite expensive and is not easy to find in the high street, but it is available in many outdoor shops. However, as these garments wick well, they can be washed and dried quickly so you will not need many.

(ii) Insulating layer

The primary function of this layer is to keep you warm. Jumpers, sweatshirts and particularly climbing fleeces may be used. Even though you may feel cold to start with, it is a mistake to put too much on too soon. You will soon get hot when you start walking and will end up hot and sweaty and then unable to take any of it off. Instead, add it as you feel you need it. It is always necessary to keep one or two extra layers to put on when you have stopped for any length of time.

(iii) Outer shell

The function of this layer is to keep you dry – not warm. A breathable fabric, such as Gore Tex, is essential. It must keep the rain and wind from getting in but also let perspiration out. It only need be put on when the rain starts and must consist of waterproof trousers as well as a jacket with a hood. Remember, just because a weather forecast promises a fine day does not guard against heavy showers, which are easily generated on apparently fine days in the mountains.

Ice Axes and How to Use Them

The situations in which ice axes are needed are becoming increasingly rare in England but this trend may not be permanent. The higher hills of the Lake District, for example, can be dangerous under winter conditions. Part of the danger is due to complacency – just because they are lower does not mean that full winter mountaineering equipment is not required. An ice axe is used either to prevent a slide or to stop one once it has started. Everyone knows that ice is slippery on level surfaces and it is even worse on steep hillsides. Hard snow is just as bad as ice in terms of its slipperiness. The chances of a successful self-arrest (stopping a slide) using an ice axe is about 50 per cent; without an ice axe this will be dramatically reduced.

There are two types of hand-held ice tools: ice axes and ice picks. Walkers will want an ice axe of about 70 centimetres in length. Shorter tools are for use by ice climbers finding their sport on vertical ice faces, where they need much more intimate contact.

As well as an axe, you may also wish to have a wrist leash, which, when tied to the axe and attached to your wrist, will prevent the axe from being lost during self-arrest.

Walkers will use the pick of their ice axe very little, mainly using the spike and sometimes the adze.

There are two methods of holding an ice axe and techniques associated with them:

(i) Self-belay

This technique is used to prevent a fall from occurring in the first place. Hold the axe with the spike pointing down and place your palm on top of the adze. Put your thumb and index finger under the upper reaches of the pick and your other fingers under the adze. Plunge the spike into the snow ahead of you and then step up to it, remove it, plunge it in again and so on. If you slip, grab the top of the shaft with your other hand and, providing that the snow is hard enough, the axe should hold you. If it does not, you will have to change your grip instantaneously to one suitable for self-arrest. Whilst it is possible to self-belay using the self-arrest grasp, it is uncomfortable.

(ii) Self-arrest

This method is used to stop a fall once it has started. Assuming you are sliding feet first on your back, grasp the bottom of the shaft with your left hand and place your right palm on the pick with your thumb and index finger underneath the adze and your other fingers under the pick (the opposite to self-belay). To self-arrest, fall to your right, *away from the shaft*, plunging the pick into the snow and pushing your body down on top of it. Push your feet (unless you are wearing crampons), knees and face down into the snow. Many self-arrests are not successful because people are too reluctant to get their faces down into the snow. If you are sliding head first, then you will need to dig the pick in as before and then be swung around so that your head is uphill before digging in your feet, knees and face. Self-arrest is a difficult technique to learn, so practise it beforehand because it could save your life.

The other purpose of an ice axe to a walker is to cut steps on steep sections. Swing the adze down ahead of you to cut the steps, and then use self-belay whilst you climb up them before cutting some more. This method is very slow and difficult and if there are long steep sections, a pair of crampons will be a good investment.

Crampons and How to Fit and Use Them

Crampons can be a great aid to a walker in hard snow and ice but are not a substitute for an ice axe.

There are four types of crampon – 10-point crampons and 12-point crampons and then each can be either flexible or rigid. Unless you have special boots and are an ice climber then forget rigid ones; for walking purposes flexible crampons are fine. Every crampon has 10 points on the bottom and most also have an extra 2 points on the front giving 12 points in total, which is recommended because it makes them more versatile.

Before choosing crampons, you will need to be sure that your boots will support crampons. Do not be fobbed off by being told that you have to buy a new pair of boots. If your boots are stiff enough so that they do not bend in half, like a slipper, they will support a pair of flexible crampons fairly well.

A flexible crampon does not have a firm frame underneath from toe to heel but instead has a movable joint in the middle, which means that it will fit any size of boot. Rigid crampons sometimes just fit particular boots and when you change your boots then you must also change crampons. Crampons attach to boots by a system of straps and this should be explained in the instructions, otherwise a shop assistant will be able to demonstrate.

There are two ways of using crampons and which you use will depend to a large extent on how steep the ground is:

(i) Pied plat (flat-footed)

On ground which is between 20° and 40° pied plat will definitely be used. Between 40° and 60°, pied plat is advised but front pointing could also be used, but above 60° front pointing is essential. 'Flat-footed' is exactly what pied plat is. All 10 points on the base of the crampon should be firmly into the snow or ice, with your boot touching the slope from toe to heel. This does put a strain upon the ankles but all 10 points must be in the snow to gain satisfactory purchase and grip.

(ii) Front pointing

This is a technique more commonly used by ice climbers but can be used over *short* distances by walkers with flexible crampons. Using this method, the two front points are plunged into the snow and that is all. This is more comfortable for the walker but it does put a terrible strain on the crampon, which, if used for too long, will cause it to break under the pressure. Front pointing can only be done using 12-point crampons.

A final point to remember about crampons: in self-arrest do not jam your feet into the snow otherwise a point is likely to catch and catapult you up into the air.

The Dangers of Snow

The dangers associated with winter conditions can be manifest on a snow-covered hill of any size. Of particular danger are the higher hills described in this book but avalanches can occur on just about any hillslope under the right conditions in the range of the danger gradient. Meanwhile, cornices can form on any sharp, windy ridge or edge.

(i) Avalanches

The risk of being caught in an avalanche is the single biggest danger to winter walkers. Avalanches occur on slopes between 25° and 60° but are most likely between 30° and 45°. Over the period of time in which the snowpack forms, several different snowfalls may occur and some of these may have existed on the surface long enough to become hard and consolidated. Also, the surface may have temporarily thawed and then refrozen, forming another type of hard layer. Wind, of course, moves vast volumes of snow around and even when there has not been any fresh snowfall, a brisk breeze may have mimicked one by blowing snow over a ridge and forming a much softer layer which can then be consolidated itself.

When there is bad bonding between layers in the snowpack an avalanche can occur. What happens is the top layers simply slide off the bottom ones and the trigger for this is generally movement on the slopes: victims usually cause the avalanches in which they are trapped. It is wise to be prudent by evaluating the risk before crossing a slope of a gradient in the danger zone. Plunging a ski-pole or ice axe shaft down into the snow will give you an idea of its strata and any hard layers to which the snow may be less well bonded.

(ii) Cornices

Cornices form when the wind blows snow up a slope and over a ridge. A lip of snow forms on the leeward side, which, although almost completely flat on top, is usually considerably undercut. Any reasonably sharp ridge can form a cornice and if there is a crag on the leeward side then it may pose a particular danger. The key is to assume that any ridge is likely to be corniced and not to risk walking too close to the edge. If this is unavoidable, however, the best thing is to probe the ground with a ski-pole or ice axe shaft before each step and if it breaks through, retreat immediately.

The key point about both avalanches and cornices is to understand the weather patterns in the days and weeks leading up to your walk and, if necessary, seek local knowledge before departure.

Heat and Sun

Before setting off walking on a hot summer's day, there are a number of medical conditions of which you should be aware:

(i) Sunburn

There is nothing unknown about sunburn but remember that the sun is normally considerably stronger in the summer than in the winter. On a long day out in the open, it is quite possible to get very badly burnt, although the degree of this will depend on your own sensitivity. The UV light that causes sunburn may also cause skin cancer if the skin is exposed for too long. Prevention is the best defence and there are many suncreams and sunblocks on the market. These contain a number of chemicals that absorb ultraviolet frequencies of light and they may also contain reflective materials, such as zinc compounds. Arms and legs that are left uncovered for the first time in the season are particularly vulnerable. Also, prolonged exposure to sunlight can also cause rashes and other minor complaints with some individuals.

(ii) Dehydration

This is often the prelude to heatstroke, which follows quickly after sweating stops. The body loses fluid mainly through sweating and urinating, although diarrhoea is another possible loss. To avoid this condition, you should regularly drink plenty of fluids, preferably water rather than other types of drinks, which I find make me more thirsty. If you stop sweating or your urine is particularly dark then you are becoming dehydrated. However, everybody sweats different amounts so the exact amount you should drink is different for each individual, although the equivalent of a cup every half an hour is the average.

(iii) Heatstroke

Heatstroke, also known as sunstroke, is the opposite of hypothermia. The first symptoms are those of heat exhaustion – tiredness and/or feeling faint. However, in heatstroke, the body temperature rises to dangerous levels, more than those experienced in an average dose of flu. The main symptom is a change in mental state. The victim may become confused or uncooperative and this is often accompanied by a rapid pulse, headache, weakness and flushed skin. Treatment should be administered quickly; take the patient to a shady area and help them cool down by fanning or splashing on water. Fluids should be given if the patient is able to drink, not only to help reduce the body temperature, but also to help with dehydration, which often accompanies and precedes heatstroke. If untreated, heatstroke can be fatal.

Geological Introduction

The geological descriptions that follow throughout the text are generally intended to be fairly self-explanatory. However, this introduction should help readers with little or no knowledge of science and geology to make more sense of what follows. The glossary contains explanations of many of the geological terms that are used throughout the book.

There are three types of rock: sedimentary, igneous and metamorphic. *Sedimentary rocks* form most English landscapes and they are mainly formed from sediments, such as muds or the skeletons of dead sea creatures, on the sea floor. These are then compacted by further sediment, which is deposited above them, and they turn into rock. The carcases of sea creatures are often mixed through the mud rather than forming the rock totally or being crushed beyond recognition. They appear in cliffs and other exposures and are called *fossils*. The knowledge of where and when they lived allows geologists not only to date the rock but also to suggest the conditions in which it was deposited. Limestones, shales and mudstones are all usually fossiliferous rocks that are formed on the sea floor.

However, sedimentary rocks do not only originate under the sea; some identical rocks are formed in inland lakes and lagoons. Others are formed on dry land or beaches. Sandstones and gritstones are examples of rocks formed on a beach. The process of compaction is the same as that under the sea but obviously this rock will contain no marine fossils. Other sandstones are formed in deserts. Where plants grow profusely, such as in tropical swamps, their remnants collapse into wet ground and do not decompose normally. Instead, they form peat, which is then compacted into coal, a fossil fuel.

Igneous rocks are lavas which may have erupted from a volcano or been forced under pressure into existing rocks; when this happens it is called an igneous intrusion. All igneous rocks begin as magma in the Earth's mantle, which is forced to the surface as a result of movements in the crust, often close to a tectonic plate boundary. The type of rock formed will depend not only on whether it formed above or below ground but also on its chemical composition. All igneous rocks are made up of crystals and contain no fossils. The size of the crystals is dependent upon the speed at which the rock cooled. If the eruption took place under the sea, the rock will contain small crystals as a result of the rapid cooling effect of the seawater but if it intruded into other rocks and cooled underground, the process would have been much slower and larger crystals would have been able to form. Finally, if the lava erupted onto the land surface, the rock will have medium-sized to small crystals. However, some igneous rocks with large crystals are now exposed in areas such as Dartmoor. Here, the rocks into which the magma intruded have since been worn away. Granite, gabbro, dolerite and basalt are all examples of igneous rocks.

Where an igneous rock came into contact with a sedimentary rock, the igneous rock would bake the sedimentary rock, causing it to melt before crystallising out. This type of rock is known as *metamorphic*. Metamorphic rocks are also formed when other types of rock are subjected to intense pressure. Marble is the metamorphic version of limestone whilst slates are the metamorphic version of shales.

Most of the sedimentary rocks that are seen today were deposited in very different conditions to those in which they now sit. Coal, for example, was deposited in tropical swamps, limestone in tropical shelf-seas and on coral reefs and some sandstones in desert conditions. The reason for this is that, hundreds of millions of years ago, Britain lay just to the north of the equator. In fact 270 million years ago, all the continents of the Earth formed one huge land mass known as Pangaea. They have since diverged due to the movement of the Earth's tectonic plates – subdivisions of the Earth's crust that are able to move independently. Britain lies on the Eurasian plate.

At their edges, plates are in contact with their neighbours. However, depending upon the motion of the plates relative to each other there can be four types of margin. At a *constructive* margin, the two plates pull apart and magma rises up from the Earth's mantle below to fill the gap. This occurs mainly under the oceans where undersea ridges, such as the Mid-Atlantic Ridge, are formed. The new segments of the Earth's crust created by these eruptions are known as oceanic crust and are much denser than continental crust. At a *destructive* margin, dense oceanic crust pushes against less dense continental crust. Here, the denser oceanic crust sinks

a) Deposition of sedimentary rock sequence

Horizontal layers of rock are deposited, perhaps in a marine setting, a freshwater lagoon, desert, tropical swamp or floodplain.

b) Folding of rock strata

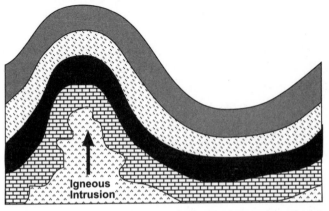

Igneous Intrusion

In the diagram, the rock strata are pushed up to form a dome (anticline) and a neighbouring syncline develops, although this is not always the case. Lateral pressure in mountain building episodes also folds the strata to form anticlines, synclines and overfolds.

c) Subsequent erosion and deposition

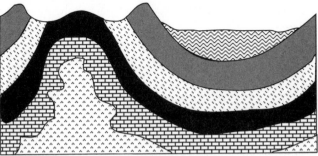

Harder rocks form cuestas, whilst softer rocks are eroded away to form vales. Deposition occurs in synclinal basins.

Figure 2: Formation of anticlines and synclines.

a) Deposition of sedimentary rock sequence

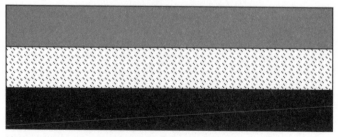

Horizontal layers of rock are deposited, perhaps in a marine setting, a freshwater lagoon, desert, tropical swamp or floodplain.

b) Subsequent transformation of rock strata and landscape

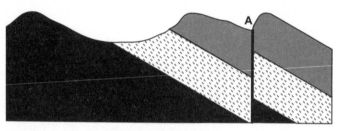

Deposition halts, perhaps because of a fall in sea level etc., and the rock strata can be deformed in various ways. Here, a mountain building episode has uplifted the land and set the strata at an angle. At the same time, the fault at A formed as the block of land on the left dropped relative to that on the right. Erosion formed a complex land surface, in which softer rocks form vales and more resistant rocks form hills and ridges.

c) Development of an uncomformity

present land surface

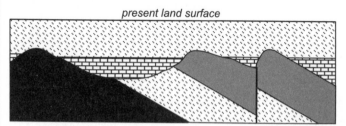

After a halt in deposition, sediments again begin to form. Perhaps, for example, the sea has covered the land. Horizontal layers of new rock now begin to form on top of the eroded landscape from (b). This interruption in deposition and strata is called an *unconformity*, which shows that there has not been continuous deposition since (a).

Figure 3: Formation of a landscape over many millions of years.

below the continental crust in what is called a subduction zone. The oceanic crust then melts causing a build up of pressure below the surface, which is relieved by earthquakes and volcanic eruptions. This is what is happening now in the West Indies, with volcanoes, such as the one on Montserrat, forming.

The third type of margin is called a *collision* boundary and here continental crust collides with continental crust. The result is the crumpling and contortion of the crust to form faults, thrust-planes, anticlines and synclines, as described below. In general, these features form as part of a range of 'fold mountains' and a period of mountain building is called an *orogeny*. The Himalayas and the Alps are both ranges of fold mountains. Finally, two plates can slide past each other at a *transform* margin. This causes violent earthquakes as the plates move. The San Andreas Fault in California is probably the most famous example of a transform margin.

Sedimentary rocks, and most lavas, form regular horizontal layers when they are deposited. Today, however, there are relatively few areas with horizontal bedding or *strata*. Mountain building crumples the crust and forms gentle dips and rises as well as tight folds and even overfolds. The formation of *anticlines* and *synclines* is shown in figure 2, which also explains how they form certain landscapes today.

When the crust breaks and moves separately, a *fault* forms. Faults can be seen where one block of land has risen or fallen relative to the surrounding land. Also, a block of land can slide horizontally relative to the surrounding crust in the same way as a transform margin above. Britain contains many fault lines, for example, the famous Craven Faults in the Yorkshire Dales (Section 2), the Church Stretton Fault in Shropshire (Vol 2) and the Great Glen Fault in Scotland. Faulting and another major principle of geology, that of *unconformity*, is explained in figure 3.

Since Britain moved to its current northern latitude, successive changes in temperature have caused the melting of ice in hotter periods and the spread of ice in colder periods, which are called *ice ages*. Britain in many ways leads a charmed life in its current position. Despite lying on the same latitude as the frozen wastes of Siberia and Labrador, Britain experiences a much milder, temperate climate. This is due to a warm ocean current, known as the Mid-Atlantic Drift, which, along with the Gulf Stream, brings tropical water northwards from the Bay of Mexico. It is in fact a convection current: warm, less-dense water on the surface is drawn northwards from the Bay of Mexico to replace cooler, denser water which has sunk further to the north around the west coast of Britain and Ireland. This cold water is then, at depth, drawn back in the opposite direction to replace the warm water that moves northwards from the Gulf of Mexico. This process is the same as what happens in a room when a radiator or fan heater is turned on.

However, for this process to work, the water must be salty. If a large amount of fresh water enters the North Atlantic, for example from the bursting of a massive continental lake or much higher rainfall, the convection current ceases and the seas around north-western Europe suddenly become much colder. Contrary to historical opinion, this change does not necessarily happen over hundreds of years but could take place in as little as 20 years if the conditions are right.

As Britain is quite a small island, its climate is very dependent on the oceans surrounding it. As a larger amount of energy is required to heat water than soil, water retains its heat in winter and remains cool in summer (water has a higher specific heat capacity). This is why Britain can never experience the extremes of temperature that can be felt in places at the centre of large continents, such as Moscow, which have freezing winters and very hot summers. Therefore, when the sea is warmed by the Mid-Atlantic Drift, Britain's climate is not only stable but warm as well. However, when the sea is not warmed, Britain's climate suddenly changes to one that is still stable but very cold.

The 'freak' events that release the amount of fresh water necessary to interrupt the Mid-Atlantic Drift occur very infrequently from a human perspective but, over geological time, they have taken place several times in the past and caused rapid changes in temperatures – as much as ten degrees Centigrade in 100 years. It is likely that such events, in connection with variations in the Earth's orbit, caused cold periods and ice ages, separated by warmer interglacial periods, such as we are in today. The last ice age was known as the Dimlington Stadial, which lasted for about 10,000 years, and, together with a minor readvancement of the ice, the Loch Lomond Stadial, this period is referred to as the Ice Age. During the Middle Ages, between AD 1450 and AD 1850, there was a cooling of the climate known as the Little Ice Age. It peaked around 1680 when 'Frost

Fairs' were held in London on the frozen Thames. This was caused by a reduction in the amount of water convected in the Mid-Atlantic Drift due to the presence of a largish amount of fresh water in the North Atlantic, which, although not large enough to stop the convection current altogether, did weaken it sufficiently to cool Britain's climate severely.

The Ice Age glaciers had a major impact on the landscape, especially in the Lake District (see Section 4). Not only was the landscape affected by glaciation but freeze-thaw weathering around the time of the Ice Age shattered rock formations and huge lakes were formed where the ice blocked the outflow of glacial meltwaters. These changed river courses as the meltwaters carved out new valleys, such as Newton Dale in the North Yorkshire Moors (Section 1). Meanwhile, the courses of the Derwent and Leven were changed in the Lake District as an effect of glacial deposits (see Section 4).

It is rather ironic that due to the effects of global warming, Britain may enter another cold period in the very near future. One of the effects of global warming will be an increase in rainfall over the North Atlantic. This, coupled with the melting of the Arctic ice sheets, will introduce a huge amount of fresh water into the North Atlantic. Scientists disagree as to whether this will actually reach the critical quantity necessary to interrupt the Mid-Atlantic Drift but it is generally agreed that it will come very close.

The Geological Timescale

When geologists talk about time, what they are referring to is time in relation to a geological scale spanning 3,750 million years of the Earth's history. As such, what they may consider to be a short period of time may be 10,000 years and quite easily more.

Names are given to separate periods in the Earth's history, some of which have easily recognisable meanings, for example Carboniferous means coal-forming (coal is a form of carbon), and Devonian refers to the time when the main rock system of Devon was deposited. Figure 4 shows the geological time scale, as well as giving an overview of the formation of the hill landscapes of northern England and the Isle of Man.

Era	Period		Age (millions of years)	Overview of the formation of the hills of northern England and the Isle of Man
Tertiary (Alpine orogeny)	Quaternary	Holocene	0	The Ice Age alters the landscape into that seen today.
		Pleistocene	2	
	Neocene	Pliocene	7	
		Miocene	24	
	Palaeogene	Oligocene	38	The formation of the Atlantic and subsidence of the North Sea Basin sets the strata of the British rocks to dip in a south-easterly direction.
		Eocene	54	
		Palaeocene	65	
Mesozoic	Cretaceous		146	Sandstones, marls and chalk deposited to form the Yorkshire Wolds.
	Jurassic		208	A sequence of limestones, sandstones and clays deposited to form the North York Moors.
	Triassic		245	Sandstones deposited over the other sediments. Today, these can be seen on the Cumbrian coast, the Isle of Man and in the Eden valley. Further folding occurs in the Lake District.
(Amorican orogeny) (Caledonian orogeny) Palaeozoic	Permian		290	
	Carboniferous		363	Limestones and the deltaic sediments of the Yoredale Beds, Millstone Grit Facies and Coal Measures are deposited. Mountain-building crumples the crust.
	Devonian		409	Granite intrusions and faulting and folding occur due to the Caledonian earth movements, forming the raised blocks beneath the Pennines.
	Silurian		439	Basement rocks of northern England deposited in a mountain chain that linked the Isle of Man and north-east England. Volcanic activity occurred in the Lake District during the Ordovician period.
	Ordovician		510	
	Cambrian		544	
	Precambrian		544 to 3750	

Figure 4: The geological timescale and an overview of the formation of the landscape of northern England and the Isle of Man.

Section 1 – The Yorkshire Wolds and North York Moors

Rivers Humber, Ouse, Swale and Wiske to Great Smeaton. Overland to the River Tees at Stockburn and then that river to the coast at Redcar. The coastline from there to the mouth of the Humber.

NAME	HEIGHT	IN SECTION	IN ENGLAND	IN BRITAIN
Urra Moor	454m/1490ft	01 of 04	92 of 184	1093J of 1552
Cringle Moor	435m/1427ft	02 of 04	97 of 184	1133J of 1552
Gisborough Moor	329m/1078ft	03 of 04	125 of 184	1328 of 1552
Bishop Wilton Wold	246m/ 807ft	04 of 04	163 of 184	1470 of 1552

The North York Moors are a landscape of heather uplands and sandstone crags. In many ways, both in terms of scenery and geology, they are not very different from the Pennines. Their rock structures and land use are similar, although the North York Moors do not attain anything like the lofty heights of the Pennines. Further to the south, the expanse of the Yorkshire Wolds is very reminiscent of southern England. This is a landscape of arable land, deeply incised by gorge-like valleys, with a prominent east-facing escarpment. The Wolds are, in fact, the most northerly of the chalklands.

The first event that had a bearing on the formation of the modern landscape occurred at the end of the Carboniferous period. This is the time when Africa and Asia collided with Europe and the Americas to create one supercontinent – Pangaea. This collision pushed up fold mountain ranges along the collision boundary and these uplands exist today as the Appalachians in North America, the Pyrenees on the French–Spanish border and the Ural Mountains in Russia. These movements had effects further north as well. Apart from a general uplift, an important upland was formed where Market Weighton is today. Known as the Market Weighton Axis, this structure was to have a major impact on the modern-day landscape.

Few changes occurred in the harsh deserts of the Permian and Triassic

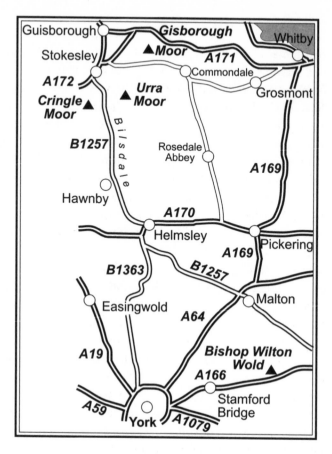

periods but, by the beginning of the Jurassic, much of Britain was once again submerged. The oldest rocks of the Jurassic are known as the Lias. These consist of a sequence of clays, shales and limestones deposited in changing ocean conditions. Colonies of bacteria and algae worked to produce iron deposits that have made many Jurassic limestones ferruginous, such as the Cleveland Ironstones. Formed in the deep ocean, with little oxygen to decompose organic matter, many of the Lias shales are highly bituminous, giving them a black coal-like appearance.

Due to the raised upland of the Market Weighton Axis, the Lias thins to a very narrow and insignificant band. So high was this upland that no further Jurassic sediments would be deposited upon it. It was the position of this axis, therefore, that defined the southern margin of the North York Moors, where the Jurassic strata end.

The Jurassic period also saw an uplift of the North Sea Basin to produce an uplifted block of land. This caused the north-east of England to be situated on river estuaries that discharged into a shallow sea to the south. It was in this sea that the limestones of the Cotswolds were deposited. Meanwhile, in Yorkshire, shifting delta channels led to a changing environment. At some points, thin limestones were deposited in clear waters, shales formed from the compaction of mudflats, coarse sandstones formed on beaches and occasional swamps formed. Organic matter from these swamps was compacted into thin coal seams or thin bands of jet. This cyclical sequence of rocks, known as the Estuarine Series, is distinctly similar to the Yoredale Beds of the Pennines (see Section 2), except that the Yoredales were formed in a similar environment a hundred million years earlier.

As the delta became more firmly established, a tough sandstone was deposited and, today, this forms the moorlands, with the Estuarine Series being exposed, slightly below the level of the highest summits, on the valley sides. Here, the bands of broken shales, looking not dissimilar to mine spoil, can form quite striking level bands along the hillsides, as seen on Cringle Moor. The Jurassic finished with a thick sequence of marine clays that are present all the way from the south coast to the Market Weighton Axis. As no deposition occurred on the axis, the clays are absent here, only to appear further north and form the wet Vale of Pickering.

At the start of the Cretaceous, the Market Weighton Axis became significant once again. Throughout almost all of the Lower Cretaceous, the Yorkshire Basin, north of the axis, was cut off and the deposition of clays continued until the ocean regressed over the axis and the Red Chalk – common further south – was deposited. The Red Chalk consists of an alternating sequence of coccolithic limestones (see below) and marls, which are coloured red by limonite. Further subsidence of the land surface allowed this sea to deepen and spread over the whole of Britain. This shallow clear sea was home to a large population of small scaly creatures called coccolithophores – a tiny plankton. Their corpses collected on the sea floor and their scales, coccoliths, compacted to form a very pure limestone sequence; this is the chalk itself. Although generally soft and very porous, unlike the Carboniferous Mountain Limestones of the Yorkshire Dales (Section 2), for example, the chalk does contain some harder beds in amongst the soft sheets of calcium carbonate. At the same time, sponges were also living in the ocean and their skeletons formed a glass-like stone called flints. As erosive forces slowly began to eat away at the chalk, the flints were left behind on the surface since the water sank into the porous chalk rather than running off and carrying the flints with it.

At this time, the Atlantic ocean was about to form and this was preceded by a doming of western Britain, causing a north-west to south-east dip and forcing the retreat of the shallow chalk-depositing sea that was covering Britain. The chalk was then eroded from much of the resulting highlands of western and northern Britain, being confined only to the southern and eastern fringes of England.

One of the anomalies of chalk landscapes is the dry valleys. These formed in the tundra conditions that existed around the time of the Ice Age. Chalk is a very porous rock and this allows it to soak up rainwater like a giant sponge, holding it in aquifers and pores in the rock. This effect makes the Wolds very dry, with springs emerging lower in the summer and somewhat higher in winter forming seasonal streams called winterbournes. However, at the time of the Ice Age, the chalk 'sponge' became frozen solid, which enabled rainwater to carve valleys into its plateau-like surface that today are dry for much of their length with some supporting winterbournes in their middle and lower reaches. The ability of chalk to soak up rainwater is the main reason why such a soft rock has been able largely to escape water erosion and form such an elevated upland.

Hence, today, the Jurassic rocks are mainly confined in Yorkshire to the area north of the Market Weighton Axis, over which the chalk extends. The Wolds are especially prominent from the Vale of York because there is no intermediate ridge formed from the tough Jurassic rocks due to the presence of the Market Weighton Axis. These two ranges of hills support very different scenery that ranges from the more lowland, agricultural landscape of the wide open Wolds to the rough uplands of the Moors, with the thick Jurassic clays forming a wide vale in between. It is by virtue of their position, surrounded by lowlands and coastlines, that the North York Moors are such a pronounced and distinctive upland area.

Access

The Wolds are crossed by a number of roads between York and the east coast, with the A166 York to Bridlington road passing over the summit of Bishop Wilton Wold. The A64 road, which connects York with the A1, cuts a line to the north of the Wolds by following the clay vale to Scarborough. The Moors can be accessed from the A1 by the A168 road to Thirsk, from where the A170 road climbs steeply over Sutton Bank before continuing past Bilsdale to Helmsley, Pickering and Scarborough. The B1257 runs up Bilsdale before climbing over a pass to reach Stokesley, to the north of the Moors. The A171 road follows the eastern and northern edge of the Moors from Scarborough, through Whitby and Guisborough to Middlesbrough. The western side of the Moors are served from the A19 Thirsk to Middlesbrough road. There are rail services from York to Scarborough and from Middlesbrough to Whitby through Esk Dale. A connecting steam railway runs from the station at Grosmont through Newton Dale to Pickering.

Accommodation

The Wolds form a largely unpopulated stretch of land. Most visitors travel to the area as part of a holiday in York or on the east coast, in towns such as Bridlington and Scarborough. The North York Moors are well established as a popular tourist destination. There is plentiful accommodation within the villages inside the National Park and in towns around the edge, such as Pickering, Helmsley and Whitby. Towns, such as Pickering and Scarborough, on the southern edge of the Moors would also provide a convenient base to explore the Wolds as well. There are youth hostels at York, Beverley, Helmsley, Osmotherley, Lockton, Scarborough, Boggle Hole and Whitby.

Urra Moor and Cringle Moor

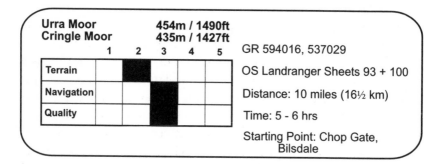

		1	2	3	4	5
Urra Moor	454m / 1490ft					
Cringle Moor	435m / 1427ft					
Terrain			■			
Navigation				■		
Quality				■		

GR 594016, 537029

OS Landranger Sheets 93 + 100

Distance: 10 miles (16½ km)

Time: 5 - 6 hrs

Starting Point: Chop Gate, Bilsdale

Sitting on the edge of the northern scarp, these two points are the highest in the North York Moors. Chop Gate on the dip slope makes a good starting point from which both summits may be conveniently linked in a

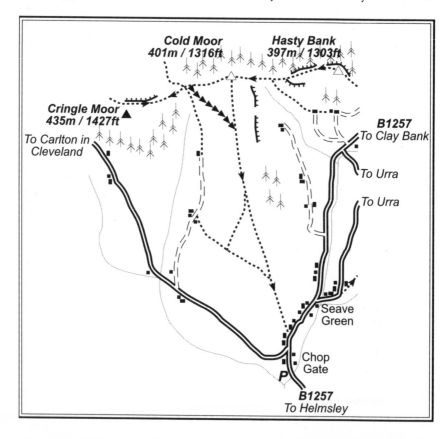

superb ridge walk, best done in August when the heather, which covers most of this area, is in full bloom.

At Chop Gate there is a free car park with toilets just to the south of the village but the best place is a lay-by in the village, just above the Carlton turn, where there is parking for a few cars. From the car park, walk up past the school to the lay-by and then onwards until there is a turn on the right, signposted 'St Hilda's Church'. Walk down it, over the river and then up the hill until the road turns sharply to the left. Just before this turn, a bridleway leaves the road on the right and curves around the front of Bilsdale Hall. After continuing through a field, it reaches the uncultivated hillside and continues upwards to a stile and an earthwork. The true path

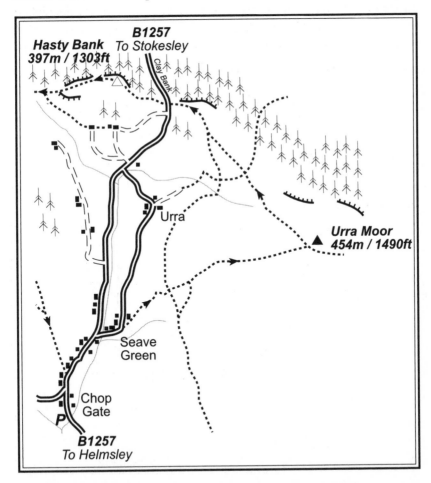

curves to the left and then back right again up a sunken roadway but the slope straight ahead provides an equally good alternative although rather less interesting. A little further onwards, a track from the right curves around to the left and from here on forms the route. Straight and hard, it continues over fairly flat ground to reach another track running from left to right, at which point, the trig point and tumulus on Urra Moor can be seen; a path to them leaves the track a short distance to the right.

Return to the track and turn right and follow it, without any deviation, over a long shoulder and then steeply down to the road at Clay Bank Top. The path, which is both the Coast to Coast and Cleveland Way, crosses straight over the road and climbs up some steps to the left of a conifer plantation. At its top, it continues up the hill after crossing a stile on the left. However, this is not Cringle Moor and after an interesting walk above its northern Millstone Grit crags, a steep descent follows to a col. However, the start of this descent is through some of these crags, the path leading down a gully on the right and around the foot of a pair of pinnacles below. After leading uneventfully over the col, it climbs steeply once more up to the cairn on the northern end of Cold Moor before once again dropping sharply to the next col. Here, it follows a wall around to the right and through a gate before once more resuming progression to the left. What follows is an even steeper hill than the previous two but it does lead finally up to the summit plateau of Cringle Moor. Again the path runs along the edge of its northern crags but, soon, a faint path runs off to the left to the large summit cairn, adrift in a sea of heather.

The route back to Chop Gate begins by retracing the ascent route back down the hill to the final col and then climbing about one-third of the way back up the opposite hillside to a gate. Just above it, a faint path leads to the right which, although completely on grass, is quite visible. Up the hillside to the left, three sunken lanes will be seen ascending obliquely across it; the path ascends to the foot of the third and then climbs up it. At the top of the small scarp, its line, marked by rushes in the heather, leads slightly back left before climbing the next hillside in similar style; it is normally quite dry throughout. The ridge of Cold Moor is now reached at a cairn and the track running along the ridge should be followed to the right, across a col and then up onto the next hilltop. After passing a group of tumuli, the track forks; take the left fork which begins to descend down to and then along the right of a conifer wood before running along to the right above the inbye wall as far as a gate giving access to a sunken lane. This, although rather wet in its upper stages, should be followed, ignoring footpaths on both the left and right, all the way down to the village, where it joins the Carlton road. A few yards along it to the left is the main road along which the lay-by is a few yards to the left and the car park a short distance down the hill to the right.

Gisborough Moor

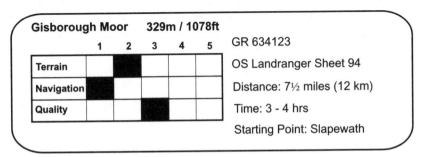

Gisborough Moor		329m / 1078ft			
	1	2	3	4	5
Terrain		■			
Navigation	■				
Quality			■		

GR 634123

OS Landranger Sheet 94

Distance: 7½ miles (12 km)

Time: 3 - 4 hrs

Starting Point: Slapewath

To the north of Esk Dale, there is a stretch of much less visited moorland. Gisborough Moor is the highest point of this block of land, much of which is strictly private. As a result of the current restrictions, an up-and-back route is recommended from Slapewath although if transport can be arranged it is possible to continue to Commondale.

A short distance to the east of Guisborough, just beyond the small village of Slapewath, there is a small lay-by and picnic site on the opposite side of the main road which is unsignposted and somewhat deserted. Indeed, it may be preferable to park in the large car park of the Fox and Hounds in the village although it may be advisable to ask first. Leave the village by returning to the main road at the eastern end of the loop before crossing it and turning off to the right beyond the bus stop into the picnic site/car park. At the far end of it, a small tarmac lane, running parallel to the main road, continues before a track running back up the slope to the right meets it. Turn up this, the Cleveland Way, before turning into a smaller path running along the hillside on the right. This is still the Cleveland Way and is now excellently signposted; the path crosses over

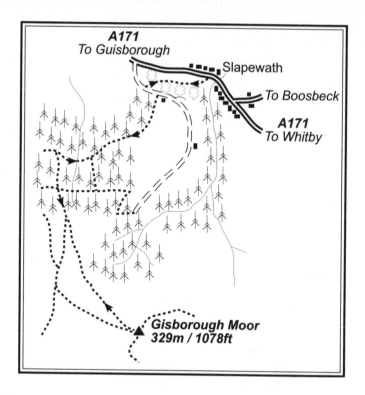

several motorbike scrambling tracks running up the hillside (it is an official site) before eventually joining a concrete farm road running up the hill. Turn left and follow it to the top of the trees, at which point the Cleveland Way and described route take off to the right.

Before too long, it enters the forestry plantations and then runs along the forest roads, which are more like green lanes than typical forest roads. By continuing along the signposted route of the Cleveland Way, a small stream is crossed after about a mile from entering the plantation; the bridge, which is easily missed, is marked by a wooden rail on the right. Soon after this point, a crosstracks is reached (note that there are earlier paths and tracks on both sides); here, turn left and after crossing another track and passing a pond on the left, the open moor is reached. The path continues to a cairn on the skyline from where the trig point (not the summit) can be seen away to the right. However, the true summit is still a distance away and is reached by following the path onwards which, if an indistinct variation along the ridge is avoided, drops down slightly into the head of a small valley on the left. It soon climbs out again onto the top of the ridge and meets a large track running from right to left; the summit is the tumulus, a short distance half right through the heather (no path), which has a small stone shelter.

At this point, unless transport can be arranged to continue to Commondale in the Esk Valley, it is best to return by the route of ascent. It used to be possible to descend to a small reservoir from a little further along the ridge to the east but this is marked strictly private and the recent construction of new shooting butts would appear to underline this. Without this option, a circular route is impossible and that is equally true in an approach from the Esk Valley, as any circle from there would involve appreciable sections of road walking.

Bishop Wilton Wold

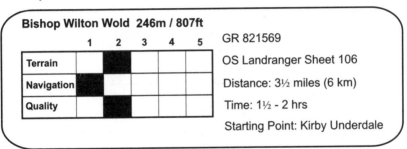

Bishop Wilton Wold 246m / 807ft

	1	2	3	4	5
Terrain		■			
Navigation	■				
Quality		■			

GR 821569

OS Landranger Sheet 106

Distance: 3½ miles (6 km)

Time: 1½ - 2 hrs

Starting Point: Kirby Underdale

For two millennia, travellers have passed over the summit of Bishop Wilton Wold. The summit, the highest point of the Yorkshire Wolds, lies almost at the intersection of two Roman roads, one of which has been superseded by the modern highway of the A166 York to Bridlington road. This broad band of tarmac, which curves over the Wolds from the top of Garrowby Hill, passes little more than ten yards from the summit and makes this by far the easiest hill summit to visit in Britain. However, a short ascent from Kirby Underdale leads to the top, although a marked absence of footpaths and bridleways means that a circular walk is not possible without making the return on the tarmac.

It is possible to park in Kirby Underdale either on the verges by the church or in the middle of the village by the shop and post office. The route begins by following a track leading to the north where the road makes a sharp right-angled turn in the village close to the shop. This track

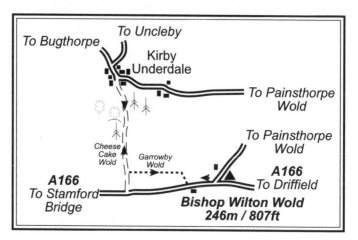

leads out of the village and into the fields behind. It aims more or less straight ahead through these, bending slightly right when it climbs steeply up towards Megdale Brow. During this section of the walk, there are good views to the right into Megdale and South Wold Dale.

Once at the top of the hill, the track, now fringed with a line of trees on the right, gradually climbs across the attractively named Cheese Cake Wold. Before too long, a track swings in from the right when the trees come to an end and the view to the right across the Vale of York appears. This is a patchwork of fields, woodlands and scattered towns and villages that stretches as far as the distant hills of the Yorkshire Dales (Section 2) and the South Pennines (Vol 2, Section 5). The giant 'golf balls' of the listening-station on Menwith Hill can be seen on the slopes on the far side of the lowlands.

Before the road is reached, a field path is signposted on the left. This climbs along the right-hand edge of the wide field ahead across the gently rising slopes of Garrowby Wold. At the far side of the field, the path moves slightly to the left and enters the small copse ahead. In this, as waymarked, it turns to the right and then proceeds along a slightly overgrown and sunken lane between two fields to reach the road almost opposite the farm of Cot Nab.

The summit is not far along the main road to the left, just beyond a road junction. The trig point lies inside the private ground surrounding the covered reservoirs on the hilltop, although the very highest point is undoubtedly on the top of one of the reservoirs. The view from the summit is very limited by the surrounding vegetation and plateau-like wolds. The descent should be made by the same route, with a pleasant view across the Vale of York being ahead throughout the walk across Garrowby Wold.

Section 2 – The Yorkshire Dales and North Pennines

Rivers Ouse, Swale and Wiske from Goole to Great Smeaton. Overland to the River Tees at Stockburn and then that river to the coast at Redcar. The coastline from there to Tynemouth and then the River Tyne, River South Tyne and Tipalt Burn to Holmhead. Hadrian's Wall from there to Gilsland and the River Irthing to the River Eden. Rivers Eden, Eamont and Lowther to Shap and the River Lune to Kirkby Lonsdale. The A65 from there to Skipton and the River Aire to Goole.

NAME	HEIGHT	IN SECTION	IN ENGLAND	IN BRITAIN
Calf Top	609m/1999ft	22 of 30	53 of 184	752 of 1552
Potts Moor	609m/1998ft	23 of 30	54J of 184	753J of 1552
Aye Gill Pike	556m/1825ft	24 of 30	64 of 184	855 of 1552
Hoove	554m/1816ft	25 of 30	65 of 184	863 of 1552
Thorpe Fell Top	506m/1660ft	26 of 30	79 of 184	979 of 1552
Kisdon	499m/1637ft	27 of 30	82 of 184	986 of 1552
Dufton Pike	481m/1578ft	28 of 30	87 of 184	1026J of 1552
Ilkley Moor	402m/1320ft	29 of 30	103 of 184	1198 of 1552
Sharp Haw	357m/1171ft	30 of 30	112 of 184	1283 of 1552

There are 21 summits above 2,000ft that are described in *England's Highest Peaks.*

The Yorkshire Dales is probably the most visited region of the Pennines. Its special landscape, packed with interesting valleys and features, due in no small part to the limestone rock, stands in contrast to the rest of the Pennines, whose moorlands are generally of less interest to tourists. However, from Derbyshire (Vol 2, Section 4) to the Scottish border (Section 3), the Pennines form a large tract of fine walking country. In this large section covering the Pennine range between Settle and the Tyne Gap, the lower summits nestle around their higher neighbours and mimic them in every way and invite exploration.

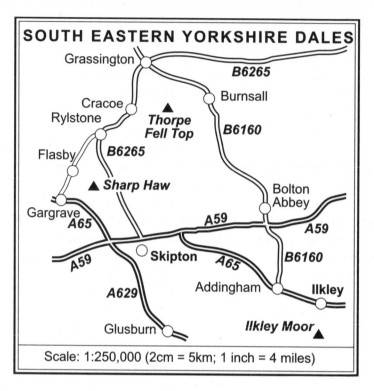

SOUTH EASTERN YORKSHIRE DALES

Scale: 1:250,000 (2cm = 5km; 1 inch = 4 miles)

The rocks that form this region are primarily Carboniferous in age, although the older rocks do, where exposed, have a profound effect on the landscape. These older Ordovician and Silurian sediments are largely unseen within the upland itself but are shown on the southern edges – in Ribblesdale, from Horton-in-Ribblesdale to the Stainforth area, and in Crummackdale (Austwick). The join is shown quite clearly by the resurgences of Austwick Beck Head and, at Horton-in-Ribblesdale, Brants Gill Head and Douk Gill Head. Further to the west, at Ingleton, the rocks are exposed once more at the top tiers of its famous waterfalls and in the Doe Valley above. The oldest deposits are the Ingleton Group (lower Ordovician in age), which consists of greywacke (fine to coarse sandy particles cemented together by clay) and highly slanting slates. A small fault, specific to the Ingleton area, then thrust down a calcareous mudstone of the Coniston Limestone Group (see Section 4), formed in the late Ordovician period and eroded elsewhere before the Carboniferous rocks were deposited. The rocks formed in the late Ordovician and Silurian period are present in Ribblesdale and Crummackdale. All these pre-Carboniferous rocks were formed as part of a huge mountain system stretching from the north-east of England to the Isle of Man and sizeable exposures can be seen both on the Isle of Man and in the Lake District. In total, these rocks are about 2,500ft (760m) thick.

An intrusion of granite at depth then pushed up the Ordovician and Silurian deposits, with cracking at the edges, to form a block of elevated land, higher than the Craven Lowlands to the south. The southern boundary is marked by the Mid-Craven Fault and the western boundary by the Dent Fault. The block underlying the Yorkshire Dales is known as the Askrigg Block, named after the village in Wensleydale, whereas a separate block underlies the North Pennines, which is known as the Alston Block.

Due to the elevation of these land masses, they escaped the early deposition of the Lower Carboniferous period but as the warm, tropical sea encroached further, the blocks were submerged. As such, the shales and reef limestones of the Clitheroe region are absent here, deposition only beginning in the Arundian period or cycle three of the Dinantian (Lower Carboniferous) era. In total, there were six cycles of the Lower Carboniferous period with different rocks or beds being deposited in each. The Great Scar Limestones were deposited in cycles three, four and five, therefore, the mid to late part of the Dinantian era. The limestones of the south Yorkshire Dales are extremely pure, about 98 per cent calcium carbonate, which gives them a very white colour, which contrasts with the deeper yellow colour of the Jurassic limestones in places such as the Cotswolds. Although limestone is a fossiliferous rock, there are few fossils visible to the naked eye in the area. There are also bands of shale amongst the limestone that, although rarely seen on the surface, do give rise to the Aysgarth Falls in Wensleydale and can be seen in pothole shafts.

However, the land to the north was being uplifted and this brought sediments southwards to form a delta across northern England. The rocks deposited lie in the Yoredale Beds, named after Wensleydale ('Uredale'). The beds consist of a cyclical series of limestones, deposited in the shallow shelf sea; clastic sediments, which in turn can be broken down into fossiliferous shales, deposited under water as the delta encroached, unfossiliferous shales and siltstones, deposited on the delta slope, and flagstones and sandstones, deposited on the delta platform, and terrigenous sediments.

These form the highest part of each cyclothem and can in turn be

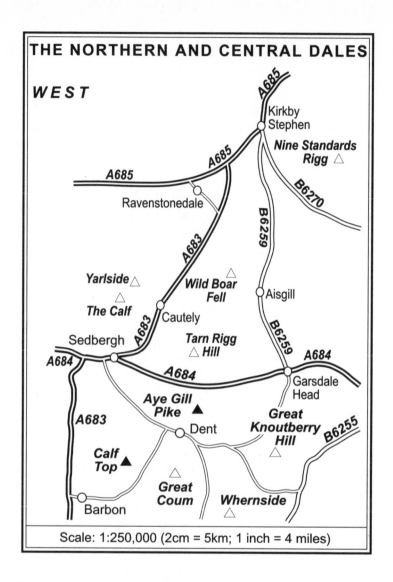

THE NORTHERN AND CENTRAL DALES

WEST

A685

Kirkby
Stephen

*Nine Standards
Rigg* △

A685

A685

B6270

Ravenstonedale

A683

B6259

Yarlside △
△
The Calf △

*Wild Boar
Fell* △

Aisgill

A683

Cautely

Sedbergh

A684

*Tarn Rigg
△ Hill*

B6259

A684

A684

Garsdale
Head

*Aye Gill
Pike* ▲

A683

Dent

*Great
Knoutberry
Hill*
△

B6255

*Calf
Top* ▲

△
*Great
Coum*

Whernside
△

Barbon

Scale: 1:250,000 (2cm = 5km; 1 inch = 4 miles)

subdivided into thin fireclay and overlying thin coal seams, both being deposited in the tropical swamps which existed on the delta top. These coal seams were mined, as witnessed by a large number of disused mine shafts or 'bell-pits' across the region. The Yoredale Beds are more extensive further to the north as deltaic conditions, spreading from the north, reached there first, whilst limestones of the Great Scar Group were still being deposited around Ingleborough.

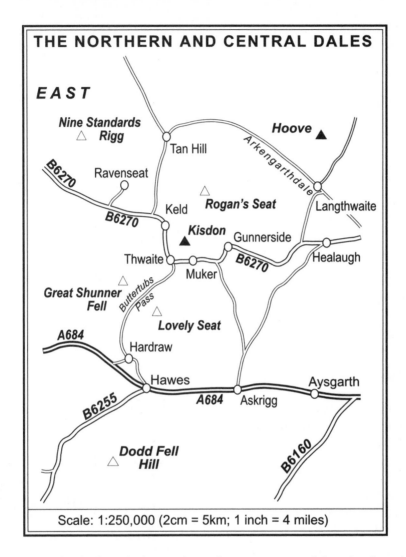

THE NORTHERN AND CENTRAL DALES

EAST

Nine Standards
△ Rigg

Tan Hill

Hoove ▲

Arkengarthdale

B6270

Ravenseat

Keld

Rogan's Seat

Langthwaite

B6270

Kisdon
▲

Gunnerside

Thwaite

Muker

B6270

Healaugh

Great Shunner
Fell

Buttertubs
Pass

Lovely Seat

A684

Hardraw

Hawes

Aysgarth

B6255

A684

Askrigg

Dodd Fell
△ Hill

B6160

Scale: 1:250,000 (2cm = 5km; 1 inch = 4 miles)

The individual cyclothems themselves were caused by the lateral movements of channels within the delta, causing erosion of sediments, as deposition would have stopped, or possibly sudden subsidence of the sea bed. Either of these would cause that area of the delta to be once more covered by a shallow sea, in which limestone could be deposited. As the delta again encroached, different conditions existed at different stages.

Shales would be deposited in the initial stages but, as the distributaries advanced, conditions would be suitable for the sandstones to be deposited

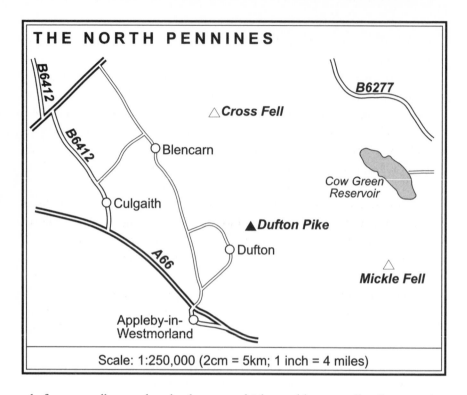

THE NORTH PENNINES

B6412

B6412

△ *Cross Fell*

B6277

○ Blencarn

Cow Green
Reservoir

○ Culgaith

▲ *Dufton Pike*

A66

○ Dufton

△
Mickle Fell

Appleby-in-
Westmorland ○

Scale: 1:250,000 (2cm = 5km; 1 inch = 4 miles)

before a sandbar enclosed a lagoon, which would eventually silt up and then become a swamp, resulting in the deposition of fireclays and coal seams. As the area once more subsided or as the delta channels moved laterally, the sea would invade once more and another cyclothem would begin. However, it should not be assumed that each layer in a particular cyclothem was built up in the same amount of time. Sandstones and siltstones would have built up relatively quickly in times of flood, whereas the deposition of limestone, which consists of the crushed remains of dead sea creatures, would have taken much longer.

In the Upper Carboniferous period, deltaic conditions became more constant and therefore the rocks become more regular. Firstly, rocks of the Millstone Grit Facies (grits, shales and sandstones) were deposited and above that the Coal Measures – sandstones with coal seams. In the south, many of these layers have been subsequently eroded but a protective coating of Millstone Grit still remains on the tops of the hills. Meanwhile, further north, the Millstone Grit is more extensive. However, although all the rocks were deposited by the end of the

Carboniferous period, the landscape at that time would have been very unfamiliar.

Apart from erosion, the subsidence of the North Sea Basin in Tertiary times pushed the western Pennines upwards, which led to a north-east dipping strata. This, apart from earlier deposition of rocks of the Yoredale Facies, also accounts for why the Great Scar Limestone, seen in Aysgarth Falls, is so very far down in the valley bottoms, appearing around 600ft (180m) and below, in direct contrast to the Great Scar Limestones of the Settle area, which attain heights of 1,450ft (440m).

This Tertiary uplift caused massive upheavals along the unstable southern boundary of the Askrigg Block as well as along the Dent Fault to the west. At the Dent Fault, the rocks to the west were uplifted to a level much higher than that of the Dales; however, subsequent erosion has removed the Carboniferous rocks from their summits (see also Section 8). As such, the rocks lying to the west of Ireby, Barbondale, Sedbergh and Ravenstonedale have a much older origin than the Carboniferous sediments deposited to the east. Hence, Calf Top and the Howgills are very different from the rest of the Dales.

At Bullpot Farm (GR 663814), the two series of rocks are thrown into a convenient juxtaposition. To the west of the farm lies Barbon Low Fell, a wet and boggy environment but by the farm itself there is a series of shake holes, potholes and swallow holes forming a part of the vast Aygill and Easegill Caverns, the largest cave system in Britain. The line of the fault can be clearly seen between Lower Easegill Kirk, where the subterranean waters of the Easegill and Leck Fell systems are forced into daylight, and Bullpot Farm. Here, on and to the east of the straight line between the Kirk and the farm, there are a series of limestone features that are not replicated on the western side; this line marks the fault. Again, by following the straight line into Barbondale, shake holes and potholes abound to its east, eventually all the way across the valley, but to the west there is nothing.

However, where there was an uplift along the Dent Fault, there was a massive down thrust along the Craven Faults to the south. The Mid Craven Fault is responsible for the formation of the fault scarps of Malham Cove and Gordale Scar and it is the oldest of the three Craven Faults. The coating of Upper Carboniferous rocks, Grassington Grits and Bowland Shales, which cover it, shows this. At Ingleton and Malham, erosion has exposed the pre-Carboniferous basement rocks above the line of faulting. These rocks are shown in Thornton Force (Twiss Valley, Ingleton) and in the existence of Malham Tarn, which would not otherwise exist upon a limestone upland. However, to the south of this at Swilla Glen (Twiss Valley) and Malham Cove/Gordale Scar (Malham), the limestones of the Great Scar group reappear.

This is due to the North Craven Fault, which runs parallel to the west bank of the River Twiss at the head of Swilla Glen, where it turns from north to north-west to the south of Pecca Quarry, and, at Malham, where the outflow from Malham Tarn sinks underground. In Wharfedale too it is present in Linton Falls and also in Ribblesdale at Catrigg Force. However, it is the South Craven Fault that finally buries the limestone. This follows roughly the line of the A65 and is prominent in features such as Giggleswick Scar, just to the west of Settle. Again, a massive down thrust occurred here and, at Ingleton, the line of the fault lies at the foot of Swilla Glen (River Twiss) and the southern edge of Storrs Common.

To the south of the fault lie the only remnants of the Upper Carboniferous Coal Measures which once overlay the Millstone Grit Facies over the whole of the area. Here, the same strata which exists on the summit of Ingleborough, 1,970ft (600m) higher, lies buried hundreds of feet underground. The fault is still unstable; the epicentre of a 1944 earth-tremor in Settle was found to lie on the South Craven Fault.

The Ice Age also changed the landscape, carving out many of the valleys seen today. The limestone scars along valley sides were also formed as a result of freeze-thaw weathering which was commonplace in the sub-arctic conditions surrounding the main period of glaciation. This is when rainwater collects in a crack and then freezes. As water freezes, it expands, which pushes the crack further apart until the rock shatters, ending up as scree and leaving a scar or small cliff face behind. However, as the glaciers retreated they left behind a coating of pebbles and soil, which is commonly known as boulder clay or glacial drift. In many valleys, this was deposited very thickly and completely covers the rock below.

Much of the characteristic Dales limestone scenery has been caused by erosion. Although limestone itself is a non-porous rock due to its crystalline character, vertical joints break it as well as horizontal planes. This means that vertical erosion can weather the rock into the clints and grikes of limestone pavements and that potholes can form but also that lateral erosion can form caves with their bases along the horizontal planes. Of course it is erosion that has removed the Upper Carboniferous rocks to expose the Great Scar Limestone below, from which the characteristic dry limestone walls can be constructed. The lime-rich soils give rise to verdant green pastures, even though the soil is quite dry, and the woodlands of ash and other lime-loving trees, particularly prevalent in Littondale and Wharfedale. However, in the valley bottom of Wharfedale, oak woods have developed on the heavier, more acidic soils relating to the older basement rocks above which the limestone has been completely worn away.

As the limestone layers in the Yoredale Beds are so thin, the potholes seen in abundance further south are largely absent to the north of Wensleydale, the exception, of course, being the Buttertubs and other shallow cave systems. What do exist, however, in both valleys, particularly in Wensleydale, are long scars and terraced slopes.

Due to the fact that the Yoredale limestones were deposited on a fairly level lateral plane, they maintain a very level course along valley sides and across the valleys as well. The terracing effect results from the difference in erosion rates between the harder shales, which protect the softer limestones below. There are cascades on valley sides as tributaries fall over the scars and small, wide waterfalls on the main valley rivers such as Aysgarth Falls (Wensleydale) and Catrake Force and Wain Wath Force (Swaledale).

The most famous waterfall of all is Hardraw Force near Hawes. Here, the water falls over the hard shale and forms a plunge pool. The limestone below the shale is then eroded, undercutting the shale, until it eventually collapses and the waterfall recedes. Most of the main tributaries have similar gorges headed by waterfalls at one or, in some cases, at several points along their length.

The area to the north of Swaledale has been extensively mined for lead, which occurs in veins, occupying fissures in the rock. These fissures occur in zones of weakness and such zones are found here but also near Alston, Grassington Moor, Hebden Gill and on Greenhow Hill near Pateley Bridge.

The lead veins were formed as a result of the same earth movements that formed the Alston and Askrigg Blocks. These uplands were formed due to a mass of molten granite that intruded into the Pennines as a result of the Caledonian earth movements, establishing the Pennine boundary faults. Boreholes in Weardale and Raydale have proved the existence of the granite below the Carboniferous sediments at a depth of 2,000ft (610m) and 1,650ft (500m) respectively.

As the granite cooled, it developed a network of joints and cracks through which solutions could flow. In the later stages of cooling, in the early Permian period, hot saline solutions, originating from a lower part of the granite that was still cooling, were forced, under pressure, through these joints and into cracks in the limestone (tension faults). In the limestone cracks, the pressure reduced and consequently the solution cooled, allowing many minerals contained in it to be deposited in veins. These minerals included galena (lead sulphide), fluorspar (calcium fluoride), barite (barium sulphate), dolomite (calcium magnesium carbonate), calcite (calcium carbonate), witherite (barium carbonate), pyromorphite (lead chloro-phosphate), quartz (silicon dioxide), pyrite (iron sulphide) and sphalerite (zinc sulphide), some formed by metasomatism – reaction of the solutions with limestone.

Certain areas, zones of weakness, possessed many tension faults and these zones became the principal mining areas. The most productive veins occur below the Grassington Grit (a rock of the Millstone Grit Facies) and around the Main Limestone (a limestone band in the Yoredale Beds), both of which acted as stratigraphic traps. These veins vary in size but are generally quite narrow (a few inches to a few feet), quite deep (hundreds of feet) and great distances in length (anywhere between a few hundred yards and a few miles). Other deposits, known as lenticles, occur between limestone beds as lateral precipitates.

The mines, mainly for lead extraction, began as small, opencast affairs, where gangs of men were leased a length of vein by the landowner; they would then quarry that vein on the surface. However, in the eighteenth century, shaft mining began as companies began operations. It was customary to sink a shaft on or close to the vein and then take off levels to the side at 60ft (20m) intervals. The mining took place on the roofs of these levels, the floor being gradually raised by wooden planking, which has now rotted and is treacherous. Adits that appear on the surface are either horizontal entrances to shafts or drainage channels to remove water from the sump or pool that existed at the bottom of the mine.

Another method of extracting lead was one that used water to create a hush. A turf dam was constructed on the moor and then the water released, tearing away the surface vegetation, rock and some lead ore. This process was repeated several times, creating massive ravines in the hillsides. Sometimes, hushes were combined with shaft mining – having removed the surface vegetation and rock, shafts were sunk in the hush to exploit the ore in the vein at greater depth. This is why it is very dangerous to walk in the bottom of a hush with which you are unfamiliar. Some of the best examples of hushes are those in Gunnerside Gill.

The lead ore that came out of the mine or hush was in the form of galena (lead sulphide) but mixed with other minerals (listed above) and rock; a profitable vein would contain over 5 per cent galena, a rich one over 10 per cent and some outstanding ones contained up to 25 per cent. The ore then had to be dressed before it could be smelted. The material would first be washed in a nearby stream to carry away the lighter material and then what was left was finally sorted by hand before the pieces of galena were broken up into a uniform size. They were finally crushed, originally using a heavy iron plate known as a bucker. Later, iron hammers and rollers were introduced, powered by water wheels that were fed by leats often from small reservoirs, such as those in Gunnerside Gill (Section 8). In the final stage, the crushed ore was allowed to settle out in water where, being heavier, it sank first before the other lighter waste material.

The final stage in the production process was the smelting of the dressed ore. This is a two-stage process. Firstly it is necessary to oxidise (burn) the lead ore thus:

Galena + oxygen $\longrightarrow$ lead oxide + sulphur dioxide

Following oxidation, more galena was added to reduce ('de-oxidise') the lead oxide:

Lead oxide + galena $\longrightarrow$ **lead** + sulphur dioxide

Zinc is obtained from its ore, sphalerite (zinc sulphide), in a similar way and iron ore was also mined in the Alston area and smelted at Stanhope, using locally quarried limestone as flux.

Lead smelting was originally done in small peat furnaces where the lead ran out from between the dross (waste) into a sumpter pot, from which it was poured into moulds. In the larger smelt mills, reverberatory furnaces were introduced which could cope with larger amounts of lead, as they were bigger and designed to be run continuously, fuelled by a coal or coke fire. In total, it could be expected to obtain 0.87 tonnes of lead from a tonne of galena. However, since an average vein contained only about 5 to 10 per cent galena, it was necessary to mine about 15 tonnes of rock to obtain just one tonne of lead. The large costs involved in mining this relatively low-grade ore and the large cost of smelting led ultimately to the demise of the industry. At its heyday in the early part of the nineteenth century, the Old Gang Smelt Mill in the Gunnerside Gill area of Swaledale (Section 8) produced over 2,000 tonnes of lead each year but by 1880 the industry had all but collapsed due to competition from cheaper Spanish imports.

Today, the best mining remains are to be found in the valleys to the north of Swaledale, such as Gunnerside Gill. However, much has been restored at Nenthead near Alston where there is a visitor centre and the old water-wheel has been restored at Killhope (Weardale).

An interesting feature of the North Pennines is the height to which land is enclosed. This surprisingly is a by-product of mining. Mine owners were obliged to provide their workers with farmsteads so all available land was enclosed and used to grow grass for grazing and hay production, grass being the only crop which could be grown easily at this altitude.

Access

The south of the area is easily accessed from the east via Skipton (A59 from York; A650 and A629 from Bradford) and the Lake District along the A65. From the south, leave the M6 at junction 31 and follow the A59 through Clitheroe, turning up to Settle on the A682 at Gisburn. Hawes is best reached from the A1 along the A684 from Leeming Bar and from junction 37 of the M6 along the A684 through Sedbergh. Further north, the B6270 runs between Richmond (reachable from either Scotch Corner or Catterick on the A1) and Kirkby Stephen along the length of Swaledale, although it is narrow and bendy in places. Buttertubs Pass links Hawes and Thwaite (Swaledale).

Dufton Pike can easily be reached from the A66 road along the Eden valley.

There are also good rail connections; there are stations at Skipton, Gargrave (about 10 miles south of Malham), Giggleswick, Clapham and Bentham (about 5 miles south of Ingleton) on the Leeds to Lancaster and Morecambe line and on the Settle to Carlisle line at Settle, Horton in Ribblesdale, Ribblehead, Dent (about 8 miles from the village), Garsdale (about 7 miles from Hawes but there is a bus service), Kirkby Stephen and Appleby-in-Westmorland – trains depart Carlisle and Leeds. At the time of writing, both lines have a Monday to Sunday service. A Sunday special between Preston (sometimes Blackpool North) and Carlisle runs along the Settle–Carlisle route from Hellifield northwards and then returns. It is possible to connect with this service from Manchester Victoria by changing at Clitheroe. There are also train services to Ilkley from Leeds and Bradford.

Accommodation

Towns such as Hawes, Settle, Ingleton and Skipton all offer a wide variety of accommodation as do many of the villages such as Dent and Kettlewell. As the section is so large, there is no one central place to stay. In Sedbergh the accommodation is more limited than that in Hawes but, as well as the town centre establishments, there are a few out of the town along the Garsdale (Hawes) road. Apart from Hawes, there are many bed and breakfast establishments in Askrigg and Aysgarth. In Swaledale, options are a little more limited in the upper valley but there is plenty of accommodation in Reeth and Richmond and 'over the top' in Kirkby Stephen. The Skipton, Sedbergh and Swaledale areas would all be good bases for the hills of the Yorkshire Dales.

In the North Pennines, if Dufton Pike were the sole objective then the Appleby area would be recommended. However, Dufton Pike can also be reached from the eastern side of the Lake District (Section 4). If you also plan to tackle some of the higher peaks of the North Pennines then the Alston area would be a better base, with the village of Garrigill perhaps being in the most convenient situation of all.

There are youth hostels at Kettlewell, Linton, Malham, Stainforth, Ingleton, Upper Dentdale, Hawes, Aysgarth, Kirkby Stephen, Keld, Grinton (near Reeth), Ninebanks (West Allendale), Alston, Langdon Beck, Dufton and Carlisle.

Calf Top

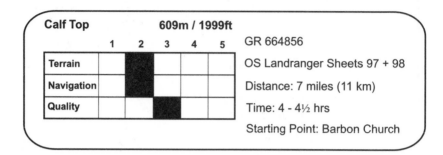

Calf Top	609m / 1999ft					
	1	**2**	**3**	**4**	**5**	GR 664856
Terrain		■				OS Landranger Sheets 97 + 98
Navigation		■				Distance: 7 miles (11 km)
Quality			■			Time: 4 - 4½ hrs
						Starting Point: Barbon Church

Calf Top is certainly one of the more major hills of the Yorkshire Dales, despite lying on the area's western limb and bounding the eastern side of the Lune valley between Sedbergh and Kirkby Lonsdale. It separates this valley from the steep-sided tributary of Barbondale, which well defines the eastern slopes of this hill. Its ridge forms a pronounced horseshoe shape, although it is from the Barbon end that the ascent is best made.

Without connecting transport, the ridge walk would be of little interest to many people as there are few field paths to relieve the trudge back down the valley on tarmac. Thus, the route described here is the up-and-back ascent from Bardon, although you may certainly like to consider extending the walk further along the ridge if you have a willing driver! The best place to park in Barbon is on the Dent road by the village church, although if this is not possible there is a large lay-by where the Dent road meets the A683 just west of the village.

The route begins by following the entrance road to Barbon Manor, which runs north from the road by the eastern end of the churchyard. This road crosses the Barbon Beck on a stone, arched bridge and then ascends slightly before swinging right in the park on the far side. It is on this bend that our route leaves the road on the left and heads pretty much straight on over the park, aiming for the right-hand side of a coniferous plantation ahead. There is no path on the ground but, once at the wood corner, the route then follows the top of the wood past various wetter areas until the far side of the parkland is reached.

Here, just above the wood, a rusty gate gives access into the agricultural field beyond above the farm of Eskholme. Our route avoids the farm, though, and swings half right aiming for three trees and a gate in the wall

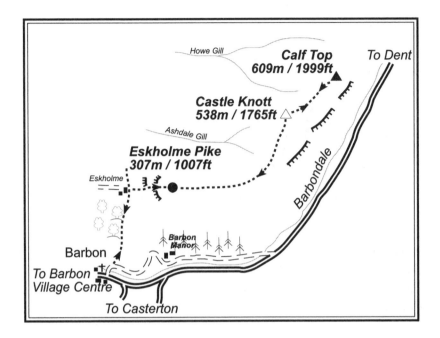

at the top of the field, which gives access out onto the open hillside. For the first stage of the ascent – as far as the summit of Eskholme Pike – there is no path. Basically just aim straight up the hillside, ignoring any initial grassy tracks that would appear to lead away to the left. The hillside is surprisingly craggy and there are many stones in amongst the grass. However, after a steep ascent, the tall pillar cairn on the shoulder of Eskholme Pike is soon reached and this forms perhaps the finest viewpoint for the Lune valley on the whole walk.

From here onwards, a fairly distinct path on grass leads onwards and up the ridge over a first bump to a second bearing a squat cairn. A little further on, the ridge begins to swing to the left and continues upwards towards the next summit – Castle Knott. This summit is again marked by a cairn and Barbondale now lies down to the right and there are good views into it on occasions, especially from the vicinity of this summit.

The path leads on and now downwards to cross the low point in the ridge at the head of the valley of the Millhouse Gill on the left. After a fairly dull trudge over this broad col, the path again starts to rise but now quite steeply and soon with the white *Nardus* grass underfoot. After a stiff climb the ridge starts to level and a wall corner is reached, where the wall turns up the ridge, having climbed up from Barbondale on the right. This can then be followed gently upwards to reach the trig point on the summit.

The summit supports a reasonably pleasant view, in which the Howgills, Aye Gill Pike on the other side of Dentdale and the sprawling mass of Great Coum on the other side of Barbondale are certainly the most prominent features. The descent is by the same route, although there are a few points worth bearing in mind. Firstly, the route swings half left at the wall corner just below the summit and, more importantly, you must climb back over Castle Knott. It is tempting to turn right from the first col and follow that ridge down but this is not the ridge leading to Barbon, so the summit of Castle Knott cannot be avoided.

Potts Moor

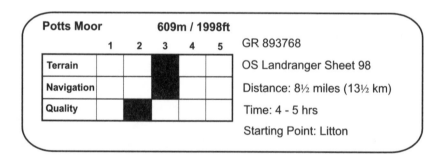

Potts Moor						609m / 1998ft
	1	2	3	4	5	GR 893768
Terrain			■			OS Landranger Sheet 98
Navigation			■			Distance: 8½ miles (13½ km)
Quality		■				Time: 4 - 5 hrs
						Starting Point: Litton

Birks Fell is the generic name given to the tract of high ground that separates Upper Wharfedale and Littondale. Depending upon which map is examined, its highest summit, Potts Moor, may or may not be just above 2,000ft (610m) but it is included here as well as in *England's Highest Peaks*.

Potts Moor is also referred to as Horse Head Moor, which is actually another lower summit of Birks Fell a little further to the north-east, but marked much more prominently on Ordnance Survey maps. It is quite possible to climb to the summit from either Wharfedale or Littondale but the Littondale approach is described here because it is the shorter and there are no particular scenic merits to either route.

Park on the road in the vicinity of the Queen's Arms at Litton on the

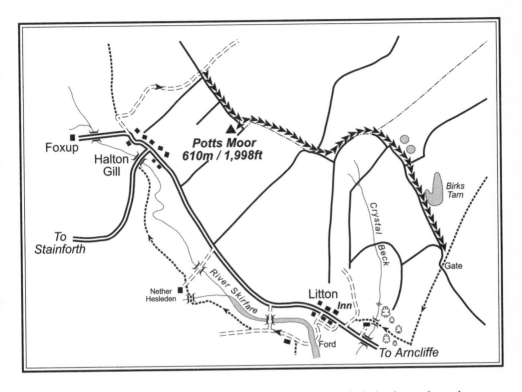

southern edge of the village. A track leaves the road slightly above the pub and this leads down through fields, turning through a right angle to meet another track coming down from the village. A left turn at this junction leads down to the river and then across the ford, which is normally dry in the summer. Turn right once over the ford and follow a track past some farm buildings, ignoring a path signposted to Arncliffe, which runs across the fields.

The track continues to run along above some conifers, before dropping down to the river at a bridge (which can be reached from Litton up the public road on the other side of the valley should the river be too full to cross at the ford). Do not cross the bridge but follow the track, which gently ascends the left-hand slope. Soon a path (signposted) runs to the right across the field and continues all the way to the house at Nether Haledon, which is reached over a bridge and through a gate.

This gate gives access to the foot of the garden in which a right turn should be made before immediately leaving through another gate at a higher level and onto the farm's access road. On the left, a sign marks the onward route but the authorities have overlooked providing a stile!

Luckily, the fence can be got over to cross a small paddock, two stiles at the other side of which give access into a larger field. A succession of ladder stiles, gates etc. and ruined barns now follows along the signposted route to the bridge at Halton Gill. Note, however, the field system on the hill above the second field and the signs of a settlement in the field itself (the circular patches in which nettles grow).

Turn right at the bridge at Halton Gill and walk up the road as far as the village green, a left turn at which leads to the edge of the village on the Foxup road. Turn right through a gate just after the last habitation and follow the track up the hill. Ignore a signposted path on the left to Beckermonds and continue up to the gate in the summit wall. Behind the wall, turn right and walk along a small path through a profusion of clints and other small lumps. When the second wall runs downhill to the right and progress ahead is barred by a fence, the summit is close at hand. Climb the fence and then climb the wall corner to reach the elevated peaty summit with no cairn or other landmark to show its significance.

Cross back over the wall corner and fence and then follow the fence, initially to the north-east, but then to the south-east as it turns through a right angle. What lies ahead now is not inviting; a succession of peat gullies and other wet places beckon which are very reminiscent in some ways of the route to the true summit of Kinder Scout (Section 3). Negotiating the difficulties, continue on until a wall bars further progress. A gate (of sorts) is in the corner and once through it, continue following the wall, which turns up to the left and shortly becomes a fence. Another fence takes off half left with a gate through it and the wall leads onwards past some peaty tarns on the left. By this stage, the wall will either be a trusted companion or an object of hate due to the now interminable slog, but, like it or not, plenty more will be seen of it yet.

Another wall ahead bars progress and this one must be climbed but this is reasonably easy and a long, slow descent follows past the waters of Birks Tarn on the left. Eventually, a broken wall is reached, just beyond which lies the Litton to Buckden bridleway. Turn right and follow it steeply downhill, through a gate to a farm in the valley of Crystal Beck. Cross the stream or dry stream bed on a small footbridge and continue along the lane ahead, which climbs over a small hill before dropping down through a farmyard to the Queen's Arms at Litton.

Aye Gill Pike

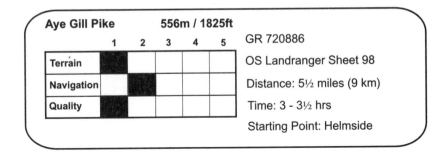

Aye Gill Pike	556m / 1825ft					GR 720886
	1	2	3	4	5	OS Landranger Sheet 98
Terrain	■					Distance: 5½ miles (9 km)
Navigation		■				Time: 3 - 3½ hrs
Quality	■					Starting Point: Helmside

Aye Gill Pike is the dominant hill that separates the deep valleys of Garsdale and Dentdale and is well defined by the low gap in the ridge above Dent Station that joins Aye Gill Pike to its higher neighbour, Great Knoutberry Hill, which is above 2,000ft. As a summit, it is typical of the hills of the western dales and is certainly of no particular interest. However, because of its dominance, it is one of those hills that, despite its lack of interest, is well worth climbing, simply 'because it's there'.

The most convenient starting point is at the small hamlet of Helmside in Dentdale. This small cluster of houses lies between Dent and Sedbergh on the main road along the valley. Its position is easily identifiable by the signposted craft shop, which also doubles as a café, with its own private car park. There is, however, limited parking in lay-bys a short distance down the road towards Sedbergh. A public footpath starts alongside the craft centre, signposted to 'Long Moor', and runs up through the car park to reach the holiday cottage beyond.

Here, the track comes to an end but a stile ahead gives access to a rough lane between a house on the left and a garage on the right. This continues to the back of the farm and, at the foot of the wood ahead, a stile half right gives access to the bottom of a field. Despite its rather peculiar start, the route now begins to unfold rather more simply. A track, running up from the buildings over to the right, climbs up the right-hand side of this field to reach a gate in the top right-hand corner, which gives access to the rough field above. Once in this larger field, follow the track ahead, forking right at a small junction to continue on roughly the same line, following a grassy path amongst the clumps of rushes.

The path continues past a small hillock on the right almost all the way to

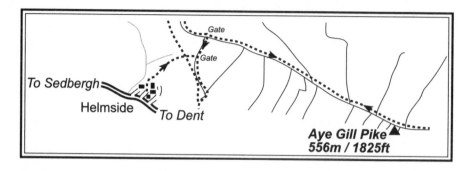

To Sedbergh
Helmside
To Dent
Gate
Gate
Aye Gill Pike
556m / 1825ft

a wall slanting from left to right. From here, the wall may then be followed to the right uphill to reach a rusty gate at the top of the field. In the field beyond, continue to follow the wall on the left, passing a signposted crosspath and some sheep pens to a further gate at the far side, which leads onto the more open hill. In fact, the hill is completely enclosed but these upper fields are rougher and, generally, larger than the fields seen hitherto.

Once through the gate, the path comes to an end as it hits the bridleway leading across the ridge between the hamlet of Lunds in Dentdale and Sedbergh. A left turn on this grassy track leads past some shake holes on the right and follows the wall on the left to reach a gate on the ridge, on the far side of which the bridleway makes a sharp left turn. However, the route to the summit of Aye Gill Pike now turns to the right and follows the wall up the ridge. A small path has developed by or near the wall and, after some initial boggy patches that are choked with rushes, the going is good, the gradient nowhere too steep and the navigation easy with the wall always on the right.

It is quite some while further on before the first obstacle is reached and this is a wall slanting in from the left. There is no easy means of crossing this, but a somewhat broken-down section slightly to the left provides the key rather than in the wall corner itself. Once past this, the wall on the right may be followed upwards along the ridge to meet a second wall branching off to the left. This crossing involves more climbing ability but the wall is relatively sound and a few well-placed throughstones make the crossing easier. With the two biggest obstacles past, the summit is not all that much further ahead. There is one steepish section before the next wall is reached. This, however, is broken down and may be crossed with ease. From here to the summit, the old wall on the right is now joined by a new fence to its left, forming a small lane between them.

This lane may be entered by climbing a short stretch of wooden fencing that has been constructed in the corner. The route, which is boggy in places, now follows this lane, crossing two other pieces of wooden fencing, before the trig point is reached just on the other side of the broken down wall on the right. The view is dominated by the hills around Dentdale – Calf Top, Great Coum, Whernside and Great Knoutberry Hill – whilst Baugh Fell on the other side of Garsdale and the Howgills above Sedbergh are also prominent.

The only practicable return is by the route of ascent since there is no way off the ridge until Cowgill, which is a long way further up Dentdale, and there are many obstacles before then. However, if transport can be arranged then a route could be completed along the ridge to Cowgill but there are no particular benefits to this continuation.

Hoove

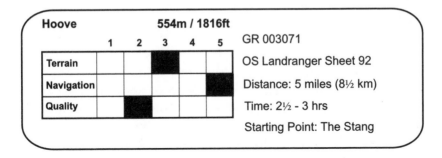

Hoove						554m / 1816ft
	1	2	3	4	5	GR 003071
Terrain			■			OS Landranger Sheet 92
Navigation					■	Distance: 5 miles (8½ km)
Quality		■				Time: 2½ - 3 hrs
						Starting Point: The Stang

Hoove lies on the very northern edge of the Yorkshire Dales on the high moorland ridge separating Arkengarthdale from Stainmore Gap. For the most part, the ridge is ill-defined standing only as the highest point of a rolling and largely unfrequented block of moorland. Hoove does not disrupt this pattern, with its table-like summit standing only a small height above the surrounding moor. The hill is redeemed, however, by its hidden secrets on the slopes and by the magnificent views from its summit, which makes it ideal for a day with good visibility.

The most interesting aspect of the hill is its northern, partly forested slopes. Here, there is a collection of potholes, mine workings and

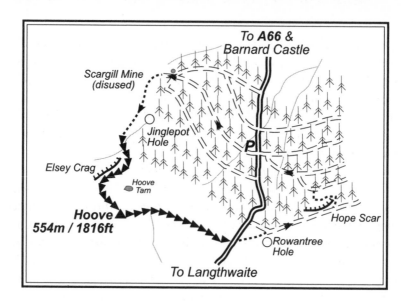

limestone scars. A pleasant but rough walk may be made from the lower forest car park on the northern side of the pass on the road between Arkengarthdale and Barnard Castle. There are two car parks on the northern side of the ridge and the lower one lies on the left not far below the hairpin when approaching from the south or on the right between steep rises when approaching from the north.

A forest track runs westwards from the car park, although this is soon brought to a sudden end by the ravine-like course of Door Gill, the bridge having been washed away. The stream bed, which is often dry due to the limestone landscape, may be crossed relatively easily just to the left of the road. On the far side, the track continues through the forest to reach a more open area close to the edge of the wood where it crosses another track by a duck pond. A short walk then leads out to a gate on the edge of the wood.

The gate is padlocked but there is a sort of semi-ruinous stile arrangement to its right and on the far side a grassy track continues to the left up and into a small dry valley. This rises upwards and past an adit on the right, which formed a part of the now disused Scargill Mine. Ahead, the valley becomes shallower and the path continues by means of a rushy groove that slants half right towards the head of the valley and a green grassy area. Ahead and to the right there are some shake holes, which are more prominent than those further to the left.

A vague track leads on across the moor some distance to the right of the forest wall. In due course, the large crater of Dovecote Hole appears over to the left and, just beyond it, the depression of Jinglepot Hole, where the stream disappears below ground. There are three interesting areas: a depression where the stream sinks in dry weather and, at the lower end, two moderately deep, gravel-bottomed crevasses from which some passages appear to lead further underground.

Back on the grassy track, this can be followed further ahead until it curves left into the wood. However, aim slightly right and follow a tongue of grass to the right of the stream and continue on this until the stream swings left higher up and passes beneath the fence above the forest. At this point, follow it left and climb the fence before striking half left up the edge of the steep escarpment of Elsey Crag where the fence becomes a wall, possibly passing some vermin traps *en route*. From here, the clear pattern of heather burning can be seen on the moor below. Towards the far end of the crags, the wall turns downhill to the right and it is from here that the route makes for the summit.

On a clear day, the trig point is clearly visible, although in mist it lies on a bearing of 172°. There are a number of peat hags to be crossed on the fairly featureless moor, although the route passes to the right of the wet fenced area around Hoove Tarn. A final climb up a steep bank leads directly to the summit and trig point, which lie at the northern edge of the summit plateau. The view is extensive – northwards into the North Pennines, westwards to the distant hills of the Lake District and southwards to Rogan's Seat on the other side of Arkengarthdale, which is only slightly overtopped by Great Shunner Fell.

The route continues almost due east from the summit, aiming in clear weather midway between the forest edge and the pillar cairn on Arndale Hill to the right. Any paths leading from the summit are merely part of the drainage system on the grouse moor and should be avoided. There are more peat hags at Hurrgill Head where there is a junction of fences; first cross the stream then cross the main fence beyond where another takes off at right angles to it on the far side. A further stretch of fairly featureless moor lies between here and the road over the moor. Depending on exactly where you reach it, you may be either slightly left or right of a bridleway leading onwards from the other side.

This track is fairly indistinct but aims for a gate into the forest, passing a little to the left of a pronounced depression. Although the rowan tree has long gone, this deep crater is named Rowantree Hole and a stream also sinks here. There is little to see but there seems to be a void beneath at least part of the infirm peaty base to the shake hole, so a close inspection is not recommended. Once inside the wood, a broad but quite rough track leads along the slope inside the trees. Ignoring a first track slanting back left, it is quite a long trudge before the next break in the trees is to be found on the left.

This gives access to the top of Hope Scar – a wonderful viewpoint and key to the next stage of the descent. Walk along its edge to the right, until, about midway, a grassy rake slants back left across the upper crag and below a steep grass slope leads down past patches of scree to a small valley below. This area is delightful and is filled with harebells and geraniums, as well as a patch of rough grass and nettles. Cross this fairly easily and then turn to the left before swinging right past a few trees to reach a lower clearing. In this, keep aiming leftwards and going downhill until a faint path appears in the grass on the right-hand side which soon turns right through a few trees to reach a more pronounced path that hairpins back to the right and then descends into the forest to reach a forestry road.

The car park is now not too distant and should be reached by turning to the left on the forest road and following that to the left and then downhill to meet another. A second left turn then leads out to the road opposite the car park.

Thorpe Fell Top

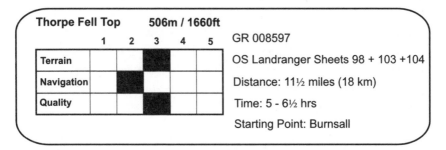

Thorpe Fell Top			506m / 1660ft		
	1	2	3	4	5
Terrain			■		
Navigation		■			
Quality			■		

GR 008597

OS Landranger Sheets 98 + 103 +104

Distance: 11½ miles (18 km)

Time: 5 - 6½ hrs

Starting Point: Burnsall

Thorpe Fell Top is the highest point of the sprawling mass of Barden Moor that lies between Embsay, Rylstone and Burnsall. The gritstone moorland is a managed grouse moor and, in late summer, when the heather is in bloom, it is a carpet of purple from edge to edge. There are few landmarks on the top of the moor and only one public right of way across the plateau. However, the moor is an Access Area, which means that the public have access except on certain days when grouse shooting is taking place or when there is a high fire risk. Dog owners should note that their animals are not allowed onto the moor. Although largely featureless, there is little problem in following the described route, even in the thickest of mists. Having said that, it may be difficult to find the summit and, if the route is lost, it is quite possible to walk for miles without finding a landmark.

Most who climb to the summit begin at either Burnsall or Rylstone as an approach from Embsay is much longer and requires the crossing of intermediate heights on the southern side of the moor. Burnsall is probably the better starting point of the two and there is car parking either on the verge, opposite the popular Wharfe View Tea Rooms, or in the Riverside Car Park (£2 for the day, payable on exit; toilets). The easiest access onto the moor is from the nearby village of Thorpe and this is reached from Burnsall by using a field path. This is reached by walking along the road towards Grassington and past the tea rooms. Where the Appletreewick road goes off to the right, the road turns through a right angle to the left and then, after the post office and craft shop, back to the right. The footpath, unnoticed by most, then leaves down a narrow lane, gated, on the left and into a field behind the cottages.

What follows is a walk across a patchwork of narrow fields, all the way to the foot of a small hill. At this point, the path curves somewhat to the

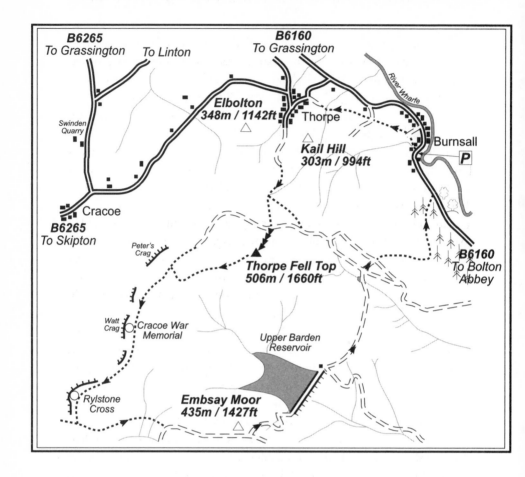

right before crossing over the wall on the left by a gated slit stile. Another field follows before a lane is crossed and a much larger field is entered. This is crossed on a grass terrace that rises across the slope before two more fields are crossed to reach a stream crossing. In the field beyond that, the path continues by the right-hand wall and above a wood before becoming more pronounced and joining a lane enclosed by limestone walls that leads all the way to the surfaced road just above Thorpe.

Here, a left turn leads down and past a farm into the village. In the centre, turn left down a lane, signposted 'Bed – Breakfast' that leads up to the end of the village where it forks. The right fork is the footpath around the back of the steep-sided hill – Elbolton – to the right whilst the left-hand fork leads up onto the moor. Thus, the left-hand track is taken and this rises up through the inbye as a walled lane, the walls now being of Millstone Grit. When the open moor is reached, a number of grooved paths lead onwards. Take the lowest and leftmost one, which soon becomes very sunken and beyond that splits at a small cairn. Of the grooves leading onwards, take the one to the left of the cairn that leads up until crossed by a grassy track from the right.

At this point, the main track swings to the left and crosses the stream but our route goes straight over and then follows the stream up to its headwaters over rough country. One particularly green area is actually a 'bottomless' swamp and thus is best given a very wide berth. Beyond this, a faint grass trod may or may not be picked up but soon a gravelled roadway will be found running from left to right. Although the summit is not yet in view, it is not far away and is reached by crossing straight over this track and climbing up half left, aiming for the highest ground, until the trig point pokes into view. It sits atop a broad gritstone slab, which, along with others hereabouts, provides excellent seating.

The next objective, the obelisk on Cracoe Fell, is now back in the direction from which we came. A small path, through the heather, runs roughly towards it, leaving the trig point on a bearing of 266°. The path leads down the slope past a boundary stone, marked C:R.T. on the nearside and D:D on the far side, to a line of grouse butts. Here, a better path is met, which, if followed to the right, leads to a dark gritstone wall and a path running along its nearside. By following this path to the left, the obelisk is soon reached over a ladder stile on the right. It is in fact the war memorial for Cracoe, sited in a novel position 1,000ft above the village.

The descent begins by continuing to follow the path onwards by the wall down to the next landmark, another boundary stone. This marks a separate boundary and is marked with a C on the near side and an R on the far side. Next is the Rylstone Cross, the present stone structure being built in 1995 to replace the previous one; again, this is reached over the wall by a ladder stile. The cross stands atop the very edge of one of the steepest places on the gritstone escarpment overlooking Rylstone and Cracoe as well as a large tract of countryside beyond. The local quarries do though stand out as ugly blotches on the landscape, even though one of the companies did help fund the replacement of the cross.

Still following the wall, the descent continues until the public bridleway across the moor is reached when it passes through the wall on the right by means of a new gate. To the left, the pathway has been improved and progress is now fast and pleasant. A sign on the right is soon passed that reads 'Deep Bog', which should deter too close an inspection. A little further on, the improved path comes to an end and a fast-flowing stream is crossed. Not too far ahead, a wooden bridge has been provided for the next stream crossing although, as the near end is surrounded by deep water, the wooden planking is in pristine condition. The stream can be crossed easily a little to the left and then rejoined around the back of another 'Deep Bog' sign over sound ground.

The path, now on grass, rises uphill before passing a shooting hut on the right and meeting with a roadway that runs down to it. A more gentle ascent follows up to and past a Millstone Grit outcrop on the left that is the summit of Embsay Moor. Just past this, a path leads off to the right, signposted 'Eastby', and then a track leads off to the left, signposted 'Burnsall'. Here, Upper Barden Reservoir comes into view down on the left and is reached by following this track down the slope and around a hairpin. The track over the dam is signposted to Burnsall and this leads to the house on the far side. By the house, a tarmac roadway begins that runs down the valley to the lower reservoir although this should soon be left for a rough trackway that contours around the hillside to the left.

A notable feature of this track is that all the streams on its left side fall into large drains that lead into a large subterranean watercourse that runs below the track. After a while, the source of the watercourse is discovered on the left and this is a small reservoir on the slopes of Thorpe Fell. Not far beyond this a crosstracks is reached and this should be crossed straight over (half right, to be exact). This track now wiggles up to reach another higher trackway. By following this to the right for a short distance, a small wooden stake is to be found on the right-hand verge. This marks the spot where a small, wet and difficult path takes off to the left. Were it not for the fact that there are footprints in it, it would be easily mistaken for a small stream bed and, after entering knee-deep heather, you could be forgiven for thinking that, if it were not marked on the map, nobody in their right mind would use it. However, a cairn is reached and after here things improve by leaps and bounds. First the path enters a groove, then dries up, then widens and passes a second, third and fourth cairn. However, just when you were beginning to think that it is not so bad, more heather is entered, only this lot is waist deep.

Without being able to see the path, progress is slow, difficult and tedious, although as this part of the moor is overdue for burning in the rotational cycle, this section will improve dramatically. Just when travel is bad enough, a bog is entered as well and here it is best to strike off to the right, over a carpet of moss and bilberry, to find a much better path running by the wall to the right. This can then be followed to the right of a lone pine tree, at which point Burnsall appears into view ahead, and all the way down by the wall, becoming increasingly stony, before entering a wood over a stile.

Footprints lead ahead here into a bog and an ensuing wet and difficult trek through a thick 'jungle'. Fortunately, though, the path does not go straight ahead but instead goes left and around the top of a big 'gully' before descending down over a carpet of pine needles to a well-constructed but boggy terrace. This should now be followed to the left to meet the road at the top of the long hill above Burnsall, which is now not a great distance to the left.

Kisdon

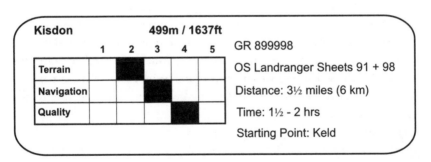

Kisdon	499m / 1637ft					
	1	2	3	4	5	GR 899998
Terrain		■				OS Landranger Sheets 91 + 98
Navigation			■			Distance: 3½ miles (6 km)
Quality				■		Time: 1½ - 2 hrs
						Starting Point: Keld

There is something about upper Swaledale that makes it one of the most beautiful of the valleys of the Yorkshire Dales. Possibly it is the combination of limestone scars, pure, rushing becks and sweeping green upland pastures. In the summer months, walkers swarm around Muker, Keld and over the hill between them – Kisdon. Few, however, venture to

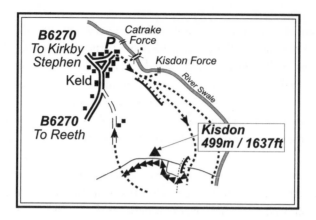

the very highest point of the hill and here, by contrast, is to be found almost complete solitude.

The villages of Keld, Thwaite and Muker at the foot of Kisdon's slopes provide the most appropriate starting points. However, Keld is the only one from which a satisfactory circular walk can be made. Hence, it is this route that is described below and it is certainly a fine little expedition, packed full of interest and surprises at every turn.

Keld, which lies off the main road up the valley down a small dead-end lane, has a car park, provided by the farm of Park Lodge, for which a charge is payable to the honesty box. There are also toilets and a shop and café nearby. The walk begins by leaving the car park and returning to the bottom of the lane in the middle of the village. Opposite, a gravelled track leads onwards and, ignoring a left fork, from which the Pennine Way joins our route, the track narrows and proceeds onwards above the Swale on the left. The next path on the left leads down to the attractive waterfall of Kisdon Force but, after returning to this junction and continuing onwards, the path runs parallel with and close to the base of an impressive limestone scar on the right.

However, before the end of the scar, there is a junction of paths. Whilst the gravelled path leads ahead on the low-level route to Muker, the Pennine Way and our route turn to the right on grass, as signposted, and continue along the foot of the scar to its end soon after. The slopes above the river on the left now become more thickly wooded again and the path ascends and descends amongst the bracken just above the top of the wood.

Towards the end of the wood, the path crosses over a somewhat broken-down wall and then continues along the hillside, curving to the right with the Swale valley, which has now turned down towards Muker. At the next wall, which is more sturdy than the previous one, the path passes through a small gate. Beyond this point, our route leaves this path and strikes up the upper slopes towards the summit. Immediately to the right, a scar bars access and would-be scramblers should be warned that although there are a number of interesting routes, the rock is rotten in places.

Walkers, however, should continue beyond the ash tree at the end of the scar and then strike up from there. On the top, a fence is hit, which should then be followed to the left, where it ends, at the point where a wall runs off up the hillside. Our route now follows this and, although rough to start with, the going becomes easier higher up, especially in the softer vegetation immediately alongside the wall. The summit is close by when a large shake hole is passed on the left and, across the wall, a pillar cairn stands at a slightly lower elevation just beyond the summit.

Ardent summiteers will be pleased to hear that the wall is easily climbable by means of a wide selection of well-placed throughstones, although a return should be made to the original side for the onwards journey. Hemmed in by the higher moorlands surrounding the head of the valley, Kisdon has no far-reaching views. However, there are few better places to admire the Swaledale moorlands and what can be seen of the valley itself.

Perhaps unsurprisingly, the descent begins by following the wall onwards. Ignoring minor wiggles, it generally curves slightly to the left and makes downwards towards a low point where one of the other bridleways from Muker to Keld ascends onto the hill. This bridleway runs to the right through a gate and proceeds to make a fairly obvious and gradual descent around the hill's western slopes back towards Keld. At mid-height, the track passes a house on the right and from this point onwards it becomes a vehicular track that, after passing through several fields, swings left towards the foot of the slope and climbs the short distance to the valley road on the far side. From here, the top of the lane leading down into Keld is only a short distance to the right, around the corner.

Dufton Pike

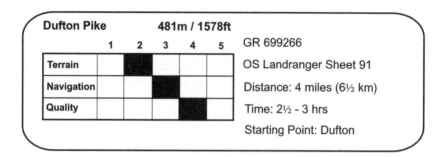

Dufton Pike		481m / 1578ft			
	1	2	3	4	5
Terrain		■			
Navigation			■		
Quality				■	

GR 699266

OS Landranger Sheet 91

Distance: 4 miles (6½ km)

Time: 2½ - 3 hrs

Starting Point: Dufton

Dufton Pike is one of the most shapely hills in England and its sharp and conical summit makes it one of, if not *the*, finest peaks in the Pennines. Despite geographically being part of the North Pennines, Dufton Pike is the most detached of three conical hills that stand just to the west of the main Pennine scarp. Despite being only of small area, its great bulk diverts the valley of Runsdale to the north before once again allowing it to flow its westwards course to join the Eden. The hill is best climbed by a traverse of its sharp north-west and south-east ridges from the village of Dufton.

Dufton can be easily reached from the A66 Appleby to Penrith road and is well signposted. In the village, there is a car park next to the toilets and recycling site. The walk begins by turning to the left from the car park entrance and walking down the village's main street to the far end, where it turns to the right. Keep straight on, passing a road on the left to find a farm track on the right that is signposted as a footpath. Keep straight on along the farm's access road to reach, after joining with the Pennine Way, the buildings at Coatsike Farm. The route runs straight through the farmyard and through a gate on the far side that leads into a rough field that now serves as a graveyard for various pieces of machinery in various stages of rusting. The track follows the wall on the left-hand edge and then enters the bottom of a charming green lane – Hurning Lane – that leads on through the fields.

There are a number of stiles to be crossed where farm tracks cross the lane, which, after serving as a farm track itself initially, soon turns into an enclosed footpath between tree-lined banks. After a while, the lane reaches a ruined farmstead, of which only one of the building's walls remain, now serving as part of the field boundary to the left of the track. Shortly

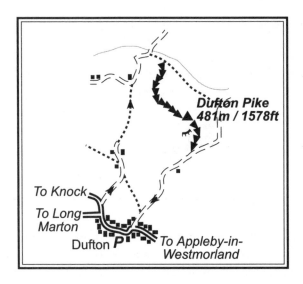

beyond this, the track passes the farm buildings at Halsteads and then enters a sloping field over which the track curves to cross the foot of Dufton Pike's north-west ridge. However, due to walls, the ridge cannot yet be followed and the track should be followed steeply down and across the slope on the far side to a ford over the Great Rundale Beck.

From here, the Pennine Way passes through a gate and crosses the stream on a clapper bridge alongside the ford. However, our route follows a track up the valley on this side of the wall that climbs slightly across the slopes of the ridge. The first wall is crossed by a stone stile next to a gate and the second wall by a lone stone stile. Once across this second wall, the open hill is reached and a way may now be made to the ridge and summit. Turn to the right and follow the way uphill and then slightly back to the right to meet a broad track that climbs across the hillslopes from further up the valley on the left. At the wall corner where the wall and track meet, a steep ascending grass path climbs across the slopes above the broad track back to the left. Although used predominantly by cattle, this path is quite distinct but soon peters out just short of a patch of stones just below the ridge crest. Between here and the stones, a way should be made up the steep slope to gain the ridge at a little levelling.

To the left, the ridge now leads upwards in a series of steps to the summit, which is now in view. However, be warned. Cattle are pastured on the hill for much of the year and they are often to be found lying on these little levellings on the ridge, which can make progress rather awkward as the ridge is narrow and there are very steep grass slopes on either side. The ridge should now be followed all the way to the sharp summit with excellent views all the way. The view from the summit is superb, although limited to the east by the North Pennine scarp. However, the view across the Eden valley and to the various crags and deep valleys on the scarp face cannot be underestimated. The summit is unmarked but there is little doubting its position, perched almost on the edge of the hill's near-vertical Rundale slopes.

The descent is far easier and shorter than the ascent and follows the hill's south-east ridge. This again falls in a number of steps and there are a number of small craglets to watch out for. However, below the highest craggy band, turn down a small valley on the right and descend to a gateway in the wall at the foot of the slope. Due to the crazy angle of the gate, care should be taken in crossing it to meet the track running down to Dufton from the disused mines at the head of Rundale. Turning to the right, the track leads down out of the rough upper fields and through a double gate into the inbye. The track then leads without any confusion all the way past Pusgill House and through a farmyard into Dufton to meet the road on a corner. Aim straight ahead down the road and then around a right-hand bend to reach the car park and starting point.

Ilkley Moor

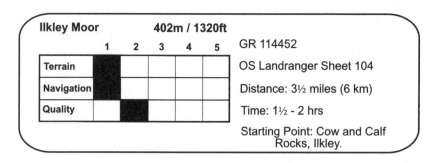

Ilkley Moor	402m / 1320ft				
	1	2	3	4	5
Terrain	■				
Navigation	■				
Quality		■			

GR 114452

OS Landranger Sheet 104

Distance: 3½ miles (6 km)

Time: 1½ - 2 hrs

Starting Point: Cow and Calf Rocks, Ilkley.

Ilkley Moor is ringed all the way around by steep slopes with crags of millstone grit whilst above them lies a gently sloping heathery moor. It is part of the larger Rombald's Moor, which forms the high ground running

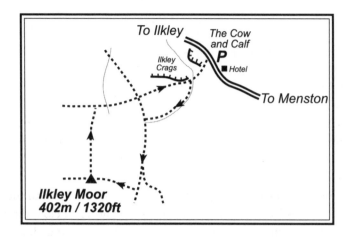

between Skipton and Menston. However, Ilkley Moor rises very sharply from the rest of the ridge, which gives it a character and an identity of its own. The name Rombald originates from the giant who was once said to live here. The legend tells how one day he leapt across the valley, leaving his heel print at the Cow and Calf Rocks above Ilkley where he dislodged the Calf Rock before landing at Almscliffe Crag near Huby. The best side of the moor is on the Wharfedale escarpment and it is from here, at the Cow and Calf Rocks, that the walk starts.

Purists may like to start in Ilkley but as any ascent from strict valley level would begin and finish as a walk through the town, it would seem more logical to start just above it at the Cow and Calf Rocks' car park just down the road from the inn. Start off not on the slabbed path from the car park but on a sandy path leading along the hillside to the massive boulder below the cliff face which is known as the Calf Rock. Behind it, it is possible to scramble up the side of the cliff through some large boulders, the route being made as difficult or as easy as is wished. At the top of the scramble, a grassy path leads on straight ahead and around the head of another amphitheatre to reach and then cross a small stream. A path on the far bank leads to the left up the gill, crossing over another path (ignore the waymark) and then on to meet the Dales Way running from right to left. Follow the path up to the left, which soon runs on a section of elevated boarding. Just after the end of this, a pair of parallel fences can be seen in the near distance, at which point a small path on the right crosses over the ditch on a rocky plank. Turn right up this path and, although distinct to begin with, it soon becomes a little indistinct but here it turns half right and then becomes more apparent once more as it swings to the left and up the hill to the mini upper escarpment. On the top, a path is found crossing from left to right and this should be followed to the right for a short distance until it forks. Take the left fork, which continues onwards up to the summit cairn and trig point just short of a pair of masts.

In total, four paths reach the summit, all 90° apart; turn right along the one that drops down to the north, crossing several smaller paths *en route*, to arrive at a distinct track running along the hillside just at the top of the main escarpment. If followed to the right, it passes a couple of large cairns and crosses a few large tracks before running along the top of Ilkley Crags. Here it forks; take the left one which drops down to the small stream that was crossed near the beginning of the walk and from there, the outwards route can be followed back to the car park, with some careful exploration of the crags and rocks recommended.

Sharp Haw

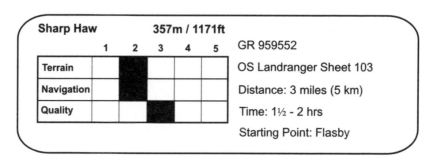

Sharp Haw		357m / 1171ft			
	1	2	3	4	5
Terrain		■			
Navigation		■			
Quality			■		

GR 959552
OS Landranger Sheet 103
Distance: 3 miles (5 km)
Time: 1½ - 2 hrs
Starting Point: Flasby

Sharp Haw is the name given to the highest point of Flasby Fell – an interesting Millstone Grit moorland on the southern edge of the Yorkshire Dales just above Skipton and Gargrave. It is unusual amongst its contemporaries in that it has a very pronounced and distinctive summit set among a moorland of rocky summits and boggy valleys that, in many ways, are more typical of the scenery of the lower hills of the Lake District. The ascent to this summit makes a superb expedition from the small village of Flasby.

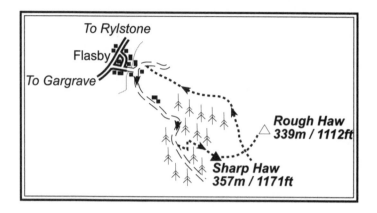

Flasby lies on the Gargrave to Cracoe road and is situated just off the main road on a small one-way loop, which is accessed from its northern end. It is possible to park a couple of cars at the lowest point of the loop where a track runs down and over the beck to the farm on the far side. In fact, it is this track that forms the first part of the route and just past the farm buildings on the right, a track runs to the right, signposted as a footpath to Stirton. This track runs up and then along and around to the left before reaching a smaller farm, through which the track passes into the field beyond.

Once in this field, the ascent begins in earnest and the track weaves a broad hairpin up to a gate in the top right corner that leads into the conifer plantation above. At the time of writing, much of the lower part of this had been recently felled so, for several years to come, the next part of the climb affords lovely views over the upper Aire valley. The track continues to climb and soon curves to the left with the contour. However, before long, a junction is reached, where the footpath to Stirton is signposted half right and slightly downhill (this is the first signposted junction since the farm in Flasby). Here, turn left and follow an unsignposted path up into the unfelled wood, with its dense under canopy of rhododendrons.

Once the path is amongst the rhododendron bushes, there is no mistaking its route and the climb could even be described as slightly claustrophobic. However, the path hairpins first left and then back right before climbing up to the top of the wood, where a wooden fence across a gate in a stone wall can be climbed to gain the open moor above. The track continues half left and the summit is now in view, although it appears much closer than it actually is. Our track starts by running roughly parallel with the wall on the left but when this turns away at a wall corner, the track strikes off across the moor by itself, aiming for the left-hand edge of Sharp Haw's pronounced summit ridge, passing amongst various block of Millstone Grit amongst the heather.

When the ridge is gained, leave the track and turn right following a steep path that climbs up the sharp ridge to the trig point on the summit. Perhaps what catches the eye most from the summit are the various rock outcrops on the moor and the complex nature of the terrain, which can easily be studied as the ground falls away so steeply from the trig point. Otherwise, to the north-east, the most prominent feature is the obelisk on Cracoe Fell (its war memorial). On the headland in front of it lies Rylstone Cross, which can be seen but is less identifiable and, of course, the summit of Thorpe Fell Top to the right of both of them. The hills around Malham also form an interesting scene, as does the Craven landscape to the south.

The descent begins by heading north from the summit down to a gap in a wall just below the level of the ridge. From here, a track leads across the next block of moor to a gate just below the rocky slopes of Rough Haw ahead. On the far side of the gate, there is usually quite a large quagmire to be negotiated and then there is a choice. If desired, the summit of Rough Haw can be taken in by climbing a path ahead up the slopes. Otherwise, turn half left and follow a track towards a stake, which on closer acquaintance is found to be topped by a band of blue paint.

A number of these stakes then lead down the hillside and they should be followed to a gate into the inbye, ignoring a couple of tracks branching to the right across the slopes of Rough Haw. Through the gate, the bridleway continues down the edge of the first field and then follows an enclosed lane all the way back down to the farmyard in Flasby, completing the circuit.

Section 3 – Kielder Forest, the Cheviots and Simonside Hills

Union border between England and Scotland from the Solway Firth to Berwick-upon-Tweed, the east coast from there to Tynemouth and then the River Tyne, River South Tyne and Tipalt Burn to Holmhead. Hadrian's Wall from there to Gilsland and the Rivers Irthing and Eden from there to the Solway Firth.

NAME	HEIGHT	IN SECTION	IN ENGLAND	IN BRITAIN
Peel Fell	602m/1975ft	02 of 08	56 of 184	763 of 1552
Sighty Crag	518m/1701ft	03 of 08	75 of 184	939 of 1552
Shillhope Law	501m/1644ft	04 of 08	81 of 184	984 of 1552
Tosson Hill	440m/1444ft	05 of 08	96 of 184	1123J of 1552
Long Crag	319m/1047ft	06 of 08	130 of 184	1343J of 1552
Ros Hill	315m/1034ft	07 of 08	133J of 184	1351J of 1552
Housedon Hill	267m/ 877ft	08 of 08	154 of 184	1431J of 1552

There is one summit above 2,000ft that is described in *England's Highest Peaks*.

The Cheviot is the most northerly of the English mountains and its foothill – Housedon Hill – is the most northerly of the separate hills. Tucked away in the far north-east of England, the Cheviot range and its surrounding hills form one of the most beautiful of the English landscapes. These hills, constructed mainly from sandstones, include popular summits, such as the Simonside Hills, alongside more infrequently visited summits, such as Peel Fell, and the most remote hill in England – Sighty Crag.

Initially, the landscape to the north of the Tyne Gap, one of the trans-Pennine breaches by the Lake District Ice (see Section 2), is not dissimilar to that of the rest of the Pennines. However, there is a subtle change on the southern edge of the Cheviot range towards a different type of

landscape and, therefore, geology. The rocks underlying Kielder Forest form the northern continuation of the Carboniferous strata of the Pennines (see Section 2). The earliest phase of Carboniferous deposition was the well-known Mountain limestones but, here, these rocks lie deep beneath the subsequent middle and upper Carboniferous rocks that followed the limestones.

The next phase of deposition occurred as a delta spread southwards into the shallow tropical Carboniferous sea from the north. The rocks deposited lie in the Yoredale Beds, named after Wensleydale ('Uredale') in Section 2. A great thickness of these rocks was deposited and they consist of a cylical sequence of limestones, shales and thin coal seams, which are discussed in more detail in Section 2. As deltaic conditions became more firmly established, the rocks become more regular. At this point, the deposition changed to the rocks of the Millstone Grit Facies, which comprise grits, shales and sandstones.

Finally, tropical swamps began to form on the delta before they were inundated by the sea of shifting delta channels. This buried their organic matter, which was then fossilised and compacted to form coal. Together with the sandstones, grits, shales and fossilised soils with which these coal seams are bedded, this Upper Carboniferous sequence is called the Coal Measures. Today, it is the Millstone Grit that forms the highest summits, appearing in occasional outcrops, such as at Christianbury Crags, which are seen on the ascent of Sighty Crag.

Slightly further north, the Cheviots support a large block of high

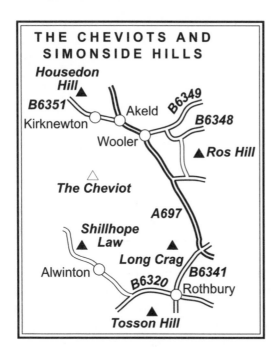

THE CHEVIOTS AND SIMONSIDE HILLS

ground, almost all of which is constructed from the satellite ridges of The Cheviot, which attains the height of 2,674ft (815m). Only one other separate summit is to be found in the range and that is Shillhope Law. The geology of the range is, as already suggested, very different from the rest of the Pennines. Originally, there were hills here, formed from the Lower Old Red Sandstones in the Devonian period and well seen in the Brecon Beacons and Black Mountains of south Wales. However, later in the Devonian period, granite intruded into much of the Pennines, including the sandstone Cheviots. Further south (in Sections 4, 8 and 9) this granite pushed up the basement rocks to form blocks of high ground and here it did likewise, forming a domed, uplifted area. This doming formed tensional cracks and the magma was forced into these, crystallising out into dykes of finely grained pink felsite. A good place to see these dykes is at Linhope Spout, where the Linhope Burn, a tributary of the River Breamish, has eroded the overlying rocks to expose them.

Large amounts of the igneous rock andesite are to be found as pebbles in stream beds, ranging in colour from grey and pink to black with red veining. This pyroclastic material and its wide distribution show that the volcanic activity was explosive. Where the andesite came into contact with the molten magma, it was baked into a harder rock containing crystals of mica and feldspar. It is this material that forms most of the rock outcrops to be seen in the Cheviots such as Braydon Crag on the northern slopes of the Cheviot and Housey Crag above the Harthope Valley on Hedgehope Hill.

By the Carboniferous period, the overlying sandstone on the granite dome had been eroded and the Cheviot granite formed an island in a warm Carboniferous sea. Fine material cemented together granite beach pebbles eroded from the dome to form a conglomerate found in the range away from the granite centre and exposed at Roddam Dene on the eastern side of the range. In deltas on this coastline, limestone and clay mixed together to form cementstone, which is to be found in bands with the conglomerate and exposed by the River Coquet in its gorge just above Alwinton. The next deposits were of Fell Sandstones, which form an outer ring around the range stretching from the Tweed down into the Simonside Hills south of Rothbury.

Since the Carboniferous period, any more recent rocks have been eroded and there has been extensive erosion of these Carboniferous sediments. The cementstones, which are easily weathered, tend to have largely disappeared around the outside giving rise to circular valleys. The Fell Sandstones have proved much more difficult to erode, and the greatest erosion of the cementstones occurs immediately behind them, leaving a sandstone ridge. The circular valley is first visible in the north where the northwards-flowing streams have been captured by the River Glen and forced eastwards to join the Till.

The River Till itself continues this capture down the eastern side of the range as far south as the River Breamish. This circular valley or, to be more accurate, trough, since it contains several valleys, has given the Fell Sandstone ridge a distinctive characteristic of having inward-facing escarpments whereas it generally slopes gently away on its eastern side. In fact, so hard is the sandstone that only two rivers flow eastwards through the ridge. These are the Aln at Whittingham and the Coquet through its narrow valley at Rothbury. These two rivers have only been permitted to do so by the weakening of the Fell Sandstones at these two points by faulting.

The Ice Age finally shaped the Cheviots and, it is believed, also robbed them of the grandeur possessed by so many other ranges constructed from volcanic rock. It is thought that at the time of the Loch Lomond Readvancement, thick sheets, mainly of sandy clay and other solid material, known as till and regolith respectively, covered the hillsides hiding much of the granite underneath except where this coating has been worn away on the highest summits. However, here there is a thick coating of wet peat, due to the impermeable nature of granite, which also hides the rock. In fact, the only rock exposures in the range is where streams have eroded the surface sufficiently to uncover the granite below or where, at the metamorphic aureole, the andesite has been baked into a harder rock. Apart from that, the Ice Age appears to have left little mark, the only corrie being that of The Bizzle on the Cheviot's northern slopes.

Access

The area can be divided into two regions – the Cheviots and Kielder. The eastern side of the Cheviot range is easily accessible from the A697, which leaves the A1 at Morpeth. The A68 cuts a line across the hills between Jedburgh and Redesdale. It is possible to reach Kielder from the A68 near Byrness by a forest road, although this is very rough and is not recommended. A good road runs up the North Tyne valley from Bellingham to Kielder and then onwards over a low pass into Liddesdale. Bellingham lies on the B6341 Hexham to Rothbury road, which crosses the A68 and A696 roads near Otterburn. The western side of Kielder can be reached by long winding lanes from Gilsland and Brampton, although a better approach is from the north from Newcastleton in Liddesdale.

There are daily rail services on the east coast main line to Berwick-on-Tweed and Alnmouth (near Alnwick). Some intercity services do not stop at Alnmouth and it may be necessary to change onto a local service at Newcastle (not Sundays). There are bus services to Wooler from Newcastle, Alnwick and Berwick and to Yetholm from Kelso. Carlisle lies on the west coast main line and is served by daily intercity services. There are stations on the Newcastle–Carlisle line at Hexham, Haltwhistle and Brampton.

Accommodation

Northumberland is a popular tourist destination and there is a variety of towns around the hills that offer accommodation. The small town of Rothbury is probably the best base for the Cheviots and Simonside Hills. Alternatively, further north, Wooler is also a good base, especially if the ascent of the Cheviot itself is to be included. Kielder is a slightly more awkward place to find accommodation. The village of Kielder is easily reached from Rothbury or Bellingham but, for the ascent of Sighty Crag, a base on the western side of the hills is required. Carlisle and Brampton are both conveniently located, although the hill can also be reached from further afield from perhaps the eastern and northern Lake District (Sections 4 and 6) or the North Pennines (part of Section 2). There are youth hostels at Carlisle, Greenhead, Once Brewed, Acomb, Bellingham, Byrness, Wooler and Kirk Yetholm (SYHA).

Peel Fell

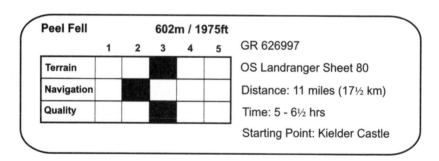

Peel Fell						602m / 1975ft
	1	2	3	4	5	GR 626997
Terrain			■			OS Landranger Sheet 80
Navigation		■				Distance: 11 miles (17½ km)
Quality			■			Time: 5 - 6½ hrs
						Starting Point: Kielder Castle

Peel Fell is the highest point of Kielder Forest and its summit rises almost to the height of 2,000ft (610m). Lying close to the Scottish border in a fairly remote setting, its summit sees few visitors, although it does lie on the Forestry Commission's 'Kielder Stane Walk'. This provides the best circuit, although it is in no way a standard forestry trail. All in all, this is a route with a real mountaineering feel about it and it should not be underestimated.

The village of Kielder is somewhat cut off in its position close to the

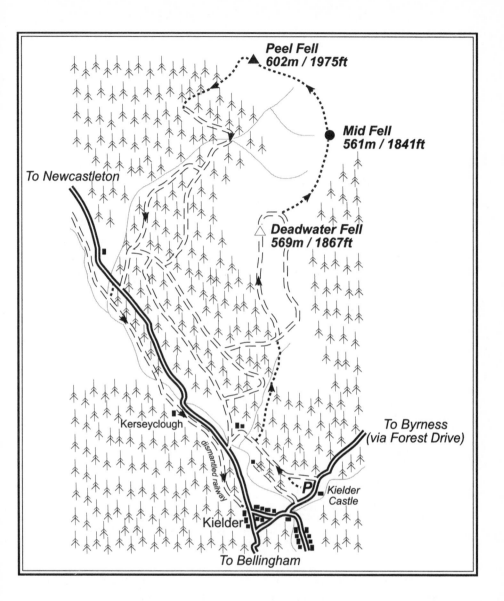

Peel Fell
602m / 1975ft

Mid Fell
561m / 1841ft

To Newcastleton

Deadwater Fell
569m / 1867ft

To Byrness
(via Forest Drive)

Kerseyclough

dismantled railway

P

Kielder
Castle

Kielder

To Bellingham

head of the North Tyne valley. A public road runs up the valley from Bellingham through to Liddesdale and a forest drive, actually 12 miles of roughish tracks, links to the A68 at Byrness. Once at Kielder, there is a visitor centre at Kielder Castle and a large car park by the castle. It is from this car park that the walk starts.

The car park lies on three tiers and the route begins by following a small path through the trees from the left corner of the car park's top tier to join a gravelled path just above the car park. This traverses to the left to reach the edge of a field and it then follows the wall up, inside the forest, to reach a forestry road by the top of the field. Turning to the left, this forestry road traverses the hillside, rising slightly, before descending back towards the valley above some more farmland on the left.

Close to the bottom of this hill, a grassy path turns to the right. Marked by a small waymarker, this ascends up a wet trackway along the side of the valley of the Lightpipe Sike. Reasonably soon, the path passes through a gate out of the forest and onto the open moor. From here on, the path becomes less distinct in the heather but it does continue. The ascent now temporarily halts as the path contours along to reach the stream at a confluence. Here, the path follows the right bank of the left tributary for a few yards before leaving it after pushing past a small tree.

Now once more back on the heathery moor, the path becomes more distinct and ascends to reach a crossing across a further tributary, following roughly a line of telegraph poles. Ahead now is a steep bank and, avoiding the temptation to turn right and follow the stream, the path climbs straight up, aiming just to the left of a telegraph pole above. From here on, once again the path becomes more distinct and, marked by stakes with some red and white tape tied to the top of them, aims for a stile back into the forest.

Just over the stile, another forestry road is reached that traverses the hillside. However, just to the right, another track continues the ascent, climbing inside the forestry fence up the right-hand side of the plantation. There is no gate at the top and the track continues above the plantation up to the masts on the summit of Deadwater Fell. With much of the climbing now complete, a rather pleasant ridge walk leads onwards to the summit of Peel Fell.

Once past the masts on Deadwater Fell, the fence on the right turns down the slope. A small path, indistinct at first, follows the edge of the fence down to reach the hairpinning track further down. The route now crosses straight over and continues down to the wet col between Deadwater Fell and the lower summit of Mid Fell. A small tarn is passed on the left and the path, following a line of fenceposts, climbs up the short distance to the south summit of Mid Fell. Again there is a wet depression, much favoured by the bog asphodel, which throws out yellow flower-spikes in the summer. Here, the path becomes indistinct but, if the fenceposts are followed, the path reappears on the other side of the bog. Another short climb leads to the excellent shelter-cairn on Mid Fell.

After now reaching its easternmost point, the ridge curves back to the west to attain the summit of Peel Fell. The path continues down and across the intervening depression before ascending to its tall summit cairn, still following the line of fenceposts. The summit is a very good viewpoint, with the wild reaches of Kielder Forest and the hills of the Scottish borders being particularly prominent. To the north-east, the bulk of the Cheviot hills is visible. The only thing that detracts at all from the view is the broadness of the summit.

Ahead, the fenceposts continue past some tarns on the right, where, in summer, the cotton grass forms a dazzling display of white. The fenceline then swings to the left as it meets the English–Scottish border. The path alternates initially between England and Scotland but soon finds that the Scottish side is preferable. Soon, the descent begins quite steeply and a prominent crag – Jenny Storie's Stone – is passed on the right. Lower down, the fence is joined by a broken-down wall on the left, which is home to at least one adder.

Soon, the path enters the forest once again but continues following both the wall and fence down a firebreak. However, at the first break in the trees on the left and at the first gap in the fence and wall, look out for a waymarked path going left. This leads through the first few trees and then joins onto the end of a grassy forestry road. This makes a gradually descending traverse of the slope to cross the Deadwater Burn before swinging sharply to the right. Here, it continues its traverse, rising slightly, before forking. Our route takes the downwards fork, which drops straight down to the road in the floor of the valley.

A long walk back to Kielder remains but the old railway line adds interest to that. To reach it, turn to the right on the road and walk for a few hundred yards, almost to the edge of the trees. Here, a path, marked by a small arrow on a squat post, points into the pine trees on the left and a small path weaves through them to reach the old railway track bed. This can then be followed to the left, through farmland, to reach the road once again at Kerseycleugh Bridge. The railway line and track, however, continue, parallel to the road for a time, before swinging to the right and making a slight short-cut back towards Kielder village.

After crossing a number of trackways, the track along the railway line comes to an end in the village and an exit can be made to the left through a gap in the sturdy wall. Opposite is the residential street of Castle Drive and that should be followed past the village shop to its far end. A left turn here leads uphill to the castle and starting point.

Sighty Crag

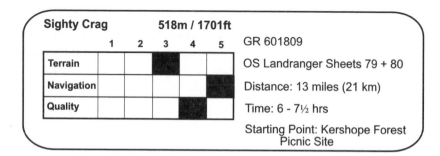

Sighty Crag						518m / 1701ft
	1	2	3	4	5	GR 601809
Terrain			■			OS Landranger Sheets 79 + 80
Navigation					■	Distance: 13 miles (21 km)
Quality				■		Time: 6 - 7½ hrs
						Starting Point: Kershope Forest Picnic Site

Sighty Crag is the most remote hill in England, thanks in no small part to the Forestry Commission. This hill lies in the very heart of Kielder Forest, far from everything and everyone. An expedition to its summit is a serious undertaking that requires stamina – it is not only long but very rough as well – and competence in map and compass work should the weather turn bad. However, the reward more than compensates for the hard work for, on the summit, you are on top of the world, with stunning views and not a sign of human life in sight or in earshot. For those interested in flora and fauna, this walk will bring delights at almost every turn.

The best line of approach is from the west, where it is possible to break out of the forest by means of a little-used footpath and get onto the rough and open moorland above. There are two ways of getting onto this path and they are either from the Kershope Forest picnic site or from the farm of The Flatt further to the south, above Roadhead. However, given the long walk in, the forestry roads from the Kershope Forest car park make for a faster climb than the rough footpaths from The Flatt. This compensates for the fact that the route from the forestry car park is actually slightly longer.

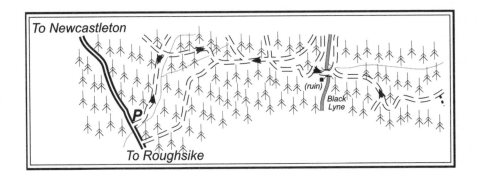

The path from the car park is signposted to Christianbury Crags. This outcrop is where the path emerges from the forest out onto the open hill, although Sighty Crag lies a good deal further beyond. The path, which is waymarked throughout with arrows, leaves the car park along the forestry road, which climbs alongside a small valley in a virtually straight line for over a mile. A right turn at a crosstracks leads down and over the stream before climbing up past a number of waymarked junctions to the top of the ridge above the Lyne valley. Only now do Christianbury Crags appear into view across the valley on the opposite skyline.

The arrows point onwards down a winding track that leads down into the Lyne valley. A right turn onto a larger forest road leads past the old habitation of Blacklyne House and then on and across the river on a concrete bridge. Just beyond this, the route turns to the right up another forestry road that climbs out of the valley. Keeping straight ahead and ignoring side-tracks, the road climbs through mature forest as well as more recently felled areas to reach an open area of heather heathland within the forest. In the middle of this open space, the main road ends but a grassy track leads on and before the next block of trees is reached, a path, waymarked with the arrows, turns off to the right and crosses the top of the heath.

After going only a short distance through the trees, a fence and wall are soon reached after crossing a stream. The path now follows between the fence on the right and the trees on the left up this wide firebreak in the forest. Underfoot, the path is very narrow and even then the going is rough through the heather and damp and boggy underfoot, although the forest wildlife, which includes foxes and red deer, adds interest if you see any. A stile is soon passed on the right, which marks the top of the path

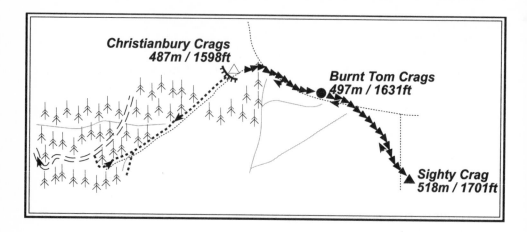

Christianbury Crags
487m / 1598ft

Burnt Tom Crags
497m / 1631ft

Sighty Crag
518m / 1701ft

from The Flatts, and the crags eventually appear into view in the distance. Occasional waymarkers encourage progress and the path continues in this way for well over a mile until it passes beyond the trees.

Things do not now improve very much, although it is a relief to be out of the trees and onto the open hill. The crags are not far ahead and the small path continues by the fence towards them. The main bulk of the crags are to the left of the fence and, with the exception of the highest point, they are easily surmounted as they run into the moor behind. The highest point is on a sandstone turret, which can be climbed by a number of tricky scrambles, although the easiest line is on its front.

The summit is now in view half right but it is still very distant and the intervening moorland rough and largely pathless. The fenceline continues north-west to the lower summit of Black Knowe where the fence butts onto another. A right turn on this leads down to the edge of a high tongue of pine wood. However, a beeline can be made from the crags across the heather and cloudberry-clad moor to the corner of the wood. From here, a small path can be followed along the left-hand side of the fence ahead up and onto the summit of Burnt Tom Crags, with the patches of bog asphodel, with clove-scented yellow flower-spikes in summer, growing ever more frequent.

Once past the top of Burnt Tom Crags, the fence swings slightly to the left. Depending on the weather, a beeline can be made for the summit of Sighty Crag ahead (153º). However, once embarked on this direct route, it is completely featureless if the mist suddenly comes in. The alternative is to follow the fence onwards as far as Sighty Crags (note the plural) and then follow a fence on the right to the summit from there. The disadvantage to this is that there are more peat gullies to cross than on the direct line lower on the slope, although if you follow the direct route, you should be aware that to begin with the ground is very wet and boggy with much standing water.

The trig point and highest rocks are on the other side of the fence, although there is a gate nearby. The view is extensive, encompassing much of Kielder Forest, part of Kielder Water, the Cheviots, Peel Fell (above Kielder), the hills of the Scottish Borders, the Solway Firth, the northern hills of the Lake District, including Skiddaw, and some of the North Pennines. Nearby and for a long distance further, there is nothing but moor and forest, and the sense of elevation is astounding.

The return should be made by the same route and the waymarking on the route through the forest is equally good in reverse. However, there is one point that is not too clear because the waymarker is somewhat hidden. Once across the ridge on the other (car park) side of the Lyne valley, look out for a curving right fork where the main forest road turns to the left. Missing this turn would not be catastrophic; the other track runs out only a hundred yards further down the road, but weary feet will be glad not to walk it.

Shillhope Law

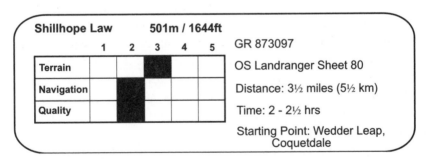

Shillhope Law		501m / 1644ft			
	1	2	3	4	5
Terrain			■		
Navigation		■			
Quality		■			

GR 873097

OS Landranger Sheet 80

Distance: 3½ miles (5½ km)

Time: 2 - 2½ hrs

Starting Point: Wedder Leap, Coquetdale

Hidden in amongst the Cheviots, Shillhope Law is a hill with little bulk or stature whose slopes fall steeply to Upper Coquetdale. This is wild and remote hill country, although the narrow road that climbs up Coquetdale

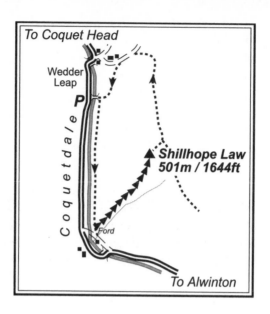

from Alwinton eases any access problems. On the other side of the valley lies the northern flank of the army's Otterburn Training Area and training without live ammunition can take place on the northern side of Coquetdale as well. However, despite Shillhope Law's lack of area on the ground, its ascent is quite strenuous and should not be underestimated.

The clearly signposted car park of Wedder Leap in Upper Coquetdale is the most convenient starting point and a circular walk may be made by walking down the valley before beginning the ascent. A footbridge leads across the Coquet a few yards above the car park and a pair of stiles leads into the field on the far bank. Here, a right turn should be made to walk down the valley, parallel to the river, to reach a stile in the field's far corner. Across this, the open hill is entered, although the path ahead is far from clear. A combination of sheep tracks leads across to a well-built sheepfold, from where a more pronounced path climbs slightly up the bank on the left to avoid a damp place by the river.

Once past this obstacle, the path drops back down to the flat ground on the riverbank and, now much clearer, continues next to the river, passing a number of rocky areas towards the next habitation down the valley. Before that is reached, a track fords the river and runs along to an old shed. From here, a track climbs up the ridge on the left of Shillhope Cleugh. After an initial steep ascent, the track levels off slightly and contours into this side valley. At this point turn to the left and strike up the largely pathless grass ridge, having now climbed above the bracken level.

The ascent is steep and unremitting except for a few very short sections. It is something of a relief when the ridge starts to level after a very hard and long climb. Higher up, more evidence of a vehicle track emerges in the grass, which soon becomes mixed with heather. However, shortly beyond the top of the ridge, a small path strikes off half left through the heather and leads to the pillar cairn, trig point and shelter-cairn on the summit. The view is not very far-reaching in any direction because of a plentiful supply of hills and ridges of the same height or higher in most directions. However, there is a good view of the hills and ridges leading up to the southern flank of the Cheviot.

Two tracks lead roughly northwards from the summit and it is the right-hand one that is required. This aims in a more north-easterly direction to reach a gate in the fence that runs just east of the summit. On the near side of the fence, a path descends the slightly boggy hillside towards a gate that leads into the inbye. On the far side of this gate, a grass track leads onwards and down to a levelling in the ridge. Here, this track forks but take the left, descending branch that leads off the ridge. This descends circuitously to reach a gravelled track that runs along the bottom of the field. A left turn here leads down to a gate by the houses at Barrowburn.

Although the track continues through the gate, keep above the fence and continue to an open gateway. Once through this, the grassy path keeps above both the wall and fence on the right and continues to a stile into a field on the right just beyond a line of trees leading down to the river. A right turn, once over this stile, leads down the edge of the slightly wet field to reach the pair of stiles by the footbridge over the river where the walk began.

Tosson Hill

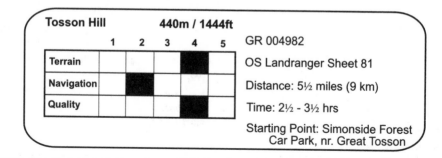

Tosson Hill			440m / 1444ft			
	1	2	3	4	5	GR 004982
Terrain				■		OS Landranger Sheet 81
Navigation		■				Distance: 5½ miles (9 km)
Quality				■		Time: 2½ - 3½ hrs

Starting Point: Simonside Forest Car Park, nr. Great Tosson

Tosson Hill is the highest point of the Simonside Hills, which rise to the south of Rothbury and Coquetdale, and are named after the slightly lower but more pronounced summit of Simonside. The hills themselves are covered in a mixture of heather, grouse-shooting moorland and forestry. The summit of Simonside makes a popular objective for an afternoon stroll, especially on a clear day when the view from its summit can be best appreciated. However, Tosson Hill is in a much wilder setting and relatively few venture out onto its less appealing summit.

There is a forestry car park on the hill's north-eastern slopes, just off the lane that connects Great Tosson with the B6342, which runs south from Rothbury, and this car park provides the most appropriate starting point. The route starts from the left-hand edge of the car park and runs through the trees to reach the picnic site. Upon reaching this, a path turns up the slope to the right and proceeds up a peat and stone track through the trees. The gradient is not too steep but the slope is unrelenting and, after crossing a traversing track at mid-height, the path ends at a forestry road.

A left turn on this road, which immediately swings back right, continues the ascent, although now much more gently. Fairly soon, the track emerges from the trees and onto the heather moorland above, with the grey sandstone crags of the summit ridge appearing ahead. It is not too long before this track comes to an end where the highest forestry road runs along the hillside. However, a path opposite leads onwards and, after crossing some flattish boggy ground, arrives at the foot of the steep final heather and bracken slopes that lead to the ridge. The path climbs straight up this slope, although it soon turns into an easy scramble as the peat has been eroded down to the underlying rocks on this steep bank.

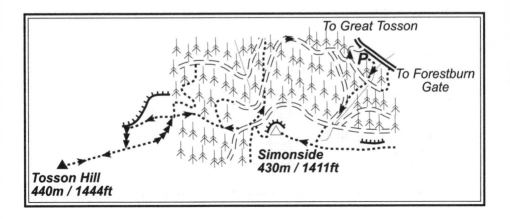

The top of the slope is soon reached, however, and the ridge path joined; a right turn leads up to the large summit cairn on Simonside. Of the two summits, this is probably the better viewpoint, due to the presence of steep drops on almost all sides. The view is not dissimilar to that from many of the other local hills, with the lower, partly forested, moorlands flanking the higher ground of the Cheviot range. On the other side of Coquetdale, the ground gradually rises to the moorland of Long Crag, whilst Tosson Hill is visible as a small outcrop further along this ridge to the west.

The path continues from Simonside by swinging half left and then dropping sharply downhill to reach the low point between it and Tosson Hill. On the col go straight over onto another forest track, although keep straight ahead when this track bears to the left. This broad path runs along the edge of the forest on the left and it should be followed, ignoring right-hand branching paths, until the fence at the edge of the forest is reached at a point marked with two tall metal poles.

At this point, it is possible to cross the fence by means of a few stones and emerge onto the open moor. A small path in the heather leads onwards to reach some sandstone crags on the northern escarpment. Keeping along the top of these crags, a small path leads onwards, although in due course this peters out in the heather. When it all starts to get a bit too rough, strike off up left through the heather to the ridge where another path will be joined. This again is quite small but it leads on across the moor to the right to reach the trig point, which stands inside a hollow cairn. From here, the absence of the forest means that more of Coquetdale is visible, with the lake formed in the disused Caistron Quarry being particularly prominent.

The descent begins by returning to the forestry fence. Thus, the small path should be followed back across the moor, although there is no need to branch left to the crags. The ridge path continues to a cairn quite close to the fence, where it ends in the heather. The two metal posts are, however, visible and a beeline half left through the heather may be made to them. Ignoring a path following the other side of the fence, continue ahead, back along the edge of the pine trees on the right. A first path on the left turns sharply back through the heather and then the forest track swings in from the right. Just after this, a second path takes off to the left.

This path should be followed and it crosses the heather strip to the top of the plantation on the left and descends through it to reach a forest road. Here, turn right and, unless you want to detour to Little Church Rock along a signposted path on the right, continue down to a junction of forestry roads. Just before this, on the left, there is a stone ring a few yards from the track. This marks the remains of a 4,000-year-old burial mound that was excavated in 1890. Continue around the hillside to the right at the junction to reach a mast in the trees on the left. Beyond this, the track merges with another and, ignoring a right turn, hairpins down the lower slopes to reach the car park.

Long Crag

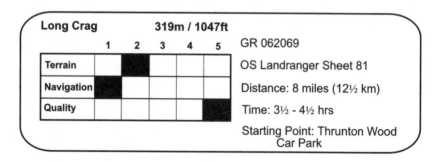

Long Crag						319m / 1047ft
	1	2	3	4	5	GR 062069
Terrain		■				OS Landranger Sheet 81
Navigation	■					Distance: 8 miles (12½ km)
Quality					■	Time: 3½ - 4½ hrs
						Starting Point: Thrunton Wood Car Park

To the north of Rothbury, there lies a large rolling tract of sandstone heather moorland forming a continuation of the Simonside Hills north of

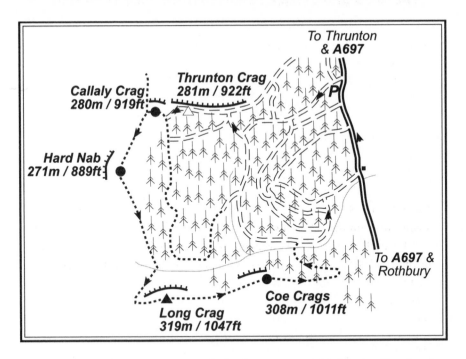

the Coquet valley. Long Crag is the highest point of this block of land and stands atop one of two north-facing escarpments. The other is the long line of Thrunton Crag and Callaly Crag. Between them lies the valley of the Coe Burn, the headwaters of which drain much of the northern part of the moor. The plantation of Thrunton Wood covers much of the north-eastern part of the moor and adds to its charm.

The best starting point for an ascent is actually the forestry car park, which is signposted down a back lane off the A697 Morpeth to Coldstream road. From the car park, three forestry trails head into the wood. Our route forms a combination of the yellow and red trails, whilst providing a shorter alternative to the longest of the three waymarked walks – the red trail or Four Crags Walk – to reach the summit. Of course, if a long expedition was desired, the red walk could be followed throughout. However, as none of this route lies on public rights of way, the Forestry Commission are entitled to close it at their discretion. They currently close the moorland part of the walks between October and March to avoid damage to the paths.

Leave the car park by the forest road that runs into the trees from the information board. This climbs gently uphill and, ignoring tracks to both the left and right, eventually ends at another track climbing up from the left. The ascent continues to the right and, before very long, this track swings right to emerge out onto the top of Thrunton Crag by a bench. The northwards view is quite superb with the ground dropping away steeply down the escarpment. Half right, the summit of Ros Hill can be seen above Chillingham, whilst the north-eastern hills of the Cheviots rise steeply out of the other side of the lowlands.

Our route now follows the orange route in reverse until just beyond Callaly Crag. Hence, a left turn is required at the top of Thrunton Crag to follow the forest track leftwards along the edge of the escarpment. In due course, the track swings slightly to the left and reaches the edge of the forest opposite a gate. Do not use this but instead turn sharply back to the right and follow the wall along for a short distance to reach another smaller gate on the left. On the other side of this, a path leads across the moorland towards the pines on the top of Callaly Crag, where there is an idyllic tarn.

The path leads across the summit with little deviation and there is little view due to the protective shield of pine trees. Beyond, the path drops slightly and reaches the top of a path climbing up the escarpment from the right in a small gully. Here, the red route is joined and this is now followed to the summit and beyond. Hence, continue straight ahead at this junction and follow the path onwards back out of the trees and uphill slightly to the cairn on the highest point of Hard Nab.

Long Crag now lies to the south across the head of the Coe Burn and the path turns southwards towards it. After continuing across the moor for a short distance, a gate is reached that leads back into the forest. However, the red route and only path continue along the edge, just inside the boundary. However, it is not far before another gate leads back out onto the open moor and the path cuts across the headwaters of the Coe Burn to reach a third gate that once again leads back inside the forest boundary, although now the hillside ahead is all open moor.

Once through this gate, the path swings to the right and follows the wall for a short distance before swinging left and beginning the climb in earnest. The path, which is quite steep in places, aims to the right of the summit and gains the ridge after a fairly unrelenting ascent. Once on the ridge, the path turns slightly left and climbs the final slopes to pass a lower cairn before crossing a slight depression and climbing again to reach the trig point. Long Crag is the best viewpoint of all with a complete panorama. The view to the south is somewhat blocked by the bulk of the Simonside Hills, although they form a shapely skyline. To the west, the Cheviot massif is dominant, whilst to the north lower hills lead towards the Scottish border.

The path now continues along the ridge, aiming for the next summit – Coe Crags. The depression between these two summits is not large, although the stony path drops slightly to the left of the ridge *en route*. Coe Crags is a very shapely peak with a final conical summit set back from the edge of some majestic crags with a scattering of small pine trees for scenic effect. Still marked with red waymarkers, the path continues its eastwards line along the ridge before swinging left and dropping down into the trees. Once inside the wood, the path swings back around to the left and spends some time making a traverse of the slopes before once again slanting downhill.

Towards the foot of the slope, the red route is joined by another, unwaymarked path and, together, they turn to the right and drop down to a footbridge across the Coe Burn and reach a forestry road on the far side. Here, the red route turns to the left and climbs over Coe Hill before dropping back to the car park. However, it is possible to minimise the distance and ascent by turning to the right on the forest road. Initially, the road follows the course of the Coe Burn on the right but soon the track turns away to the left and traverses the hillslopes. After being joined by another couple of tracks on the left, it swings to the right when joined by a third track and continues out to the road opposite the few small houses at Coeburn. The car park now lies about half a mile up this road to the left and is soon reached after a slight ascent.

Ros Hill

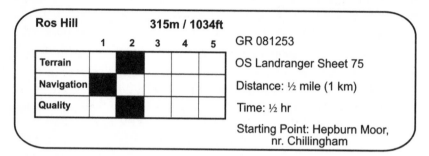

Ros Hill	315m / 1034ft				
	1	2	3	4	5
Terrain		■			
Navigation	■				
Quality		■			

GR 081253

OS Landranger Sheet 75

Distance: ½ mile (1 km)

Time: ½ hr

Starting Point: Hepburn Moor, nr. Chillingham

Ros Hill is the highest point of the moor above Chillingham, with its castle and famous breed of wild white cattle. The cattle have been enclosed since the twelfth century and live entirely naturally, fending for themselves from their rough grazing and moorland enclosure. They are of particular interest to scientists because, although they are genetically very similar after 900 years of inbreeding, they do not produce deformed calves. However, due to their wide enclosure, there are no footpaths on the hillslopes, making a long walk from the valley impossible.

It is possible to park midway up the slopes on the road that runs across the moor from Hepburn, just to the south of Chillingham. Here, there is a Forestry Commission car park and their red trail takes a circuitous route to the top of the hill, involving some fairly rough moorland walking, and returns down the road. However, what is recommended is to park on the wide verges on the highest point of the road and follow the National Trust footpath from there; this still involves a couple of hundred feet of ascent.

The footpath is marked by a red arrow at its start and it climbs through first heather and then bracken around the back slopes of the hill. To make a small circuit, ignore a first left-hand turn when on the

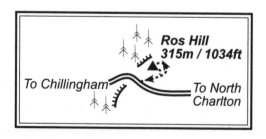

back of the hill and instead go straight on and around to the summit. For the descent, the other path, which has a few steps, can be followed back down.

The summit is marked by a trig point and nearby there is a rather unusual walk-in toposcope built into the wall with four separate plaques. The view is panoramic and, on a clear day, a total of seven castles can be seen from the summit, which lies in a 3,000-year-old hill fort, giving the summit the name of Ros Castle.

Housedon Hill

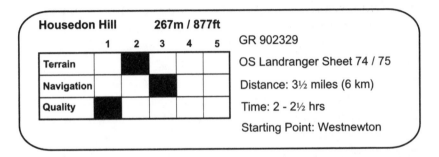

Housedon Hill	267m / 877ft					
	1	2	3	4	5	GR 902329
Terrain		■				OS Landranger Sheet 74 / 75
Navigation			■			Distance: 3½ miles (6 km)
Quality	■					Time: 2 - 2½ hrs
						Starting Point: Westnewton

Despite being the most northerly separate hill in England, Housedon Hill is infrequently visited. The main problem is due to a lack of access but it also suffers from its proximity to the Cheviot range and the other far superior hills described in this book. To the south, it is separated from the Cheviot hills by the valley of the Bowmont Water, whilst, to the north, the ground falls away from the cluster of hills of which Housedon is the highest, to Flodden Field. This was where the Scots, allied with the French, invaded England in 1513 as a spin-off from the Hundred Years War, only to be driven back by Henry VIII's army.

The best approach is from the south, from Westnewton, from where a road runs up to Hethpool in the College Valley. A short distance on the Akeld side of the turn, a footpath takes off to the north across fields and there is room to park a couple of cars on the verge opposite this entrance. The track is signposted to Crookhouse and West Flodden and the track curves across the field to reach a bridge over the Bowmont Water after

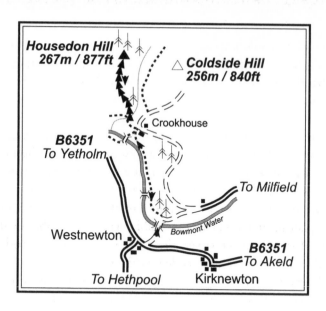

passing through a gap in the old railway cutting. Once across the river, the track curves back to the right and approaches a pine wood.

On reaching the foot of the wood, turn back left and pass through a gate. A right of way then leads along the field, through thistles, by the fenceline at the base of the wood. It then keeps straight ahead through the next field, where it comes close to the river again, although a bridge on the left should be ignored, and through the third field. Once over a small stream at the far side of the field, the path curves to the right and climbs the bank to reach the left-hand edge of the buildings at the farm of Crookhouse.

However, there is no way to enter the buildings and the path turns to the left below the wall and runs along to a stile at the end of a green lane. To reach this, it passes through a bed of thistles and, in the summer months, the green lane is a bed of nettles from end to end, so it is a good idea to bring a stick. The green lane is only a few hundred yards long and it leads out onto the open hill. A grass track swings to the right and leads across the head of a small stream. The right of way turns down to the left and passes through further beds of impenetrable vegetation on its way up the valley.

Fortunately, our route now lies up the ridge ahead, off the right of way. The grassy track leads ahead and climbs through the bracken just to the left of another stand of pine trees. When it stops, aim left and pass through the weaker bracken higher up the slope to reach the rabbit-cropped turf of the higher ridge. The route now lies straight up the crest, avoiding a fenced area on the right to reach a gap in a fence and wall and cross the ridge obliquely.

Once over this boundary, turn to the right and finish climbing the ridge to the lower south summit. The very highest point (the north summit) lies just across a small depression and actually across a further fence on the edge of a larger pine plantation. Due to the trees, there is no view to the north and that to the south is limited to the Cheviot range only. The summit plateau of the Cheviot is visible, as are a number of the steep foothills of the range. However, the scene is not exactly superb and an expeditious descent is recommended by the same route, remembering to aim half left towards the foot of the ridge to avoid the worst of the bracken, nettles, thistles and other unpleasant vegetation.

Section 4 – Eastern Lakeland, Kendal and the Shap Fells

The River Crake from the coast to Coniston Water and the A593 through Yewdale to Skelwith Bridge. Rivers Brathay and Rothay to Grasmere, Dunmail Raise, Thirlmere and St John's Beck to Threlkeld. A66 to Penrith, River Lowther to Shap and River Lune to Lancaster.

NAME	HEIGHT	IN SECTION	IN ENGLAND	IN BRITAIN
Great Mell Fell	537m/1761ft	10 of 20	70 of 184	901 of 1552
Little Mell Fell	505m/1657ft	11 of 20	80 of 184	980 of 1552
Grayrigg Forest	494m/1620ft	12 of 20	83 of 184	994 of 1552
Wansfell	488m/1601ft	13 of 20	84J of 184	1010J of 1552
Hallin Fell	388m/1273ft	14 of 20	106 of 184	1226 of 1552
Lambrigg Fell	339m/1112ft	15 of 20	117 of 184	1309 of 1552
Top o'Selside	335m/1100ft	16 of 20	118J of 184	1315J of 1552
Gummer's How	321m/1054ft	17 of 20	128 of 184	1337J of 1552
Hutton Roof Crags	274m/ 899ft	18 of 20	150 of 184	1423J of 1552
Claife Heights	270m/ 885ft	19 of 20	152 of 184	1428 of 1552
Whitbarrow	215m/ 706ft	20 of 20	173 of 184	1501 of 1552

There are nine summits above 2,000ft that are described in *England's Highest Peaks*.

The region covered by this section contains landscapes that are both typical of the best Lakeland scenery and more Pennine-style moors. There is no doubt that this is the most popular part of the Lake District. It is easy to see why with hills, such as Hallin Fell, that are the epitome of Lakeland scenery – craggy hills with partly wooded slopes alongside long lakes. Many of the hills, however, lie in the southern part of the district, away from the high mountains in the equally beautiful environs of Windermere and Coniston Water. Meanwhile, limestone hills, such as Whitbarrow and Hutton Roof Crags, provide a striking contrast.

The Geology of Lakeland (Sections 4, 5 and 6)

It appears most appropriate to link the whole of the district together when discussing geology because although there are many separate hills here, they are found in a quite compact area with the same basic rock formations.

The Lake District is formed from a massif of sedimentary and volcanic rocks deposited during the Ordovician and Silurian periods. The oldest rocks to be found are the Skiddaw Slates, formed from lower Ordovician sediments. However, the series is not completely formed from slates for, in amongst them, there are beds of flagstones and grits: one band in particular with a high quartz content has been termed the Skiddaw Grit. The rocks are highly cleaved and shaly which, unlike their counterparts in Snowdonia, renders them worthless to the construction industry. It also forms the typically smooth outline of the northern fells (Section 6) around Loweswater, Whinlatter and the Skiddaw massif. The smooth outline is a result of the softer rock, for as it weathers, the rock breaks up into scree, which now covers the slopes and is seen to advantage on Barf and Lord's Seat (Section 6). Occasional igneous intrusions are to be found amongst the other sediments high in the series, immediately prior to the overlying volcanic rocks. Where crags do form, such as on Grasmoor (Section 6), they are formed from the bands of igneous rocks and grits, rather than the slates.

These volcanic rocks were deposited about 500 million years ago, in the Upper Ordovician period, when Lakeland lay close to a tectonic plate boundary. At that boundary, a collision occurred between a section of dense oceanic crust that sank below the less-dense continental crust, into which it collided, supporting what is now Lakeland. This is termed a subduction zone and, as the oceanic crust sank into the Earth's mantle, it melted, causing a build-up of pressure. To relieve this, underwater volcanic vents became active and threw out magma and ash, forming a chain of islands, similar to the West Indies or the islands around the Pacific Rim today.

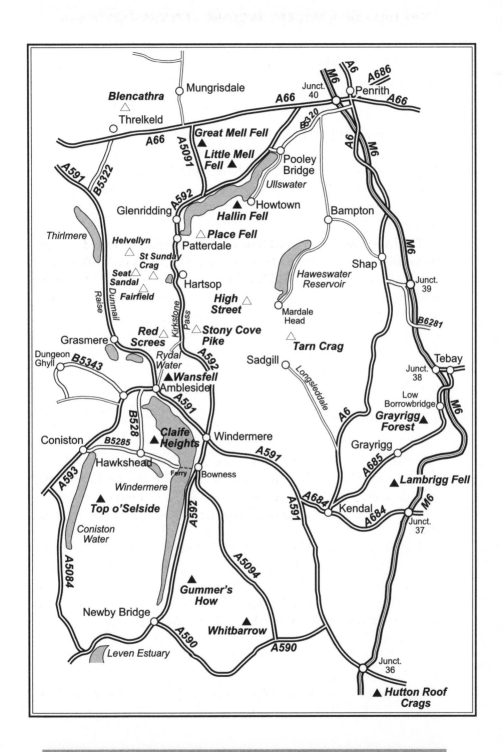

The magma that was thrown out can be divided into two forms, basic andesites, containing less than 50 per cent silica (silicon dioxide), and acid rhyolites, containing more than 50 per cent silica; the higher rocks of the Borrowdale Series, as these Ordovician volcanics have been called, become increasingly rhyolitic in their composition. Being deposited under water, bands of sediment, ranging from fine mudstones to coarse grits, which accumulated between eruptions, are to be found. Due to the heat and pressure, the mudstones underwent considerable metamorphosis, transforming them into true slates. However, not all the slates of the Borrowdale Series are formed from mudstones, for amongst the layers of lava were also deposited large quantities of volcanic ash, which have since developed into green false slates, such as those quarried at Honister (Section 6). These layers of ash have often eroded much more than the lava-based rocks with which they are interleaved. This has led to a terracing effect on many hillsides, which is well seen on the Borrowdale slopes of Bleaberry Fell. These rocks, where now exposed on the surface, form the rugged, craggy hills and mountains for which Lakeland is best known.

In fact, the Borrowdale Series can be divided into several distinct groups. The earliest to be deposited was the Falcon Crag group, followed by the Ullswater basic andesitic group, the Sty Head garnetiferous group, the Scafell ash and breccia group, the Shap andesitic group and finally the Shap rhyolitic group. It is the Falcon Crag group that shows the lava and ash layers to their best and it is this rock that is exposed on the Borrowdale slopes of Bleaberry Fell. However, the Ullswater basic andesitic group differs little in its composition but its well-cleaved ashes form the 'false slates' mentioned earlier at Honister Crag (Section 6). The Sty Head garnetiferous group is quite thin but is characterised by garnets, glassy red gemstones formed from silica, which are found in it. These garnets are thought to have been formed in the original volcanic activity and not as a result of the later intrusions that deposited so many other minerals.

The Scafell ash and breccia group contains very little lava but mainly pyroclastic material, ranging from coarse angular particles to the finest volcanic dusts; in the south, the ashes were compressed into slates, such as those found at Tilberthwaite, near Coniston (Section 5). The Shap andesitic and rhyolitic groups comprised the final volcanic activity, both being similar in structure to the rocks of the Falcon Crag group. At the

ABOVE: The escarpment of the North York Moors boasts a number of sandstone crags, such as these on Cringle Moor (Section 1).

BELOW: A winter's sunset over Potts Moor (Section 2) from near Oughtershaw.

ABOVE: The moorland summit of Hoove (Section 2) from Hope Scar.

BELOW: The northern escarpment of Long Crag (Section 3) from Hard Nab.

ABOVE: The Cheviot Hills from the Summit of Shillhope Law (Section 3).

BELOW: Great Mell Fell (left) and Little Mell Fell (right) from Hallin Fell (Section 4).

ABOVE: The summit of Gummer's How (Section 4) commands an excellent view of southern Lakeland and Windermere, as seen here on a winter's afternoon.

BELOW: The limestone summit ridge of Whitbarrow (Section 4) consists of many knolls and scars, as seen here from the southern end of the ridge.

ABOVE: Windermere from Skelghyll on the slopes of Wansfell (Section 4). The hill to the right of the lake is Claife Heights and Gummer's How can be seen in the distance on the left of the lake.

BELOW: Afternoon sunshine on Harter Fell and the Dunnerdale Fells from the summit of Hard Knott (Section 5).

ABOVE: The craggy slopes of Lingmoor Fell (Section 5) from Elterwater Common.

BELOW: An autumnal scene around Yew Tree Tarn from the slopes of Holm Fell (Section 5).

ABOVE: The craggy slopes of Mellbreak (left) and Crummock Water from near Scale Force (Section 6).

BELOW: The summit of Lord's Seat (Section 6) from Barf.

ABOVE: Looking north along the west coast of the Isle of Man from Bradda Hill (Section 7).

BELOW: The hilly crest of the Isle of Man (Section 7) from Cold Fell in western Lakeland.

same time, a small number of igneous intrusions were injected into the rocks of the Borrowdale Series and can be seen as sills and dykes, varying in composition from basic to rhyolitic. Some larger masses exist, including the Ennerdale and Buttermere granophyre, a pink rhyolitic rock consisting of feldspar (aluminosilicates of potassium and sodium), quartz (silicon dioxide) and chlorite (aluminium, iron and magnesium silicates), well seen on the Bleaberry Comb slopes of the Buttermere Red Pike, visible from Mellbreak and Blake Fell (Section 6).

However, by the end of the Ordovician period, the intense volcanic activity had come to an end and, in the Silurian period, sedimentary rocks were once more being deposited; the first of these were the Coniston Limestones. Like in the upper beds of the Skiddaw slates, some rhyolitic lava flows are to be found amongst the Coniston Limestone group as the volcanic activity became less intense before dying out altogether. Limestones actually play a very small part in the series, which mainly consists of calcareous mudstones, often containing much fine volcanic dust, interstratified with limestones of varying degrees of purity. As such, where the Coniston Limestone appears on the surface, it supports much more lush vegetation than the surrounding acidic soils overlying the Borrowdale Series.

Other Silurian deposits followed, namely the Stockdale Shales, the Coniston Flags and Grits, the Bannisdale Shales and the Kirkby Moor Flags. These rocks are easily weathered and, as such, tend to form the more subdued relief of southern Lakeland and they are well seen on hills such as Claife Heights and Gummer's How (Section 4).

In the Devonian period, it would appear that no new rocks were deposited but, during this period, considerable earth movements occurred. Considerable lateral pressure was exerted on the rocks and this caused extensive doming and folding but also shattering of the rock, resulting in the formation of faults. With continuing pressure, blocks on either side of the fault slid independently from each other; this is a tear fault and these are well seen amongst the Coniston Limestones where the rock bands are, in places, displaced for over a mile. Along the line of these faults, fault-breccias (sections of broken rock fragments) came into being where the movement shattered the rock.

Near horizontal faults appear to exist between the Skiddaw Slates and the Borrowdale volcanic rocks and between the Borrowdale Series and the

Coniston Limestone as well as amongst the Borrowdale rocks and the Silurian beds; evidence for this is provided by the existence of fault-breccias. These earth movements uplifted the sea bed, halting the deposition of sediment, and forming dry land.

The other effect of the uplift was the development of the distinct cleavage in the Skiddaw Slates, mentioned above. Further uplift was caused by a granite intrusion, also of Devonian age, which is exposed near Shap (Section 4), on Carrock Fell (Section 6) and in and on the slopes of Eskdale, Miterdale and lower Wasdale (Section 5). The granite has been exposed here more due to erosion than any other factor but it did have effects on the existing rocks. The greatest was the penetration of hot mineralising solutions under pressure into cracks, developed as a result of the pressure earlier in Devonian times. As the solutions entered these cracks, the pressure was reduced and correspondingly they cooled, depositing their minerals in veins. In the past, these have been extensively mined; particularly notable are the copper-bearing veins above Coniston (Section 5), the iron mines of Eskdale (Section 5) and the lead and copper mines of the northern fells and Newlands (Section 6).

By the Carboniferous period, the district had once more been submerged under a shallow sea but this time a warm tropical one. Tiny organisms and corals thrived on shelves and their bodies sank to the bottom to be compressed into limestone, similar to that seen in Section 2. As in the Pennines, this limestone was then covered in the upper Carboniferous by layers of rocks of the Millstone Grit Facies (grits, shales and sandstones) and then Coal Measures as deltaic conditions and then tropical swamps became prevalent. Further uplifting followed but, unlike earlier, little folding took place and instead an elevated plateau developed. Semi-arid conditions now prevailed in the Permian and Triassic periods in which sandstones were deposited, including the Penrith Sandstone (Permian) and the St Bees and Kirklinton Sandstones (Triassic). These sandstones can also be seen on the Isle of Man (Section 7), which has a somewhat similar geological history. Mid-Cretaceous and Tertiary folding once more uplifted the district but these movements, along with the earlier ones, notably the granitic intrusion, began to allow the landscape to form into what can be seen today.

The movements had formed a domed plateau; the central dome existed somewhere in the Scafell Pike–Great End area (Section 5) but an axis runs eastwards from the dome, roughly through High Raise (Section 6), Red Screes (Section 4), Stony Cove Pike (Section 4) and Harter Fell (Mardale – Section 4). This initiated a rough radial drainage pattern. Around Scafell Pike (Section 5), it is truly radial, the valleys of Borrowdale (R. Derwent), Buttermere, Ennerdale, Wasdale, Eskdale, Dunnerdale and Langdale radiating out like the spokes of a wheel. To the north of the east–west axis, Thirlmere, Ullswater, Mardale (Haweswater) and Swindale developed while to the south lie the Rothay (Grasmere), Troutbeck, Kentmere, Longsleddale and Borrowdale (Borrow Beck, nr. Tebay). These valleys began to erode the slopes of the dome, cutting straight valleys through the Triassic, Permian and Carboniferous deposits to hit the lower Paleozoic rocks. The exception to the rule of straight valleys is Ullswater, which has a bend in it; this is due to the fact that it runs along the line of a fault; Thirlmere is also a fault-valley.

As the valleys deepened, so the plateau surrounding them lowered also, the post-Paleozoic rocks being confined only to small patches on the summits of the highest hills and as concentric rings around the edges of the dome. Soon, all evidence of their existence in the centre of the dome had vanished. However, the Skiddaw group (Section 6) interrupted the radial drainage pattern. This ground had formed a separate and indeed higher dome, which had initiated its own radial drainage; the erosion not only stripped it of its post-Paleozoic deposits but also much of its Silurian and Ordovician deposits, leaving only the lowest layer in the Paleozoic deposits, the Skiddaw Slates, exposed. Another dome existed on the Howgill Fells (Section 2) where today the Silurian deposits can be seen at heights well over 2,000ft (610m), whereas in Lakeland they reach only lower elevations.

The rocks of the Lake District were now exposed in a more or less similar way to how they are today. Therefore, it seems appropriate to discuss their exposure on the surface before discussing the glacial and post-glacial alterations to the landscape. As already mentioned, the district at the end of the Tertiary period represented a large dome with other smaller ones surrounding it and minor anticlines and synclines within the various beds of rock. To recap, the formations began with the Skiddaw Slates (Lower Ordovician and possibly earlier) and they were followed by the Borrowdale Volcanic Series (Upper Ordovician), the soft Silurian sediments and finally the Carboniferous limestones and coals and Permian and Triassic sandstones.

The easiest way to visualise the effect of the erosion upon the area is to imagine the top of the dome simply being cut off. In the north of the region, the Skiddaw Slates are to be found, north of a line drawn between Buttermere, Dale Head, Grange-in-Borrowdale and Penruddock (this is something of an over-simplification as minor variations occur). Between this line and another, drawn between Millom, Coniston, Waterhead (Ambleside), Troutbeck, Kentmere and Sadgill (Longsleddale), lie the Borrowdale Volcanics. To the south of that line lie the Silurian rocks. Around the edge lies a surround of Carboniferous limestones (except on the west coast between Egremont and Millom) and Carboniferous coal measures lying on the Cumbrian coalfield around Whitehaven. Around these Carboniferous deposits, Permian and Triassic sediments are to be found in the Eden Valley and around Penrith but these are absent on the coast between Whitehaven and Maryport where the Carboniferous rocks form the shoreline. Again, the Permian and Triassic deposits are not to be found in the south-east where the Pennine Faults (see Sections 4 and 8) have elevated the land exposing the underlying Paleozoic rocks. Around Langdale, a syncline has exposed all of the rocks of the Borrowdale Series on the surface.

It is important to note that the Lake District that existed then had much fewer, if any, lakes, fewer crags and more rounded summits. It was the Ice Age that carved out the landforms seen today and it would have begun with a gradual build-up and compaction of snow into ice. This occurred first in valleys but as the quantities grew, it spread over connecting ridges, forming a huge ice sheet over the whole district. It is difficult to establish how much of the erosion caused by the Ice Age is attributable to this building-up phase of glaciation, as the huge power of the later ice sheet would have removed all its effects.

At the end of the period, the ice would have gradually diminished, exposing the ridges and summits and then eventually the valleys also; the last pockets would be in corries, where little glaciers would survive for a short time. It was probably not quite this simple; minor fluctuations in temperature would have caused sporadic advances and retreats and possibly a major thaw followed by another subsequent build-up, removing the effects of the earlier period. What can be certain is that the ice was shed by the central east–west axis across the district mentioned above. It did breach this at two points, firstly at Kirkstone Pass and more dramatically at Dunmail Raise.

Northwards and westwards, the movement of the ice was inhibited by the Scottish ice, which was forced around the Lake District and to the east up the Eden Valley through the Stainmore Gap (Section 3). In the centre of the district, where the ice was able to move freely, most erosion occurred whilst to the north, in the Skiddaw group (Section 6) and to the west in the Howgill Fells (Section 2), where the Scottish ice inhibited the flow, glacial changes have been quite minor. Like present-day winds, the movement of the ice differed at different altitudes: in the valleys it was constrained, being forced to move in the radial pattern mentioned earlier whilst at higher altitudes it is thought that it moved much more freely.

One example of the erosive action of the glaciers are rounded rocks known as roches moutonnées. These are exposures of rock that are smoothed and polished on the side that faces up the valley whilst they are rough and irregular on the side facing down the valley. This is attributed to the scouring action of the ice as it passed over it and then a plucking action as it moved away. They occur often on all types of rocks and notable examples exist near Quay Foot Quarry in Borrowdale.

The glaciers had the effect of widening and deepening valleys. As there was more ice in the main dale than in tributary valleys, the main valley deepened much more, leaving the tributary to emerge, once the ice had retreated, high on the valley side. These tributaries are known as hanging valleys, notable examples being the Watendlath valley on the eastern side of Borrowdale above Derwentwater, Gillercomb on the western side of Borrowdale at Seathwaite and Bleaberry Comb opposite Buttermere. The latter is much shorter than the other two and has a corrie at its head.

Corries are formed mainly on the northern and eastern slopes of the fells where the snow collected most and small glaciers remained once the main ice sheet had retreated. These small glaciers plucked away at the depressions on the hillsides in which they formed, deepening their bases and steepening their walls. Notable examples are on the Buttermere side of the High Stile ridge (Section 6), on the eastern side of Helvellyn (Section 4), at the head of Mardale (Section 4) and above Coniston (Section 5).

Many corries have tarns in them, where the ice has deepened the floor, but in some cases they have silted up completely. At the mouths of other corries, moraines (collections of debris deposited by a retreating glacier) have formed a natural dam, deepening the tarn. The action of the ice in neighbouring corries has sometimes formed sharp arêtes between corries, Striding Edge and Swirral Edge on Helvellyn (Section 4) being prime examples. Corries, or combes as they are sometimes called, are similar to hanging valleys in that their outflow streams fall steeply down to valley level in a series of cascades, Sour Milk Gill near Buttermere (Section 6) being a fine example.

Valley glaciers were also irregular in their movement and, on occasions, deepened the valley at a particular point in which a lake may have subsequently formed. Many of the long ribbon lakes found in the Lake District are also dammed by moraines at their outflow. Another characteristic of glacial valleys is their U-shape in cross-section. This is a direct consequence of the widening, deepening and removal of interlocking spurs by the glacier. As the glaciers began to move more slowly or retreated, they deposited rock material in moraines which appear as small grassy hillocks often with damp, marshy ground in between them. An excellent example lies just above Black Sail Youth Hostel in Ennerdale (Section 6).

Other material has been deposited as boulder clay in valley floors and in some cases this has choked the valley so much that it has caused a diversion of the river. There are two good examples of this; the first is the Wythop Valley near Bassenthwaite Lake. This small valley, which supports only a small stream, begins high on the hillside on the eastern side of Bassenthwaite Lake near Beck Wythop. It then descends gradually down to Cockermouth, away from the lake, where it meets the present course of the River Derwent. Originally, this valley was the outflow of the River Derwent but because it became so clogged up by glacial drift (boulder clay), the river cut itself a new course and deepened its new valley. However, what has happened at the foot of Windermere is even more striking. At places such as Haverthwaite and Backbarrow, most would express surprise that such a big river as the Leven (Windermere's outflow) is flowing down such a narrow valley. The reason is that its original valley, a wide, almost dry dale, containing the village of Cartmel, became so clogged with glacial drift that the Leven broke over a low col into a neighbouring valley which supported only a small beck; the Leven has not had time yet to widen this valley sufficiently to satisfy its own requirements.

Where corries have not formed on the fellsides, many Lakeland ridges can easily be seen to be asymmetrical. Although not perfect due to corries, the Helvellyn range is a good example: on its western side it throws down quite dull convex slopes to Thirlmere whilst it is much steeper and rockier on its eastern side. Great Rigg, a member of the Fairfield group, and Red Screes (Section 4) are prime examples, their north-western slopes being convex whilst their south-eastern slopes are distinctly concave. This is due to the fact that the strongest ice currents were to be found on the eastern sides of the valleys so it is here that they did most erosion, the original rounded outline remaining relatively undisturbed on the western slopes. Although most Lakeland ridges follow this pattern of convex slopes on the south or west and concave slopes on the north or east, Blencathra (Section 6) and most prominently Illgill Head (Section 5) are exceptions to the rule, having steep slopes on the south and west and subdued relief to the north and west. In both places, there is evidence that there were exceptionally strong ice currents on these steepened slopes.

After the Ice Age, freeze-thaw weathering has produced scree slopes; particularly notable are those on the southern side of Wastwater (Section 6). Also, large quantities of peat have formed on the acid, wet hillsides from dead organic matter.

Access (Section 4 only)

The west coast main line passes to the east of the district, with Intercity services to Oxenholme and Penrith. A branch line between Oxenholme and Windermere has regular daily services in summer; in winter it still runs daily but the service is more limited. There are direct trains between Windermere, Manchester Piccadilly and Manchester Airport, again subject to the above restrictions. There are regular bus services linking Windermere with Ambleside, Grasmere and Keswick. The A591 links Kendal and Keswick via Ambleside and Grasmere (approachable from the south from Junction 36 of the M6), whilst the A593 links Ambleside and Coniston. A weekend bus service runs between Penrith and the head of Haweswater. The A592 crosses Kirkstone Pass and runs between Windermere and Penrith via Patterdale (approachable from the north from Junction 40 of the M6).

Accommodation (Section 4 only)

There are plenty of bed and breakfast establishments and hotels in Ambleside and Windermere, with fewer around Patterdale and Glenridding. Either Ambleside or Grasmere is probably the best base; in Grasmere there are plenty of hotels but a few bed and breakfast establishments also, including a couple up the Easedale Road and a couple along the Red Bank Road. There are youth hostels at Thirlmere, Langdale (Red Bank), Grasmere (Butterlip How and Thorney How), Ambleside, Windermere, Coniston (Holly How and Coppermines), Hawkshead, Patterdale, Helvellyn (actually above the village of Glenridding, at the foot of the mountain) and Kendal.

Great Mell Fell and Little Mell Fell

The Mell Fells are two of Lakeland's most distinctive hills and are almost exact replicas of each other in terms of shape and stature. Great Mell Fell is the higher and its slopes are clothed richly in an assortment of pines and deciduous trees. Little Mell Fell, by contrast, is bare but is slightly larger in extent than its neighbour, throwing down two ridges to the north. Both hills rise from the relatively flat and bleak moorland separating Ullswater from Mungrisdale, although they are separated by a deep valley through which waters flow southwards eventually to plummet down to Ullswater at the dramatic cascades of Aira Force. Although each hill is best climbed separately by its own up-and-back route, they are considered here together more as a pair since both hills can be climbed together in a fairly leisurely day if desired. However, if time is pressing then Great Mell Fell is far superior to its more lowly neighbour.

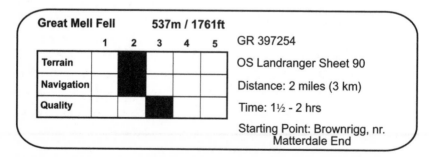

Great Mell Fell	537m / 1761ft					
	1	2	3	4	5	GR 397254
Terrain		■				OS Landranger Sheet 90
Navigation		■				Distance: 2 miles (3 km)
Quality			■			Time: 1½ - 2 hrs
						Starting Point: Brownrigg, nr. Matterdale End

The starting point for Great Mell Fell is at the foot of its south-east ridge on the Matterdale End to Penruddock road. A track takes off to the west when the road comes in tight under the hill's slopes and there is room to park a few cars on verges hereabouts. The route starts by following the track past a first stile on the right to a second one. Both these stiles lead onto the steep and wooded lower slopes of Great Mell Fell and, from the second, a path follows the fenceline half left that separates the open hill and wood from the lowland fields. On the right, there are the scars of a small quarry and the path continues by the fence until out of the wood, from where onwards the hillside on the right is bracken-clad.

Look out for a small path in the bracken, which begins to climb the steep hillside on the right. This path leads eventually to the summit after many twists and turns but is a delightful route to follow. The steepest bit is at the beginning and the gradient soon begins to slacken slightly and a right fork should soon be taken (the main track) to follow a groove up the hillside and out of the bracken. The groove then continues across grass and the path should be followed up it until the ridge itself is gained. At this point, the main path swings to the left and begins to climb the ridge, passing a number of gnarled and windbeaten trees.

Ahead, a band of pine trees stretches across the ridge and forms a small wood. The path becomes a little indistinct on the ridge before them but its line can be followed with care and the route is much more obvious in descent. In a patch of rushes a hundred yards short of the wood, follow the main path around to the left and then along and up towards the left edge of the wood where it turns into a tractor track. It turns to the right into

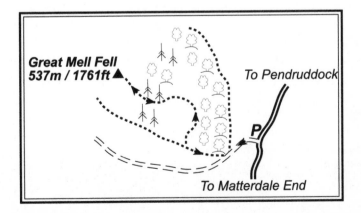

the trees and then ignoring branches to the left, the track continues to the top edge of the wood, from where the path again leads onwards past more lone and battered trees. Once past the last tree, the path splits: the main branch goes right but the smaller path ahead can be followed if desired. Both paths rejoin just short of the summit, which is marked by a small cairn on a slightly raised summit mound.

The view is quite extensive, as is often the case from monolithic hills. Little Mell Fell, of course, features prominently, as does, most spectacularly, Blencathra. Much of the rest of the view is dominated by the Helvellyn, Fairfield and High Street fells and Ullswater is only visible in part. However, it is certainly an attractive view and the Lakeland fells are seen from a somewhat unusual perspective. The return is best made by simply reversing the route of ascent back down the ridge, taking care to turn to the right just above the lower wood to follow the groove back down the steep lower slopes.

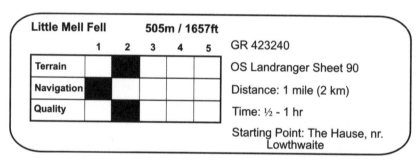

Little Mell Fell	505m / 1657ft					GR 423240
	1	2	3	4	5	
Terrain		■				OS Landranger Sheet 90
Navigation	■					Distance: 1 mile (2 km)
Quality		■				Time: ½ - 1 hr

GR 423240

OS Landranger Sheet 90

Distance: 1 mile (2 km)

Time: ½ - 1 hr

Starting Point: The Hause, nr. Lowthwaite

Little Mell Fell has only one practicable route of ascent and that is from the south at a pass known as The Hause. This can be reached by car from Great Mell Fell by driving towards Matterdale End and then taking the first turning on the left. The Hause is then the point where the road crosses the ridge ahead and there is a small lay-by on the right. The route begins by crossing a stile by a gate on the left just a few yards further on from the lay-by. A path crosses a field to another gate and stile that give access onto the open fell.

A steeply rising path continues half left and this is signposted as a permitted path. After climbing steadily for a while, it levels off somewhat and begins a rising traverse to the left. Continue along this path but look out for a small grass path on the right that climbs the final slopes to reach

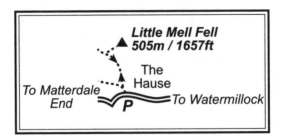

the summit and trig point. Ironically, for its relatively drab appearance, Little Mell Fell is the better viewpoint. There is a much improved view of Ullswater, on the other side of which stands Hallin Fell with Martindale and Boredale beyond. In addition, the view of the northern fells has now opened up to encompass more summits, including Skiddaw itself.

Despite there being three paths leading away from the summit, neither of the other two are continuous enough to make a practical alternative for a descent down the steep slopes, so the route of ascent should simply be reversed back to The Hause.

Grayrigg Forest

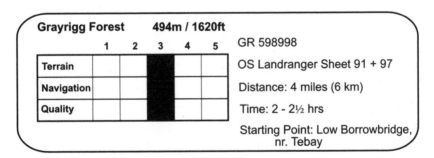

Grayrigg Forest	1	2	3	4	5
Terrain			■		
Navigation			■		
Quality			■		

494m / 1620ft

GR 598998

OS Landranger Sheet 91 + 97

Distance: 4 miles (6 km)

Time: 2 - 2½ hrs

Starting Point: Low Borrowbridge, nr. Tebay

On the south-eastern limb of the Shap Fells, a prominent and steep-sided ridge extends on a north-west to south-east axis, separating the valleys of Bannisdale and Borrowdale. Named the Whinfell Ridge, this axis is much more reminiscent of the nearby Howgills – on the other side of the Lune Gorge – than the bulk of the bleak Shap Fells, with which the ridge is

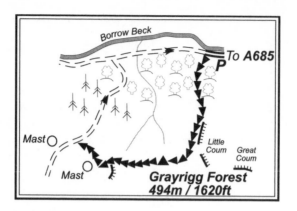

technically joined. Indeed, parts of it are wooded, much of it is enclosed by large and rough upland fields, whilst around the summit of Grayrigg Forest, and more particularly its more eastern top – Grayrigg Pike – the slopes drop sharply into two dramatic combes, each with its own gracefully curving head and a narrow and low ridge separating the two. By ascending along the edge of the more western combe – Little Coum – both may be savoured, together with the dramatic views of the Lune Gorge at the foot of the slopes.

Once upon a time, before the construction of the west coast main line and, most obtrusively, the M6 through the hidden 'corridor' through the hills of the Lune Gorge, the hamlet of Low Borrowbridge was no doubt a place of tranquil serenity. However, today, the River Lune, railway, motorway and rebuilt A685 Kendal to Tebay road jostle for position in this deep and narrow valley. Low Borrowbridge is the starting point for this route and there is a lay-by for parking just down a lane to the west from the A685 almost opposite the road into the hamlet underneath the M6 and railway viaducts. From the lay-by, a gated tarmac lane, which is a bridleway, leads on up the unspoilt valley of Borrowdale, which still has much of the rural Lakeland charm that its more famous namesake at Keswick has lost. The lane is reserved for the return to the car park after the descent, whereas the ascent starts almost immediately. Once through the gate and into the wood beyond, turn to the left and follow the fence on the left-hand edge of the wood steeply uphill, crossing some very wet and boggy ground underfoot.

The top of the wood is not marked by any fence but rather the trees simply give way to a steep and grassy hillside. There is a gate in the wall on the left but ignore this and instead follow a grassy trod rising half right from the gate up the exceedingly steep hillside, curving to the right to avoid a series of stepped craglets by the wall ahead. Once above these, the grass track rather loses its identity but continue by the wall to attain height rapidly with ever more impressive views of the Lune Gorge behind allowing for many stops to 'admire the view' (!). After some time, the wall turns to the right through slightly more than a right-angle and, just before this, where the wall is broken down slightly on the left, cross the makeshift wire fence plugging the gap to reach the other side. Depending on the weather, there are now two options. In clear weather, continue ahead, following a grassy groove on the left of a small valley to emerge soon close to the edge of Little Coum ahead. This edge can then be followed around to the right to reach the wall running up the ridge on the upper Coum's right-hand side. In mist, however, turn to the right and follow the uphill side of the wall along before turning left and following a branching wall uphill, which is the one mentioned above.

A slight descent follows on the ridge before the final climb to the summit. Ahead is a series of broken crags on the flank of Little Coum and, at a point of your choice before reaching these, the wall on the right must be crossed. There is one point where the wall is particularly low for those not into acrobatics. On the other and less dramatic side of the wall, a vehicle track runs up through the rough grass. However, when the wall swings left to follow the edge of Little Coum past the crags, aim straight up the hillside to gain the ridge a short distance ahead and then turn to the right to reach the trig point on a knoll that is only very slightly higher than its surroundings.

The view from the summit is particularly superb, with the grassy Howgill Fells perhaps being the most eyecatching scene in view. To the north of Tebay, the limestone uplands around Crosby Garrett and Crosby Ravensworth can be seen, although their lower elevation does little to promote their interesting uplands. They merge into the bleak and uninspiring mass of the Shap Fells, traversed by the twin carriageways of the M6. Further west, the high ridge of the High Street fells is somewhat upstaged by the conical summits on its southern limb around Kentmere. The Coniston fells also appear prominently, as do the wind turbines on the seemingly insignificant height of Lambrigg Fell to the south.

The descent route lies along the ridge to the north-west past a pair of prominent landscape features not already mentioned – the Whinfell masts. Before reaching them, however, the ridge should be followed down to the col at the head of the next valley on the right. Once over this, the ground rises steeply but make an ascent around the right-hand flank so as to avoid the craggy slope directly ahead. There is one final obstacle before reaching the first mast – a high wall. This one is very greasy and requires much care to cross safely. The best crossing point is on the very highest point of the ridge where the drop on the far side is least and can be safely swung down. Once across it, turn half right and pass the mast on your left and continue that line downhill towards the head of the next tributary valley. Before reaching the valley bottom, however, a grass track will be crossed that, although invisible during the descent from the mast, is quite hard to miss. A right turn on it leads down to a gate through a wall and off the rough hill.

The track runs through some rushes, following a wire fence on the right, towards the head of the wood ahead. Take time here to admire possibly the most charming view seen all day – that of the rarely seen curving valley of Borrowdale with its typically Lakeland combination of crags and scree fans, woods and flat, fertile fields on the valley floor. The track continues to wind down through the wood to reach the bridleway running up the valley a short distance above the valley floor. This track may then be followed to the right and it soon becomes tarmacked for the final walk down the valley to the lay-by, accompanied towards the end by the rushing waters of the Borrow Beck.

Wansfell

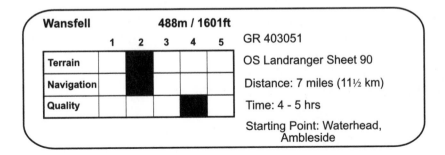

Wansfell						488m / 1601ft
	1	2	3	4	5	
Terrain		■				
Navigation		■				
Quality				■		

GR 403051

OS Landranger Sheet 90

Distance: 7 miles (11½ km)

Time: 4 - 5 hrs

Starting Point: Waterhead, Ambleside

Wansfell is a commanding height between Ambleside and Troutbeck and makes for a popular outing from these places. Its summit is the southerly termination of the most westerly ridge descending from the High Street range, from which the fell only narrowly gains its detachment. The low point at Woundale Raise is crossed by the Windermere to Kirkstone road and the uninspiring view from there is characteristic of the northern and eastern slopes. However, a fine walk may be completed most conveniently from Ambleside to combine the summit with the classic view from the southern slopes.

There are a number of places to park in Ambleside, although the most appropriate is the pay and display car park at Waterhead, which can be approached from the lower road from the traffic lights at the head of Lake Windermere. There are toilets, and a short flight of steps leads up from the back of the car park to the main road into Ambleside. This should be followed to the left and past the garden centre on the left at the outskirts of the town.

Shortly beyond this, fork right up a minor road that runs parallel to the first and past the top of another car park, which is accessible from the main road and would serve as a good alternative to the one at Waterhead. Not far beyond this car park, a lane leads steeply to the right and this should be followed before branching left on a connecting road which leads to a second lane leading uphill. This one now leads up to the top of the houses, from where a track leads on and into the woods above.

The track now takes an ascending line across the hillside above Ambleside on the left. Beyond the end of the wood, it continues along the foot of a field high above the lower valley of Stock Ghyll and its waterfalls.

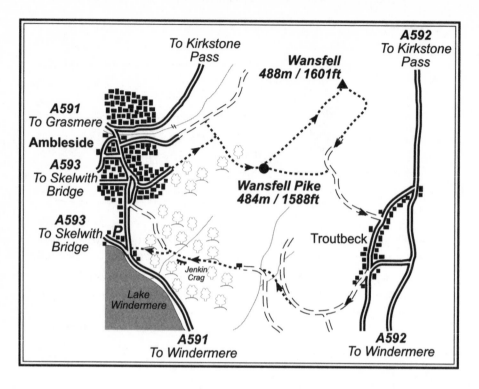

In due course, the track comes to an end where a paved path climbs up the hillside from the left to the right. This is now the main Wansfell path from the town centre and it may be followed steeply uphill to the right. After being carefully restored, this steep path is a joy to walk as the views increase all the way upwards. There are a few rocky sections but surprisingly soon the rocky cone of Wansfell Pike is underfoot at the southern end of the Wansfell ridge.

Although not the very highest point, this charming rocky eminence is certainly the one that most people visit. Windermere is dominating in the view, flanked by Claife Heights on the right and, more distantly, by Gummer's How on the left. However, the best views of Windermere are to be had from Skelghyll on the route back to Ambleside. The Coniston and Langdale fells feature best in the view, although the Fairfield group and Red Screes dominate the north-western skyline. To the north, Stony Cove Pike lies to the right of Kirkstone Pass, whilst Ill Bell is the most dominant of the Kentmere fells.

The very highest point of Wansfell, which is known as Baystones, lies at the northern end of the summit ridge. It is reached by following the Troutbeck path over the ladder stile in the summit wall and then turning to the left alongside the wall. A number of bumps are crossed before a second ladder stile is reached over a transverse wall. Beyond this, the path swings slightly away from the wall to cross two quite sharp eminences before splitting. Ignore the right branch and go ahead until the path becomes more distinct again and leads up to the cairn on the northern summit, from where the view of Windermere is significantly reduced.

A few yards further north, a wall marks the end of public access on the fell. This wall should be followed downhill to the right where there is a faint path. After a quite steep descent on grass, the wall turns sharply to the right and continues along until a ladder stile leads left into the head of Nanny Lane. This walled lane leads all the way down in a series of turns to the road in Troutbeck village, joining with the direct path from Wansfell Pike en route.

Once on the road in the village, turn to the right and continue on until the post office is reached on the right. Immediately beyond this a track, signposted 'Robin Lane', forks to the right. This rough lane leads past a final house on the right before climbing around the hillside and joining with other tracks from the left to come to a point below a pillar on the hill on the right. Here, where the track has stopped climbing, leave it and fork left through a gate signposted 'Skelghyll and Jenkin Crag'. This path leads clearly down the edge of a field and around crossing two streams to meet the tarmac drive leading to the farm at High Skelghyll. A track, however, leads onwards from the farm and soon enters Skelghyll wood. Throughout the stretch from Robin Lane to the wood the views of Windermere are superb, with the rarely seen Blelham Tarn close to the far bank. However, once in the wood the renowned viewpoint of Jenkin Crag is passed on the left. There is access but the views are no better than those from Skelghyll and are somewhat reduced by the surrounding trees.

It is now no great distance back to Waterhead and the main track continues from the crag before forking. Either fork leads to a small bridge across a charming stream that cascades down the hillside through the wood. Once across it, follow the main track downhill and then to the right. However, look out for a path on the left after the right turn and follow this path over a crosspath and downhill to the bottom of the wood where it enters a field down a ladder. The path then slants half right to another stile on the other side, from where an enclosed path leads down between the houses to the road at the traffic lights. From here the car park can be reached either down the road opposite or by the flight of steps along to the right.

Hallin Fell

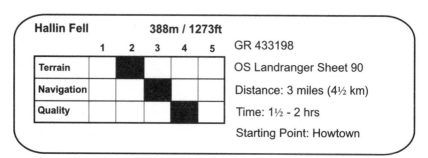

Hallin Fell			388m / 1273ft			
	1	2	3	4	5	GR 433198
Terrain		■				OS Landranger Sheet 90
Navigation			■			Distance: 3 miles (4½ km)
Quality				■		Time: 1½ - 2 hrs
						Starting Point: Howtown

What Hallin Fell lacks in either bulk or stature it makes up for by virtue of its commanding position. It juts out into the water just where Ullswater bends, making it visible for the length of the lake and enhancing its distinctive profile. The hillsides rise steeply from the surrounding valleys to a craggy hill that is quite separate from any of the surrounding higher peaks. This is the trippers' hill and many walk to its summit from the head of the Howtown hairpins. However, a pleasant ramble may be made up the northern slopes from the shores of Ullswater to complete a short but interesting circuit.

Howtown is the best starting point and this can be reached by road from Pooley Bridge down Ullswater's eastern shore. At weekends and popular periods, it is possible to park in the field by the pier for a small fee by permission of the Outdoors Centre, although there are plans to make the car park permanent. Otherwise, it is possible to park on the road through the village to Martindale, or the walk can be combined with a cruise on the steamer from either Glenridding or Pooley Bridge.

From the car park at the northern end of the village, a path leads along the shore the short distance to the pier, which stands on a promontory at the mouth of the beck. The lakeside path crosses this on a bridge and

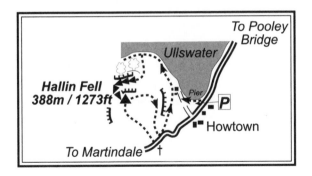

continues close to the shore to reach the track leading to the house at Waternook. However, the path slants across this and climbs steps to reach the open fell just above the house. Once here, continue on the 'lakeside' path by turning right and continuing along above the shoreline fields. After a while, the fields cease and the path drops gradually down to reach the lake by Geordie's Crag at the foot of Hallin Fell's north ridge. Here, the path, following the lake, curves left and then continues towards the wood ahead, skirting a small bay in the process.

However, just before the bay, a small path turns uphill to the left through bracken. This ascends a small valley before turning steeply uphill to the left once through the denser bracken on the lower slopes. After a short steep climb, it swings right and climbs more gently past the top of the wood and then above it to reach a pleasant grassy platform above the crag at the top of the wood. From here onwards, the path becomes more indistinct. It continues through the bracken linking together other little grass platforms and becoming increasingly like a sheep track. Before long, it swings to the left and then back right to pass close to a small tree and then cross a small stream.

Cross over this wet area and continue ahead as the sheep track aims into a small valley ahead, which runs parallel with the lake below, of which there are excellent views. However, almost immediately leave the defile by means of a small path on the left in bracken, which climbs to a small open rocky area amidst the bracken. Here, climb up a tongue of grass above it and continue through the now shorter bracken to reach a shelf, still following a small path, and climb the shelf to the right to reach the edge of the bracken. Broken crags lie on the left but the grassy shelf continues to rise ahead and it should be followed until it comes to an end above a level area on the fell's west ridge. Turning sharply back to the left, the summit lies just over a minor bump on the ridge and is marked by a tall and wide square obelisk.

The view is understandably dominated by the expanse of Ullswater and the steep hillsides of the High Street fells to the south and east, which block any views in those directions. However, to the north-west, Great and Little Mell Fell appear above Gowbarrow Fell and the craggy east faces of the Helvellyn range are clearly in view just to the south-west. There are a number of routes down to the low pass between Howtown and Martindale but it is scenically best to go straight ahead (north-east) at the obelisk on a grassy path. Ignoring a first right fork, it drops away from the summit before curving back to the right on a shelf. It then continues before the main path swings to the right to avoid two cairned knolls, which could easily be incorporated in the route if desired. Beyond these, the path starts to drop steeply towards the church in the pass to a cairn at mid-height.

Go straight ahead at the cairn to drop down the track leading from the pass to Waternook just a few yards from the road. This track may then be followed down and across the hillside, past some benches, to reach Waternook, from where the outwards route should be reversed back to Howtown pier and the car park.

Lambrigg Fell

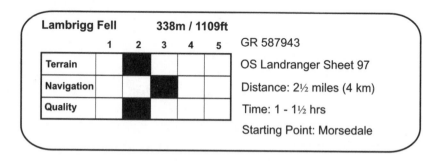

Lambrigg Fell	338m / 1109ft					
	1	2	3	4	5	GR 587943
Terrain		■				OS Landranger Sheet 97
Navigation			■			Distance: 2½ miles (4 km)
Quality		■				Time: 1 - 1½ hrs
						Starting Point: Morsedale

Lambrigg Fell forms a sprawling mass of moorland between Kendal and the M6 and it is traversed by both that motorway and the Kendal to Sedbergh road. These two arteries of communication are joined, just to

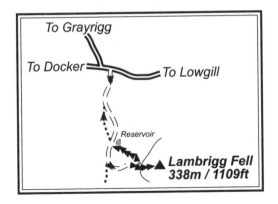

To Grayrigg

To Docker

To Lowgill

Reservoir

Lambrigg Fell
338m / 1109ft

the east of the summit, by a small wind farm whose turbines stand almost as high as the ill-defined and unmemorable summit. However, as a viewpoint, the hill is excellent, lying in a superb location for close-range views of both the Howgills and Lakeland fells, together with the Yorkshire Dales. Combined with the rumbling of the unseen trains on the busy west coast main line, this hill harbours a number of surprises that make it well worth climbing.

The best route of ascent is from the minor road linking Docker and Lambrigg Head, which runs across the northern slopes of the fell. Almost opposite the stately entrance to Morsedale Hall, there is a public telephone and it is possible to park on verges in dry weather and in lay-bys further to the east. There is also an old quarry in which it may also be possible to park. A few yards to the west of the telephone box, a gate gives access to a track and bridleway that climbs through the first field to a gate leading into the one above. At the top of this second field, a pair of gates gives access to the open hill through a sheep pen.

Ahead, the main track curves to the left but a smaller path follows the wall on the right through an initial boggy patch but then strikes off up the hillside when the wall turns to the right. In due course, it merges once again with the main track just below an unseen reservoir up to the left (although its perimeter fence can be seen). This reservoir will be seen during the descent. For the time being, continue on the track as it climbs further up to a gap in the ridge running across the fell from east to west. After passing through this gap, the track curves left and, ignoring a small path forking right at a cairn, it ascends up to the ruins of an old stone building.

At this building, the track becomes much less distinct but it does continue over grass for a short distance further ahead to gain a minor ridge. A left turn on this followed by a right turn onto a small path in the heather leads over a first rocky ridge to reach a second higher ridge, which is the point marked 338m on the Ordnance Survey maps. However, this seems to be slightly lower than the next ridge, which is generally accepted to be the true summit. This can be reached by continuing ahead and making a steep descent of the heathery slope to reach an old wall by a boggy hollow on the left. This wall can be crossed most easily at its lowest point immediately to the right of the boggy area. Ahead, more grassy slopes lead up and over a rocky eminence to the true summit beyond, from where the M6 motorway and wind turbines can be seen just below and to the east.

Eastwards, the green valleys of Garsdale, left, and Dentdale, right, can be seen amongst the drab-looking hills of the western Dales. By contrast, the steep grass slopes of the Howgills with their high ridges form a more interesting block of land. To the west of the unseen Lune Gorge and to the north lies the summit of Grayrigg Forest, whilst the skyline of the Lakeland mountains appears particularly impressive around Kentmere, Langdale and Coniston. The descent begins by returning to the wall crossing from where an alternative route may be made down to the reservoir.

Once over the wall, turn to the right and skirt the boggy hollow before following the hillside around to the left. Keep above the first boggy area on the right before turning to the right beyond it and then aiming half left over a damp area to reach a low gap in the small knolls ahead. Once through this, the reservoir comes into view below and a route should be made down the damp slopes ahead to reach the left-hand side of it and the track. From here, the descent is made by reversing the route of ascent, although be careful to fork left at a small cairn in the heather to follow the direct path back down to the inbye gate.

Top o'Selside

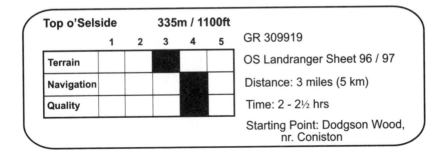

Top o'Selside			335m / 1100ft			GR 309919
	1	2	3	4	5	OS Landranger Sheet 96 / 97
Terrain			■			Distance: 3 miles (5 km)
Navigation				■		Time: 2 - 2½ hrs
Quality			■			Starting Point: Dodgson Wood, nr. Coniston

Selside is the steep and wooded slope rising from the less frequented eastern shore of Coniston Water and Top o'Selside is the name given to the highest point of the rough and rarely visited moorland above. Much of this moor, especially to the north and east, has been covered by a cloak of pine trees forming part of the Grizedale forestry plantations but the area around the highest point itself has been spared. The ascent may be made by a very pleasant route from the lakeshore that is to be preferred to any more circuitous approaches from Nibthwaite to the south.

The starting point is the National Trust's Dodgson Wood car park on the eastern shore of Coniston Water. This is the fourth woodland car park when approaching from Coniston or the third when approaching from Nibthwaite. A path leads away half right from behind the small information sign to reach a stone-built building in the wood, which has an outside toilet that is open to the public. Our route, however, passes below the building and then curves left behind it to a gate and stile leading onto the main wooded hillside.

From here, the white arrows and waymarkers indicate the twists and turns of the permitted path to Low Parkamoor that our route now follows up a series of hairpins and across three becks in the wood to reach a stile leading out of the top of the wood. The footpath now follows a wall on the left up the hill and then a stream to reach a track running across the hillside to the house at Low Parkamoor on the left.

Our route, however, keeps straight on, following a grass path that continues by the wall ahead to join with a gravelled track that swings in from the right and then continues along the same line. This track should now be followed onwards, although take care to look out over the wall on

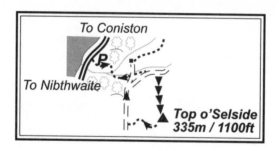

the left for the ruined farmstead of High Parkamoor not too much further ahead. Beyond this, our route leaves this track on the right bank of the first small stream that crosses the track where it bends to the left just after a sharp right bend. From here to the summit, the route lies across rough country.

Start off by following the right bank but soon cross to the left before a dense area of bracken. A wet patch beyond this may then be skirted on the left before returning gradually to the stream bank further over to the right once the wet ground is past. Continue then to follow the stream and the small wet valley beyond, which curves slightly to the left, to pass over a small col into another boggy hollow on the gently sloping hillside.

Follow the left-hand bank of this stream uphill, where it flows through a small ravine-like runnel. This leads to a further boggy terrace, from where the stream should be followed up and past a small arête of naked rock rising a few feet from the wet hillside. A boggy plateau cutting across the ridge is thus reached and the summit lies on the knoll slightly left, marked by a small cairn.

The view from the summit is very good, although Coniston Water itself remains almost completely hidden. However, there is an excellent view of the lake on the descent. The Coniston fells are understandably prominent, as is the Fairfield group, Red Screes and the southern outliers of the High Street range. The scene is almost stolen by the idyllic waters of the rarely seen Arnsbarrow Tarn that lies on the moor just to the south-east of the summit.

The descent begins by following a small grass path to the right from the summit. This takes a roundabout route downwards but its route is always obvious; at any forks, simply take the most distinct path. It turns sharply right at the top of a steep bank and then back to the right, revealing a charming view of Coniston Water. However, a better view still can be reached by continuing on the path until it swings left and then continuing ahead to the next rocky eminence. From here, only the very head of the lake remains hidden.

Returning to the path, it can then be followed down the hillside to reach the track running between Nibthwaite and Parkamoor. A right turn on this gravelled track soon leads along to a waymarked fork from where the left, grassy branch should be taken which leads slightly down to Low Parkamoor, from where the route of ascent may be reversed back down the stream and wall sides and then through the wood back to the car park.

Gummer's How

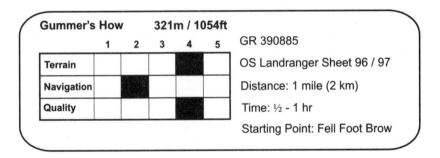

Gummer's How	321m / 1054ft				
	1	2	3	4	5
Terrain				■	
Navigation		■			
Quality				■	

GR 390885

OS Landranger Sheet 96 / 97

Distance: 1 mile (2 km)

Time: ½ - 1 hr

Starting Point: Fell Foot Brow

Gummer's How is perhaps the hill that best characterises the scenery of south Lakeland. It is a craggy eminence, rising from a wooded ridge with a view dominated by lakes and forests. It is not in many ways dissimilar to the slightly lower summit of Claife Heights on the other side of Lake Windermere and slightly to the north. However, given a high-level starting point and its excellent views, Gummer's How is deservedly a popular stroll that is best left for a fine day.

There is really only one way to climb the hill by any practicable route and that is to make use of the high-level forestry car park on the road between Fell Foot at the bottom of Lake Windermere and Bowland Bridge in the Winster Valley. When approaching from Windermere, this car park is on the right and it can be quite busy in summer.

The route begins by ascending the road for a few yards before turning off to the left through a kissing gate on a signposted footpath. This leads

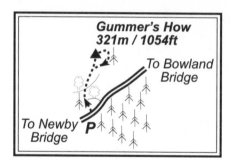

towards the rocky summit through a charming woodland of pine and deciduous trees before the ascent begins in earnest on a restored path to reach a craggy band. Here, a tendency to go right should be ignored and, instead, the rocks should be climbed direct, turning more to the left if anything to reach the continuing path above, which soon swings right on grass to reach the trig point on the summit.

Given the shortness of the route, it is well worth exploring the summit area to gain the best views. A good viewpoint for the lake is to the left at the top of the hill's craggy western slopes, whilst the scars and woodlands of Whitbarrow are also prominent in the view from the trig point to the east.

Once the view has been admired, there is a choice of descent routes. Either the route of ascent may be reversed or alternatively a slight variation may be made. In the latter case, leave the summit in a north-easterly direction aiming for a group of larch trees. However, turn to the right just before them and drop down to reach a stony path that can be followed to the right and through a small stand of pine trees to reach the ascent route at the bottom of the craggy band. From there, reversing the route of ascent, the path leads back through the lower wood to the road and car park.

Hutton Roof Crags

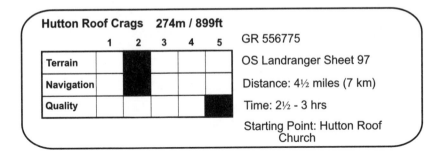

Hutton Roof Crags		274m / 899ft		
	1	2	3	4	5
Terrain		■			
Navigation		■			
Quality					■

GR 556775

OS Landranger Sheet 97

Distance: 4½ miles (7 km)

Time: 2½ - 3 hrs

Starting Point: Hutton Roof Church

Few motorists travelling along the M6 motorway can fail to notice the bulk of Hutton Roof Crags, or, more accurately, the dominating limestone escarpment of its northern outpost – Farleton Fell. Together, these two fells and the summit of Newbiggin Crags form a relatively small but nevertheless dominating limestone upland between Burton-in-Kendal and Kirkby Lonsdale. This alone makes the summit a worthy destination but those who venture onto the hill itself will soon realise that this is no ordinary upland. The whole of the hill is covered by combinations of limestone pavements and parallel scars, a combination which is known as a 'rake'. And between them, thick scrub has developed making the going rough and tough.

Without local knowledge, reaching the summit can soon become a frustrating and dangerous assault course requiring both rock climbing and wilderness travel skills as, even if the summit can be seen, reaching it can be all but impossible. Readers of this book should, however, have no such problems as there is an easy but intricate route to the top and this is described below.

There are a number of places where parking is possible in Hutton Roof village but the best place is by the church, which is a short distance out of the village on the Kendal road. However, if this area is very busy, such as on Sunday mornings, for example, then it is possible to park elsewhere in the village and gain access to the open hill by taking the small rough lane between houses that leaves the main road almost opposite the junction with the Kirkby Lonsdale road in the middle of the village. However, if starting at the church, follow the Burton-in-Kendal road around the back of the church and hall before crossing a stone stile built into the wall to

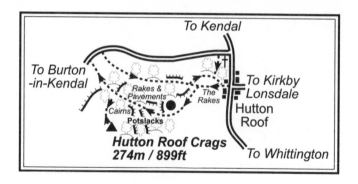

enter the paddock behind. A path slants uphill across this before entering a wood and then continuing through it past moss-covered rocks to reach a stile out onto the open hill at the far side. Once on the hill, a left fork followed by a left turn leads downhill to the back of Hutton Roof village and the end of the rough track mentioned above.

However, just before reaching the village, turn sharply to the right and follow a steeply rising path. This shortly passes a large perched boulder on the left before meeting the lowest of the rakes. There are, in total, three of these on this lower part of the hill and once over the third little ridge a path is met ascending from the right. Here, go roughly straight ahead and follow a path that curves around the back of a small knoll ahead before reaching the edge of the slightly craggy escarpment on the right. Shortly, however, fork left just before a craggy turret to the left of the path and when the Kent estuary comes into view ahead. This fork curves to the left and follows a small valley just below the scar to the right and, towards the far end of the scar, reaches another fork. Here, go straight on and ignore a further branching path to the right, instead following a small path that curves around the far side of the false summit at the eastern end of the crags. (Incidentally, it is not possible to traverse this summit due to the rakes and pavements on the far side so if it is to be visited then make a return to this point.)

Once around the far side of the eastern summit, the path begins to descend into the hollow of Potslacks. This area is the roughest and most difficult part of the ridge and, although the summit is quite nearby, there is no direct route to it. The path, however, follows the one line of weakness and descends along a grassy groove between pavements and then cuts such an easy line through the rakes and crags that it hardly does them justice.

Hence, it is well worth having a quick look to the left of the path in the trees to see the scars and pavements amongst the tangled scrub.

The path reaches its lowest point in a grassy hollow and then begins to ascend through small craglets, still following its line of weakness, as witnessed by the bigger scars and obstacles on either side. Soon, however, the path reaches its highest point next to an area of sloping pavement on the left and a rare break in the scrub; there is a small cairn on the left on the foot of the pavement some 12 yards before the path goes quite steeply downhill. This almost unnoticeable break is the key to reaching the summit and, at the top of the short slope on the left, another small cairn is to be found at the edge of a more extensive area of pavement, which can be crossed easily to reach a group of three large cairns, with the central one, which has an upright stone on the top, being the next landmark.

The summit is still not in view but can now be reached relatively easily. To set the correct course, first locate a short upright stone in the pavement about five yards beyond the central cairn and on a bearing of 192° from it. Continue on this line past first a juniper bush then another short upright stone to leave the pavement by passing between a small thorn bush on the left and a squat hazel on the right. Here, a path is picked up, which, although invisible from the cairn, leads on through the dwarf bracken and grass to a more stony area. Here, the path becomes more prominent and continues to the next area of pavement, where, as cairned, it follows the line of a broad, grassy grike. However, when the path reaches the next area of pavement, which lies atop a grassy bank, no such waymarks are visible. However, the trig point has now appeared into view so aim across the pavement towards it, pushing through a line of scrub, to follow the path beyond up the final grass slopes.

The summit is a little bit disappointing in that it lies at the centre of a fairly innocuous grassy meadow. The false summit is in view to the east and, since even the crags and difficult pavement of Potslacks remain hidden, it looks easily attainable. The view is, however, very good with the western Dales, Howgills and Lakeland peaks all being in view. The armchair-like profile of the western slopes of Calf Top is particularly eyecatching, as is the flat-topped profile of Ingleborough further to the right. The coastal scene is also quite panoramic, although not unbroken due to the low coastal hills, such as Warton Crag above Carnforth.

The descent begins by returning past the three cairns to rejoin the path that was followed through Potslacks. A left turn on this leads down the hill to the north-west and past the dominating scar of Uberash Breast on the left. Further down, the main path should be followed throughout, ignoring minor branching paths in the grass on the right to emerge onto the lane between Hutton Roof and Burton-in-Kendal through a gate. Once on the road, a right turn leads uphill to the road's highest point where a ladder stile on the right marks the start of the path back along the hillside to Hutton Roof.

On the far side of the stile, the path climbs initially quite steeply up the slope before curving to the left and following a terrace along the hillside through the scrubby woodland below the main rakes themselves. In due course, the path emerges from the scrub and contours along a more open grassy hillside, from which there are superb views into the deep valley on the left. Soon, the path starts to climb again and it finds itself rising, next to a craggy edge on the left, back to the top of the rakes immediately above Hutton Roof village. However, look out for a left turn onto a path that drops down the escarpment and soon, after curving to the right below the escarpment for a short while, reaches the wood behind the church. After a short descent alongside the wood, the path forks. Here, the left branch leads back to the stile and the path through the wood to the church, whilst the path ahead leads back to the centre of Hutton Roof village.

Claife Heights

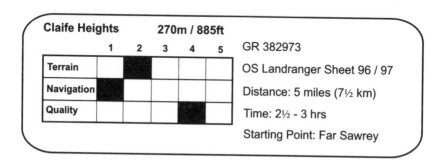

Claife Heights	270m / 885ft				
	1	2	3	4	5
Terrain		■			
Navigation	■				
Quality				■	

GR 382973

OS Landranger Sheet 96 / 97

Distance: 5 miles (7½ km)

Time: 2½ - 3 hrs

Starting Point: Far Sawrey

Claife Heights is the name given to the highest point of the upland separating Esthwaite Water, near Hawkshead, and the long ribbon of

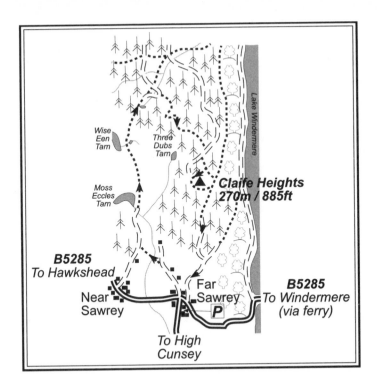

Map labels:
- Lake Windermere
- Wise Een Tarn
- Three Dubs Tarn
- Moss Eccles Tarn
- Claife Heights 270m / 885ft
- B5285 To Hawkshead
- Near Sawrey
- Far Sawrey P
- B5285 To Windermere (via ferry)
- To High Cunsey

water that is Lake Windermere. Latterbarrow is the most easily identifiable summit of the range, with the monument on its open hilltop being easily seen from Hawkshead and Tarn Hows. However, the summit of the range is an infrequently visited craggy knoll above Sawrey that rises out of the very beautiful forest plantations along the western side of Windermere. With a surprise around almost every corner and excellent views in a number of places, this walk should be reserved for a fine and warm day.

Sawrey is divided into two villages – Near and Far Sawrey – with the former being associated with Beatrix Potter. The route begins from the village of Far Sawrey, where it is possible to park in the village hall car park at the eastern end of the village, on the road to the ferry across the lake to Bowness-on-Windermere. Although there is no fee, donations are welcome in the box by the gate. To the west, the road leads past the Sawrey Hotel and then rises slightly. Here, a bridleway goes up a surfaced lane to the right and is signposted to Moss Eccles Tarn and Claife Heights. This lane runs up through the lower fields before entering an area of parkland where there is a small beck on the left.

The lane leads up to the house on the right so bear left at the signpost and follow a grassy track across the beck, where there is a footbridge. It then continues as an enclosed track past further fields to emerge, through a gate, into the foot of a rocky and rougher field. After fording another beck, Moss Eccles Tarn appears into view on the left. All the small lakes on this hillside are in fact artificial but all are very pretty and the rocks on the left make a pleasant place to sit and admire the tarn.

However, the track continues upwards from the tarn, swinging left in front of a gateway in a fence at the top of the first slope. It is no great distance from there, through another gate, to reach the tranquil setting of Wise Een Tarn from where there is a charming northwards view towards the Langdale Fells. The track curves to the right and passes below the brick-faced embankment to another smaller lake on the right. Ahead, at the far side of the field, a gate gives access to the forestry plantations. Another damp area, with a partially silted tarn, is passed in the trees on the right as the track, now turning ever more into a forestry road, continues across the ridge.

Not long after the wet area, from which the Belle Grange Beck issues, waymarkers point the bridleway down a path that slants to the left. However, our route follows the road onwards, which swings to the right and crosses the tumbling waters of the beck. Soon after, the road swings sharply to the left and another right of way is joined. This is the waymarked linear walk between the car park by the ferry crossing near Far Sawrey and Latterbarrow and Hawkshead. Throughout its route, the path is marked by white-topped stakes and these can now be followed to the right from point number eight.

As the forestry track drops slightly off the ridge, an ascent is called for to regain it and soon the path emerges from the trees to reach a regenerating area. It then curves up the slopes ahead to reach a magnificent viewpoint for Ambleside, the head of Windermere and the fells around the Rothay valley. The large gap in the hills at Dunmail Raise is also prominent. A slight descent then follows as the path crosses a boggy patch on a raised walkway and, after only a slight rise, descends to join another forestry road.

Still following the white-topped stakes, the route goes right and then very soon left at point number five. It is now that the final climb to the summit begins as the path rises steeply. A right turn when the path ahead starts to descend leads up to the very highest slopes. A small path on the left, signposted as the route to the viewpoint, leads up to a clump of rocks, from where a route may be found through the bracken to the right to the trig point and summit on a slightly higher clump of rocks. The view from here is dominated by Bowness on the other side of the narrow strait of Windermere. Beyond, greener hills continue towards Staveley and Kendal, whilst Gummer's How is visible to the right above the far shore of Windermere.

A return should be made back past the viewpoint to rejoin the main path. The white stakes continue to the left and lead down to a footbridge across the head of another hidden boggy hollow on the left. A short climb leads to a further rocky outcrop where the path swings left to climb to a second rocky outcrop – High Pate Crags – where an even steeper left turn is made. A descent then leads down to the Belle Grange to Far Sawrey bridleway.

Now, at point number four on the white walk, a right turn leads down over the rocky band of Low Pate Crag and, after a while, out into the upper inbye fields. The track, now no longer marked with white-topped stakes but nevertheless very clear, curves through the fields to reach, after some time, point number three. Here, the route leaves the white walk and turns through the gate on the right and follows this track down the hill to reach the road in Far Sawrey opposite the village hall.

Whitbarrow

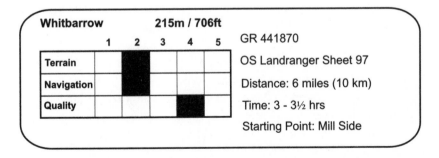

Whitbarrow	215m / 706ft					
	1	2	3	4	5	GR 441870
Terrain		■				OS Landranger Sheet 97
Navigation		■				Distance: 6 miles (10 km)
Quality				■		Time: 3 - 3½ hrs
						Starting Point: Mill Side

Whitbarrow is one of the most interesting and unusual hills within the Lake District. It differs from many of its neighbours by being the only

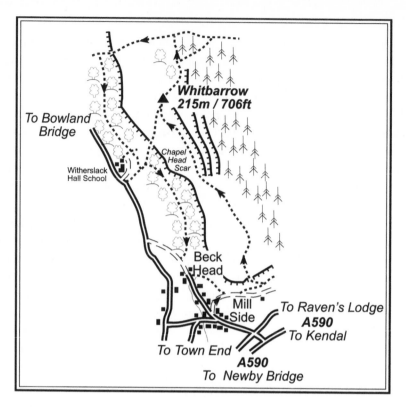

significant summit within the National Park that is constructed from a massif of Carboniferous mountain limestone. On two sides, vertical scars and steep woodlands abound to give this lowly summit a dramatic elevation above the low-lying valleys of the Winster and Lyth, which Whitbarrow separates. The summit itself lies on a ridge of about two miles' extent that is formed from a mixture of small copses, broken patches of limestone pavement, knoll-like summits and small and diminutive scars.

A good starting point for a circular walk is the village of Mill Side at the foot of the hill's south-western slopes. From here, a small dead-end lane leads up to the tranquil hamlet and there is limited parking by the telephone box where this lane leaves the main road through Mill Side. Just beyond the telephone box, a lane slants to the right past some houses and ascends to the bottom of the wood below the scar. Once there, the track swings to the right and continues inside but close to the bottom of the wood en route to Whitbarrow Lodge.

However, before its gates are reached, look out for a path running into the wood on the left. This makes a traversing ascent of the hillside and soon, after passing a small resurgence on the left, reaches a bench from where there is a good view to the right through a break in the trees. Ahead, the path continues to an old quarry but our route, as indicated by a white arrow, turns to the left and hairpins back through the wood on a very narrow path. This climbs to reach less steep ground close to the top of the wood and above the main escarpment. Here, the path passes through an old wall but then immediately turns almost back on itself and crosses the wall once again.

Immediately ahead, the route is not clear but keep straight ahead and soon the path develops once again, leading out of the trees and onto the scrubby upland beyond. After climbing for a short distance through the bushy vegetation, the path swings left and continues over cropped grass to the southerly summit on the Whitbarrow ridge, which is marked by a large but slightly untidy cairn. Ahead, along the ridge, another subsidiary summit can be seen, beyond which is the main summit, marked by a well-built pillar cairn. However, that is some distance away and by far the most striking object in the view is the curving cliff of Chapel Head Scar half left. The path continues along the slightly heathery ridge to attain the other subsidiary summit, beyond which it continues without branching to cross a transverse wall that crosses the ridge.

From here, the National Nature Reserve in which the summit lies is entered. The next part of the walk is probably the most delightful section as the path descends past some patches of limestone pavement and past a number of trees with a small but very attractive scar on the right. Once past this area, the path swings slightly to the left to gain the foot of a long grassy 'ramp' that leads up to the pillar cairn on the summit. From here, the views are extensive and encompass much of the fells of southern Lakeland in an unbroken sweep from Coniston through the Langdale Pikes and Red Screes to Kentmere. In the foreground, the wooded foothills form a charming landscape of hidden valleys and rocky summits, with Gummer's How lying just slightly north of west.

From the summit, our route continues along the ridge a little further before descending into the woodland on the left at the foot of the scar and then returning through the trees to Mill Side. To begin, take a path slanting half right from the summit that descends to reach, in due course, a further small scar, which it follows. At the end of the scar, this natural barrier is replaced by a sturdy wall that marks the boundary between the open upland on the left and the plantation on the right.

Thus, ignoring a path crossing the wall, continue on a cart-track close by the wall through a small copse to reach a second transverse wall crossing the ridge. Staying on the nearside of the wall, follow a small path to the left that runs alongside the wall to reach an old mine level on the left at the top of the scar. The path then proceeds to make use of a boulder ruckle – Bell Rake – to descend the scar and then enters the wood below, inside which a gate leads off the hill.

The path continues inside the wood to reach a signposted junction where a left turn should be made. This leads on to a track that continues through the wood to reach the environs of Witherslack Hall School, which could be seen from the ridge above. There are a number of forks in the wood but bear slightly left at all of them to reach a crosstracks on the edge of a more open area, which is actually the school's playing field. However, keep straight on and continue to a stile that leads out of the wood and into an agricultural field.

At this point, a left turn leads along the edge of the field to reach a gate into the next block of woodland, ignoring a stile on the left en route. From this gate, a track climbs gently ahead into the wood, passing another small resurgence just to the left of the track. Soon, however, the track swings back to take a course roughly parallel to the scarp and runs through the woodland, which can be very wet and boggy after rain. Ignoring all branching tracks, the main track comes to an end on the edge of the wood where it meets the bridleway continuing onwards from the road-head in Beck Head. This can be reached by following the track a few hundred yards to the left and no great distance further is the charming resurgence in the village where the beck issues from the base of a small scar. It is then only a short and very pleasant walk down the road to Mill Side.

Section 5 – South-western Lakeland

The River Crake from the coast to Coniston Water and the A593 through Yewdale to Skelwith Bridge. River Brathay and the Great Langdale Beck to Mickleden. Stake Pass and the Langstrath Beck to Rosthwaite. The River Derwent and Styhead Gill to Sty Head Pass. Lingmell Beck to Wastwater and the River Irt to the sea at Ravenglass. The coast from there to the mouth of the Crake near Ulverston.

NAME	HEIGHT	IN SECTION	IN ENGLAND	IN BRITAIN
Illgill Head	609m/1998ft	05 of 12	54J of 184	754J of 1552
Black Combe	600m/1970ft	06 of 12	57 of 184	769 of 1552
Whitfell	573m/1881ft	07 of 12	59 of 184	811 of 1552
Hard Knott	549m/1801ft	08 of 12	67 of 184	877 of 1552
Lingmoor Fell	469m/1540ft	09 of 12	89 of 184	1052 of 1552
Kirkby Moor	333m/1092ft	10 of 12	122 of 184	1320 of 1552
Holm Fell	317m/1040ft	11 of 12	131 of 184	1348J of 1552
Muncaster Fell	231m/ 758ft	12 of 12	169 of 184	1483 of 1552

There are four summits above 2,000ft that are described in *England's Highest Peaks*.

The area enclosed by this section includes many picturesque summits, such as Holm Fell, alongside high, dominating peaks, such as Illgill Head, which holds its ground against any of its higher neighbours. The hills described here, are, by and large, situated on the south-west ridges descending from the higher mountains around Scafell and the Crinkle Crags. As such, quite a few of these summits provide rougher and more difficult expeditions than the hills of Eastern Lakeland (Section 4), which by contrast tend to be lower and more individual. As the geology of each part of the Lake District is very similar to the others, the geology is discussed wholly within Section 4 on page 126.

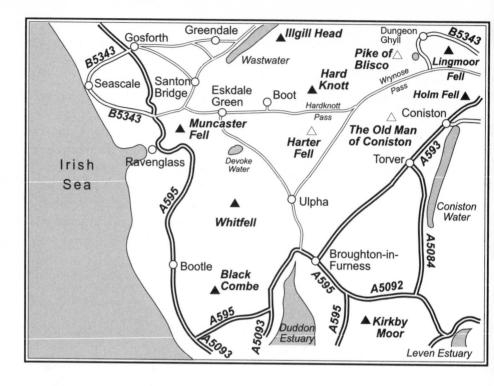

Access

There is a rail service to the coastal towns, stations of use to walkers being Ulverston (bus to Coniston and Ambleside), Kirkby-in-Furness, Silecroft, Bootle, Ravenglass (from where there is a narrow-gauge steam railway up Eskdale to Boot), Drigg, Seascale and Sellafield. There is a frequent daily train service between Manchester Airport, Preston, Lancaster, Ulverston and Barrow-in-Furness. There are regular Monday to Saturday trains between Barrow-in-Furness and Carlisle, servicing the western part of the district. A branch line from Oxenholme, on the west coast main line, runs to Windermere and there are regular daily services in summer, but in winter, although it still runs daily, the service is more limited; there are direct trains between Windermere, Manchester Piccadilly and Manchester Airport, subject to the above restrictions. A bus service connects Windermere, Ambleside and Grasmere, whilst a summer service runs between Ambleside, Elterwater and Old Dungeon Ghyll (Great Langdale).

By car, it is more difficult to reach the western side of the district than the east. The A590, A5092 and A595 together run around the coast, linking Junction 36 of the M6 with Ravenglass, Workington and Carlisle. The A591 leaves the A590 at Kendal and goes through Ambleside and Grasmere on its way to Keswick. Coniston can be reached along the A593 from the A590 to the south and Ambleside to the north. The only other way from east to west is across the mountain passes of Wrynose and Hardknott. This route has severe gradients (up to 1:3) and countless very sharp, acutely angled hairpin bends; it links Little Langdale (normally reached over Blea Tarn Pass from Great Langdale), Dunnerdale and the head of Eskdale, although it is closed in wintry conditions.

Accommodation

On the eastern side, there is accommodation in Coniston, Ambleside and Grasmere (see Section 4) but for many of the hills it will be necessary to be in the west. There are several inns and a hotel in Eskdale as well as a few bed and breakfast establishments around Eskdale Green and there is a hotel at Wasdale Head. The area around Millom and Bootle is more industrial. However, the hills in this area can be easily reached from Eskdale. There are youth hostels at Wastwater, Eskdale, Coniston (Holly How and Coppermines), Hawkshead, Elterwater, Langdale (Red Bank), Grasmere (Butterlip How and Thorney How) and Ambleside.

Illgill Head

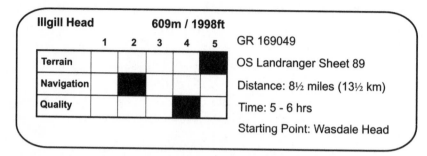

Illgill Head	1	2	3	4	5
Terrain					■
Navigation		■			
Quality				■	

609m / 1998ft

GR 169049

OS Landranger Sheet 89

Distance: 8½ miles (13½ km)

Time: 5 - 6 hrs

Starting Point: Wasdale Head

Often admired but rarely seen at close quarters is an apt description of the tallest scree slope in England. For almost two miles along the south-eastern shore of Wastwater, England's deepest lake, the crags and gullies throw down stony slopes for over 1,600ft. On a summer's day, the gravelled pull-ins on the side of the road along the opposite shore of the lake are filled with vehicles whose owners have stopped to admire this, probably the most fantastic of all England's mountain scenes. However, after walking the footpath along the foot of the scree slope and then returning over the summits along the top of the crags, many will be left with very different sentiments. This route should not be attempted in reverse – you have been warned!

The starting point is the National Trust car park at Wasdale Hall, close to the top of the lake and reached over a somewhat ugly concrete bridge, signposted to the campsite. Non-NT members may be able to park in a lay-by opposite on the main road and thus avoid the daily parking fee levied by the Trust. The walk starts from the far end of the car park and leads onwards through a gate and over the beck flowing from Hollow Stones. When over it, almost immediately turn left along a broad track, signposted 'Lakeshore Path', which is also the driveway to Wasdale Head Hall Farm. In due course when the road swings to the farm, the footpath leaves over a stile by a telegraph pole into a muddy field; two gates further on the open fell is reached after the warning notice about future hazards.

To begin with the lakeshore path is very pleasant as it runs along the grassy hillside, gradually rising slightly above the lake. After a while, it crosses a broken-down wall and a little further on still it meets the first rocks. These are mainly small stones and, like most of the rocks along the path, they are quite stable. The path now continues with alternating grass

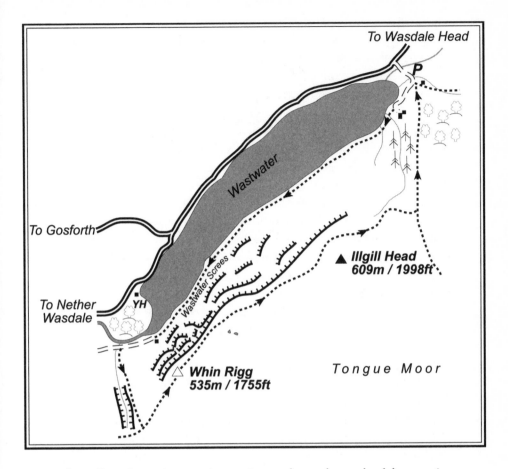

and small rock sections as it continues along above the lake, passing through a number of small copses of silver birch and mountain ash. This continues for most of the way along the lakeshore but in due course the 'killer' section appears into view.

This part is not easily mistaken for any other as the rocks increase dramatically in size and the footpath disappears altogether. Despite vain attempts to cairn a route through the chaotic jumble of boulders, two 'routes' have developed, an upper and a lower one. There are no real advantages in going further up so when the path splits, keep on the lower branch. Once onto the stones there is little to say other than that they soon become very greasy and dangerously slippery after rain. About halfway along a much larger boulder will be met but it is quite easy to cross towards its top or it is possible to descend and pass below it by the water's edge.

The crags above now may be impressive but they are out of bounds to climbers and scramblers. The rock quality is very poor and rotten and the vegetated, north-facing cliffs make for dank and desperate expeditions. However, the most promising route of ascent is the ridge of Broken Rib, which can be seen at the far end of the 'killer' section of scree. The better quality of the rock is seen clearly by the way that it has resisted erosion much better than any other part of the scree. However, there is no real way of circumnavigating its vegetated lower buttress to reach the better quality climbing higher up so no real routes have been established. Apart from the obvious danger of rock falls due to the disintegrating face, the obvious effort required to reach the Rib up the shifting screes in between mean that the route is quite simply not worth the bother.

When underneath Broken Rib, the worst of the screes finish and a pleasant path once again leads onwards all the way to the pumping station at the foot of the lake. Onwards, the route continues down its access road until the inbye gate is met. In front of it, turn left and climb uphill alongside the wall before swinging with it around to the right and following along above it. After crossing one small stream, the main path rising up through the inbye is met at a stile just before the mouth of the huge ravine of Greathall Gill. Like the screes, its bed is too strenuous and vegetated to provide an alternative way of reaching the high ground. The footpath is now steep but after a while it does slacken off as it passes the huge crater-like head of the gill just before meeting the ridge path at a cairn.

The ascent, though, is not complete and the rising path to the left leads upwards to the first and lower summit at the top of the screes – Whin Rigg. A steepish descent then follows to a depression containing a tarn, just before which the path is forced around the head of one of the spectacular scree gullies of the slopes. When in the depression fork left and walk outwards to a pair of promontories. The first descending ridge is the top of Broken Rib, although its narrow and exposed upper section does not make for a pleasant excursion. The next, higher and slightly undercut, headland is also a very good viewpoint for those with a head for heights.

The path then leads back slightly inland through a fascinating area in a partial and ongoing state of collapse. The ground is peppered with holes and grooves in the rock, separated by small ridges, as the whole part of the hillside slowly detaches itself from the ridge on its onwards progression to the lakeshore far below. When the main path is rejoined, a steep hill now beckons to the disputed summit of Illgill Head, the highest summit of the screes. The first cairn reached is certainly the largest and does have a claim to be the highest point; certainly Wainwright thought it was. Quite where the trig point has gone to is a mystery but the author certainly could not find it. The Ordnance Survey, however, believes the next summit across a damp depression to be higher, by a full 20 feet. On this next collection of knolls, the contender is not the one with the shelter-cairn but the first, unmarked one.

After making a personal decision, leave the north-eastern (second) summit and continue onwards down the obvious path along the steepening ridge. The slopes make for an excellent descent as they lie at just the right angle to allow speedy progress. A broken-down wall is met and then crossed before following down its far side to the foot of the steep slope. Here it bends a little to the left and, ignoring a branching path to the right, the path by the wall should be followed. This path leads across wet ground and then crosses a small stream to meet the Old Corpse Road between Boot (Eskdale) and Wasdale Head at a cairn on the other bank. Now, this old trackway can be followed downhill and over a double bridge as it leads down to a gate. This leads into the grounds of the small house belonging to the Fell and Rock Climbing Club before meeting the route of ascent only a few yards from the car park.

Black Combe

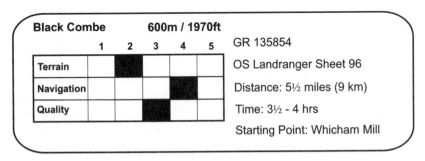

Black Combe			600m / 1970ft			GR 135854
	1	2	3	4	5	OS Landranger Sheet 96
Terrain		■				Distance: 5½ miles (9 km)
Navigation				■		Time: 3½ - 4 hrs
Quality			■			Starting Point: Whicham Mill

Black Combe is probably the most unfrequented of the high Lakeland fells. Despite being almost 2,000ft in altitude, most of those who walk in

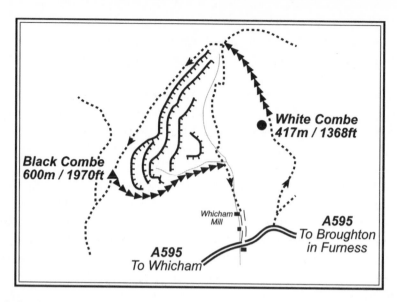

Lakeland will never have heard of it before. Although the fells behind Skiddaw are thought of as outliers, Black Combe is most definitely out on a limb. In fact, it is the highest point on the long, high and featureless ridge that separates Eskdale and Dunnerdale, which has its beginnings on the highest of the Crinkle Crags. Lying on the coast, it has an unequalled coastal panorama and the silhouette of Southern Lakeland is also quite excellent. This said, however, on a misty day, it is very much like a piece of bleak Pennine-style moor.

The best place to begin the ascent is the farm at Beckside on the main A595 road between Silecroft and Broughton-in-Furness. On the southern side of the road, by the bridge over the beck, there is a large lay-by with room for about five cars if all are parked carefully. The route begins by walking north-east along the road and up the hill. This part of the walk is quite awkward as the road is narrow, bendy and often very busy with large lorries making their way to the towns of Workington and Whitehaven further up the coast. When the road starts to descend slightly and bends sharply to the right, leave it for a gate on the left, which is not visible until the entrance is reached. Behind it is an initially muddy green lane that runs up through the inbye, its banks carpeted with bluebells and wood anemone. In due course, the open fell is reached through the second gate on the left.

Here is the first point of divergence. A tempting path runs to the right along above the wall but, rather than taking this, follow the other wall up the hill for a short way until a slanting sunken green drove road is found running off up the hill to the right. Following this, there is the choice of its sheltered bottom or its right-hand bank, although in a few places, the verdant growth of the rushes makes progress in the bottom of the groove difficult. In summer, the drove road cuts a swathe through the ocean of green bracken that covers the hillside hereabout. As height is gained, the seawards view opens up with the Duddon Estuary and then the small reservoir at Baystone Bank comes into view before it is hidden once again by the rocky turret of Hook Knott.

Ignore any tracks that branch off left up the hill and maintain the gentle uphill gradient of the drove road until, after some distance, it hairpins more steeply uphill. Beyond the hairpins, the ascent continues and at a further fork below the upper slopes of White Combe, aim right again. In due course, the rushy groove comes to an end and onwards there is no path (contrary to what might be believed from the Ordnance Survey map). A bearing of 288°, which is more or less straight on, leads up safely back onto the ridge, just a little to the right of the large summit cairn of White Combe, which can be visited if desired. Ahead is the first full view of Black Combe's fine crags, which are very reminiscent of those at Cautely in the Howgill Fells.

The onwards route goes to the right along the ridge (in mist, 338°). In due course, the crest of the ridge may be left as it rises up to the nameless lump ahead, called Stoupdale Head by Wainwright. It is very easy to contour around on its left-hand slopes to meet the track that has been rising up from Whitecombe. Here, go straight over and, soon, a path that forked from it lower down is met. This can now be followed onwards over Whitecombe Head and then up the slope on the far side. With altitude, the path becomes less distinct but in clear weather the very edge of the crags on the left may be followed. In due course, the trig point is found, surrounded by a large shelter.

A direct descent back down to the valley on the left is now impossible because of the large crags on this side but in clear weather a path will be picked up by following along their edge. In mist, it is better to walk south initially (178°, to be precise) until a small tarn is found in a depression. There is also a sturdy section of stone wall here and, if the wind is coming from the east or west, it would provide a better shelter than the hollow cairn on the summit. Here, turn left through 90° (east) and descend until the small path mentioned above is found. This leads along the ridge, which now swings to the left before the path vanishes. Keeping on the left-hand side of the ridge, just in from the escarpment, a small boggy hollow, Eller Peapot, is passed on the left. Continuing the descent, a small tarn is then passed before the next knoll is reached.

Here, it will become clear that the main ridge has been left but this is all right. Descend the steep grass and short heather slope to the left of the small stream right down to the main valley floor. Although the map shows a profusion of crags here, there are none but there are some further down the main ridge that are not shown. However, when the stream in Blackcombe is reached, it can be followed to the right or, if the legs are willing, a short ascent up the opposite slope leads to a grassy path. Down to the right, though, both meet the main path in Whitecombe in the vicinity of some spoil from an old copper mine. In fact, if you are following the upper path, you will pass close to a small quarry, used for prospecting. On the main path, turn right and, after crossing the stream on a footbridge, the inbye is reached and then the tranquil cottage at Whicham Mill. Further on and through the farmyard at Ralliss, the main road is met opposite the lay-by.

Whitfell

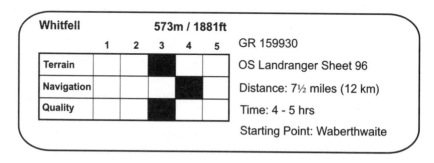

Whitfell			573m / 1881ft			
	1	2	3	4	5	GR 159930
Terrain			■			OS Landranger Sheet 96
Navigation				■		Distance: 7½ miles (12 km)
Quality			■			Time: 4 - 5 hrs
						Starting Point: Waberthwaite

Lying only a little lower than Black Combe, Whitfell is the next major summit to the north on the long and undulating ridge running south-west from the Crinkle Crags. It stands in a fairly remote setting, away from

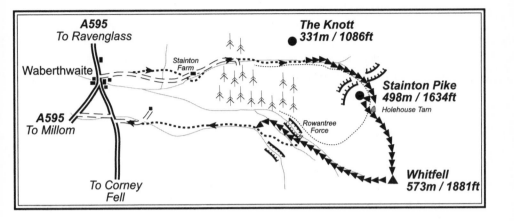

footpaths and the itineries of many of Lakeland's fell-walking visitors. However, like many of the peaks on this long ridge, its views to the Scafell group and upper Eskdale are quite superb and matched by a charming coastal seascape. Whitfell gives possibly the best view of all these hills. Its most interesting slopes are to the north, where a host of enchanting satellite summits – Stainton Pike, Yoadcastle and Woodend Height – continue in a line along the ridge towards Devoke Water. It is through this hinterland of crags and tarns that the most interesting approach lies and not from the road across Corney Fell to the south from where most of Whitfell's visitors ascend.

It is possible to park on verges on the Corney Fell road at Waberthwaite above the initial steep rise from the coast road and also at the beginning of a small dead-end road just to the north of where the Corney Fell road joins the coast road. Almost opposite this latter parking place, a track, signposted to Stainton Fell, leads up the left-hand side of the farmyard at Broadoak and up the hill beyond. After a gentle ascent, the track levels and swings to the right. However, the right of way crosses the ladder stile ahead and then slants half left across this first field, aiming roughly for the rocky turret of Yoadcastle on the ridge ahead (Stainton Pike is the conical summit further to the right).

On the far side of the field, a stile leads over a fence just below the point where the boundary changes to a wall. Aim straight on across the next field to reach a small gap in the belt of mainly coniferous woodland on the other side of the field through which a track leads; a stile at the far side gives access to a third field. Ahead, the farm buildings at Stainton may now be seen and the right of way aims across to the access road just below them. Here, a ladder stile leads over a wall and a footbridge beyond crosses the beck. The right of way avoids the farmyard by staying close to the right bank of the stream and passing through a broken-down wall by a second footbridge on the left to reach a further stile.

This stile gives access to the rough riverbank ahead and a way should be made up its right-hand side to a third stile above the farm. Once over this, aim left when possible to pick up a track rising from the farm. This can now be followed gently uphill, aiming for the gap between two blocks of forestry ahead. Just before reaching them, the track swings to the right but ignore this and continue ahead and in due course through a gate to gain the field in the gap. In this field, the track swings right and crosses the stream before climbing by its other bank to the top of the field where the track swings right. Ahead, through a few yards of low bracken, is a stile.

Once over this stile only one further rough field remains before the open fell is reached. Stay on the right bank of the beck and follow it up, ignoring tributary valleys joining from the right. In due course, the final ladder stile is reached. From here onwards, the stream banks rapidly become very rocky and choked with bracken so cross the stream and escape left onto the grassy hillside alongside the small valley. Continue upwards, parallel to the stream and past the rocky spur of The Knott, which lies over to the left. When the valley ahead begins to get boggy cross back over the stream to the fence on the now grassy right-hand bank.

The upper valley consists of one huge boggy hollow in the hillside but our route follows the fence, which, although very wet in places, avoids the very wettest areas down in the bottom of the valley. The best route stays close to the fence throughout, where tussocky vegetation for the most part provides a safe passage through the worst of the boggy places. In due course, the terrain starts to improve and the fence is soon rising steeply past a rocky area that can be avoided on the left. Not all that far beyond, the fence turns to the right and climbs up through a grassy break between the crags of Stainton Pike to reach a more level plateau-like area behind the pike.

Despite Stainton Pike's impressive appearance from the valley, it merges fairly inconspicuously into the moor beyond. It is, however, an impressive viewpoint for the coast and can easily be visited by crossing the fence on the right either before or at the little-known sheet of water called Holehouse Tarn by the fence. From the near end of the tarn, Whitfell still appears quite high and distant. However, appearances are deceptive and a line should be made direct for its summit (164° in mist), giving the line of rushes at the end of the tarn a very wide berth to avoid a dangerous bog. This line leads slightly to the left of the slightly rocky ridge linking the pike with Whitfell. Before the lowest point is reached, a sheep track will be joined which leads across the pass and almost all the way to the summit.

Whitfell's summit is marked by a large cairn atop a natural mound of rock at a slightly higher elevation than the trig point to the left. The view is superb, although the presence of Black Combe to the south interrupts the coastal view. Particularly impressive are the estuaries at Ravenglass and the railway bridge that strides across the sands and saltmarshes at Eskmeals. Inland, the mountain skyline is superb. Starting from the east, the horizon passes over the Coniston fells before there is a distant glimpse of Fairfield over Wrynose Pass. Then there are the Crinkle Crags with the pyramid of Harter Fell in front, Bowfell, Esk Pike, Ill Crag, Scafell Pike, Scafell, Great Gable, Kirk Fell, Pillar, Scoat Fell and Haycock before the ridge descends slowly down to the somewhat less scenic view of the Sellafield plant.

The descent begins by aiming towards the headwaters of the Rowantree Gill on a bearing of 254°. These waters may be followed down on the left bank past a number of cascades to the point where the stream drops suddenly down Rowantree Force into a gorge. After admiring the cascades, turn left away from the stream to hit the next small beck and then follow that down to flatter ground. Before this stream enters a boggy patch, turn to the left and walk just above the bog to cross a further stream descending from the gully on the hillside to the left. Keep above a further patch of rushes to pick up the intermittent bridleway that descends down from the hillside.

To the right, this path crosses the stream and then turns to the left to reach, in a few yards, a large circular embanked area that forms a part of the ancient settlements on this low moor. A little further on, there are a few hummocky areas and then the path splits. Here, do not go right or left back across the stream but aim just slightly left and then down the right-hand bank on a grassy path. Beyond this, there are two further forks where right turns are needed to reach a patch of cropped gorse. Aim down through this to reach a rough track just above the inbye wall. This track, which is very intermittent, may be followed to the left, close to the wall to reach the gate at the end of Fell Lane. A short walk down this enclosed gravelled track leads out onto the Corney Fell road only a short distance above Waberthwaite, which lies to the right.

Hard Knott

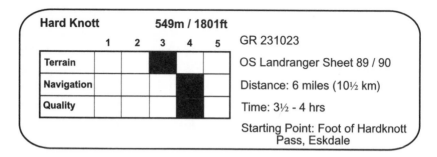

Hard Knott			549m / 1801ft		
	1	2	3	4	5
Terrain			■		
Navigation				■	
Quality				■	

GR 231023

OS Landranger Sheet 89 / 90

Distance: 6 miles (10½ km)

Time: 3½ - 4 hrs

Starting Point: Foot of Hardknott Pass, Eskdale

At the foot of Hardknott Pass, just above the trees which form a small copse on the first incline of the pass, there is a car parking area between the road and gill. The route begins by walking initially up the tarmac until a gate and ladder stile are found set back on the left. The stile should be crossed but rather than continuing straight on, a small path should be followed uphill, parallel to the road but on the other side of the wall. When the wall turns to the left along the hillside, a small slit gives access to the path on the other side which soon rejoins the road.

The road should now be followed uphill past what remains of the Roman fort over a comparatively level area. Just before the next set of hairpins, a path on grass takes off to the left, avoiding the road and making some small hairpins of its own to meet the road once more above the steep section. The large cairn marking the top of the pass is now not a great deal further up the road.

Here, leave the road, following a grassy path around the back of the cairn and then steeply up the hillside to the left until it enters a wet hanging valley. When at this point, leave what indistinct remnants of the path are left and climb up the slope on the left to reach the ridge just to the left of what appears to be the summit cairn; alas the cairn on the next knoll is a little higher.

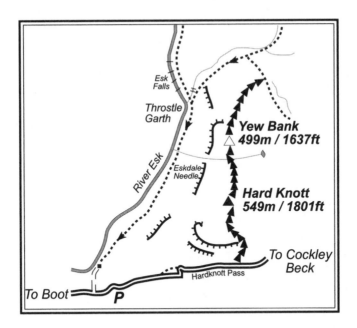

On reaching this point, a further disappointment is found, for this is not the summit either. Care should be taken to avoid crags in making the small descent to the pair of wet depressions between this and the next rocky cone, a fine view appearing of the rocky spire of the Eskdale Needle down on the left whilst crossing the second. The next summit contender supports no cairn and appears just very slightly higher than the next knoll, which is graced by a cairn. Appearances are deceptive, however, and when that cairn is reached, there is no doubting that the summit has now finally been reached.

A grassy path leads north from the summit, running initially on the left-hand side of the ridge before moving to the right-hand side. After a while a steeper descent follows to a very wet hollow containing a small tarn, at which point the path disappears completely. The ridge rises slightly on the other side but keep on the tussocky grass on its right, Mosedale, side before following the ridge's graceful curve around to the right to cross the path climbing up Mosedale from Cockley Beck at the low Mosedale–Lingcove col.

Here, turn left and follow the indistinct grassy path leftwards before meeting the path running just above the beck. At this point turn left and follow the path as it soon descends steeply down out of the hanging valley to meet the Esk by the packhorse bridge at Throstle Garth.

The path continues on the left-hand side of the valley, with a fine view back up to the Eskdale Needle on the skyline at the top of Hard Knott's crags on the left. The path reaches the inbye at a gate and ladder stile, the path degenerating into a muddy quagmire just before. Over the stile, tyre tracks can be followed onwards and through the next gateway. At the one after, leave the track and pass through a kissing gate on the right onto the river bank.

After a few hundred yards a bridge is reached. Here, keep straight on, passing by the farm buildings at Brotherikeld, and follow that farm's driveway out to the main road at the foot of Hardknott Pass; the car park is now only a short distance up the hill to the left.

Lingmoor Fell

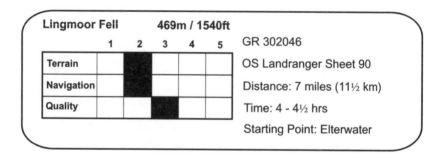

Lingmoor Fell		469m / 1540ft			
	1	2	3	4	5
Terrain		■			
Navigation		■			
Quality			■		

GR 302046
OS Landranger Sheet 90
Distance: 7 miles (11½ km)
Time: 4 - 4½ hrs
Starting Point: Elterwater

Lingmoor Fell is the prominent, craggy hill separating Great and Little Langdales but much of its grandeur is lost to its higher neighbours, the Langdale Pikes, Bowfell, the Crinkle Crags, Pike o'Blisco and Wetherlam. However, as is so often the case with lower hills, Lingmoor Fell provides an excellent viewpoint for its neighbours' majestic buttresses.

Little Langdale does not lend itself to an approach so the best place to start is Elterwater. In the village itself, parking is restricted but the best place is a small car park on the left (when approaching from the Ambleside direction) on the Colwith/Little Langdale road just before the bridge. If this is full, the next nearest car park is in an old quarry on the common on the Ambleside road out of the village, while the main signposted car park is even further afield, on the other side of the Ambleside to Dungeon

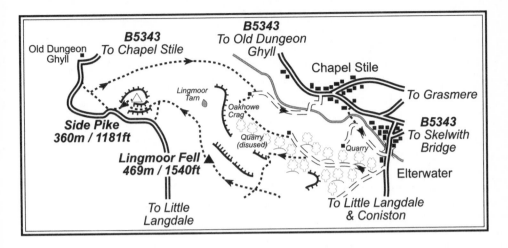

Ghyll road, just up the Grasmere road on the far side of the common.

Begin by returning to the village (if necessary), cross the river bridge and follow the Little Langdale road onwards past the youth hostel on the right. Shortly after that, the Elterwater Hall Hotel will be found on the left and, just past its entrance, on the right, a road leads off. After bending sharply to the right initially, it climbs up a steepish hill before bending off to the right about halfway up. At this point ignore the bridleway ahead to Little Langdale but follow the tarmac around to the right. A few more houses are passed but after a while a signed bridleway will be found running off to the left, up into the wood. Take this and follow it onwards, keeping straight on where it is signed to the left. This broad track is in fact the old quarry road and when, after gently curving upwards, it leaves the trees, the lower quarry workings are to be found. However, follow the track onwards out onto the open fell and continue up towards the higher quarry. Before reaching that, however, directly above a prominent dark-green yew, a waymark should be followed which points back up left on a wide path through bracken which, after hairpinning a few times, leads up to and through the ridge wall.

The view of Little Langdale and Wetherlam now opens up ahead but Lingmoor Fell's summit, Brown Howe, still lies some distance away to the right. A path runs this way, keeping roughly parallel to the wall and climbing over several rocky outcrops. It is some time before the actual summit opens up ahead and more peaty depressions must be crossed to get there. In due course, the wall turns sharply to the right and climbs up a very steep slope; the path continues along to the left. Follow the path initially but look out for a small hairpinning path which climbs the steep slope on the right. This path, on stone to begin with but on grass higher up, leads alongside the summit fence as far as the cairn which lies on the far side of it (stile provided).

Staying on this side of the fence, a small path leads onwards over several rocky knolls with fine views down to the right into the heathery hollow which supports the reedy waters of Lingmoor Tarn. Keeping close to the fence/wall all the time, the path curves around the side and base of a further knoll before descending down into the col between Lingmoor Fell and the rocky summit of Side Pike, crossing a stile over the fence en route; cross over the grassy col with its well-built wall. Towards the far side, a stile is reached.[1] Although very close, there is no direct route from the col to the summit of Side Pike (scramblers may like to note two cracks on the right-hand side of the V-shaped gully eating into the face which provide an ascent onto the right-hand grassy spur descending from the summit). The eastwards-facing rock is, however, greasy after rain). For walkers, cross the stile and follow a small path around to the left which runs onto a ledge on the left-hand face of the pike. The only obstacle is then reached, a classic 'Fat Man's Agony' between a large substantial flake and the rock face; those walkers with a chest of much more than forty inches may like to avoid this traverse completely by following note 1 (see below). After the squeeze, the path rounds the corner on the ledge and then escapes upwards to the ridge on more open steep grass slopes. When the ridge path is reached, the summit is a short distance up to the right.

To descend, follow the ridge path downwards, weaving an intricate line amongst small craglets with the odd rock step. It becomes less distinct lower down but is more obvious once more when it begins to run through bracken. At the foot of the slope, just above the Dungeon Ghyll to Little Langdale road, it meets a path running from left to right; turn right and follow it along and down the hill.* Just before the path enters a conifer wood, turn right along a permissive path which cuts across several fields and crosses several ladder stiles. On the other side of the final one there is a footbridge, and once over this follow the stream down left to the back of Side House. Do not enter the farmyard, however, but turn half right on a clear track which, after passing out of the field, begins to climb quite steeply up the fellside. It does, however, level off and then descend back once more to valley level where it enters a small walled lane and runs around the back of a pair of hillocks. Quite soon after this, a house is reached and a left turn should be made at this point down its drive to the river. Rather than crossing the footbridge, however, stick to following the drive along the near bank until it too crosses over the river on an arched stone bridge. When it finally turns leftwards up to the road, keep straight on along a footpath which runs up to Thrang Farm. Follow its driveway before swinging around to the right along the back of the school to reach the main road just above the Wainwright Inn. Turn right on the road and pass the pub before turning right to cross the river on a footbridge. A path now runs along the river bank before ascending slightly to join the quarry road, which leads back to the bridge in Elterwater village, where the outwards route is rejoined.

Note: 1. To avoid Side Pike, or the 'Fat Man's Agony', completely, turn left before the stile down the main path which leads down to the road at Bleatarn House. Follow the path above the road which drops sharply back down the hill into Langdale. Rejoin the described route above at the *.

Kirkby Moor

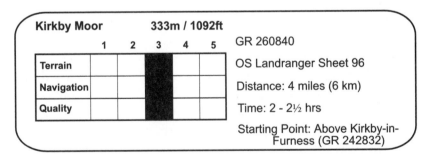

Kirkby Moor					333m / 1092ft
	1	2	3	4	5
Terrain			■		
Navigation			■		
Quality			■		

GR 260840

OS Landranger Sheet 96

Distance: 4 miles (6 km)

Time: 2 - 2½ hrs

Starting Point: Above Kirkby-in-Furness (GR 242832)

Were it not for its distance from the tourist centres of the Lake District and its more Pennine-like appearance, Kirkby Moor would no doubt be a popular walking area. It is a prominent landmark on the coastal road around the south of the Lake District, with its wind farm and quarried

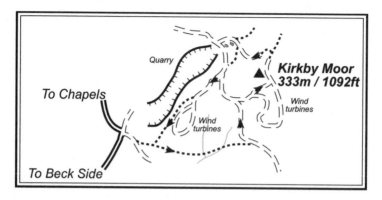

western slopes. However, much of the south of the moor is unspoilt and relatively pathless, which makes for a good and interesting walk best left to a clear and sunny day. It would be a shame, after all, to miss the charming coastal vista that is in view at almost every twist of the route.

The starting point is above Kirkby-in-Furness and can be reached along a small lane from either Chapels, Beck Side or by another lane from Wall End that joins the former at a caravan park. It is possible to park on the roads and tracks around a right angled bend (the second such bend when approaching from the caravan park and the first from Beck Side) where there is a noticeboard recommending routes to the wind farm.

Alongside the noticeboard, a track climbs steeply up through some trees to a gate onto the open hill. A clear track swings right alongside the wall and continues by it along the southern edge of the moor. However, after about a hundred yards from the gate and where the denser bracken on the left comes to an end opposite a row of high vertical slates on the wall-top on the right, a grassy track forks to the left. This makes a somewhat indistinct line across the moor to pass above a clump of rushes just before reaching a pronounced valley containing a stream (this, however, is not the first stream that the track crosses). Just over to the right are the remains of a stone circle, although to the untrained eye there is little more than a low circular parapet of earth enclosing a small depression.

Rather than crossing directly over the small valley, the track, following a slightly sunken 'groove' runs alongside the stream before crossing it just above a confluence. On the far side of the tributary stream, three wide grooves lead on but the one furthest right is the only one that is continuous. It follows the left-hand side of the valley opposite and, now quite pronounced, the track continues to reach a second tributary stream and cross it. Once again, there are a number of grooves ahead that climb the hillside and the second from left (roughly straight on) should be chosen. This soon peters to little more than a sheep track and, when it becomes very indistinct, simply aim straight up the hillside towards the left to reach shortly the clear track of the Kirkby Slate Road.

The wind farm is now increasingly prominent to the left and the track leads along the hillside towards the turbines. It soon hits one of the wind farm's access tracks and a right turn leads up the hill towards the summit. A left turn on another track when the ridge is reached soon leads past the summit cairn on a knoll just to the left of the track. The view across Duddon Sands to Black Combe and Whitfell is very impressive, whilst in most other directions away from the coast the scene is relatively uninspiring. However, both the Duddon and Crake estuaries, separated by the Furness peninsula, add interest to the scene.

From the summit, the access track leads on to the most northerly of the wind turbines and there ends. However, a small track leads on through the heather and soon splits. Here, aim left and follow the curving trackway down and around the hillside past some old quarry workings to a set of reservoirs above the active slate quarry. As soon as the first reservoir is reached, the right of way turns sharply back to the left along its bank to the left corner. From here, a small path leads uphill through the bracken half right to a yellow-topped waymarker.

The path leads ahead crossing the wettest areas on a series of raised walkways to reach the edge of the quarry spoil around which the waymarkers lead until the path joins the highest of the quarry roads. The route now follows the road ahead until the waymarkers point the route right alongside the fence marking the quarry boundary. Four more wind turbines are passed on the left whilst the waymarkers define the route, which soon leaves the fence and runs parallel to it slightly further to the left.

In a short while, the route swings left, as waymarked, and then back right to reach a man-made depression on the edge of a grassy area. Here, the waymarkers end but a sheep track leads through the short bracken and patchy gorse down a ridge. Soon, the path becomes more distinct and rejoins the outwards route just above the wall. A short walk to the right then leads back down through the gate to the road corner.

Holm Fell

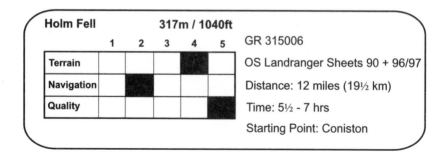

Holm Fell			317m / 1040ft			
	1	2	3	4	5	
Terrain				■		
Navigation		■				
Quality					■	

GR 315006

OS Landranger Sheets 90 + 96/97

Distance: 12 miles (19½ km)

Time: 5½ - 7 hrs

Starting Point: Coniston

Holm Fell is a very obvious outlier of the Coniston Group and catches the eye of most travellers along the A591 Coniston to Ambleside road. Its tree-covered slopes rise from the beautiful waters of Yew Tree Tarn with small craglets in plenty on its steep slopes. Holm Fell is a beautiful example of a small fell that is as majestic as any of the great mountains which surround it.

The best place to start a circular walk is the village of Coniston itself although up-and-back routes can easily be accomplished by all the family from Yew Tree Tarn and even Tarn Hows, and those interested should see notes one and two respectively, below. The National Park's car park is situated close to the church in Coniston although out of season it may be possible to park on the road outside. Begin by walking to the right down the Hawkshead road from the car park and then taking the second road on the left. This curves back around to the left and after passing the football ground on the right, a bridge is to be found on the same side. Signposted 'Footpath', the route crosses the bridge and then turns left along the far bank of the river in front of a gate marked 'Private'.

From here, it climbs slowly uphill, through fields, before passing through a small copse and then descending once more to reach a walled track running from right to left. A left turn leads down, along the side of the beck and then over the bridge to reach a farm. Walk down through the farmyard and out along the headland of the first field, then through a gate (unwaymarked) and across the next two fields. After passing through the fourth gate in total since the farm, turn left and follow the edge of the field up, past a line of yew trees (a rarity in agricultural land as their red berries are highly poisonous to livestock – and humans!) to

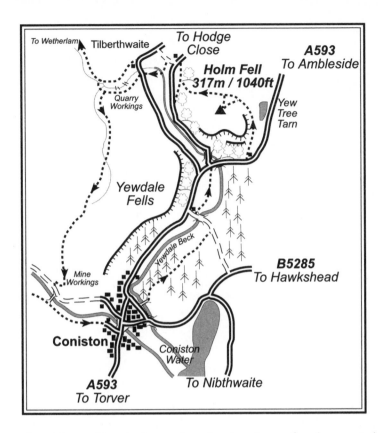

meet the main road just in front of a rather handsome farmhouse. A short distance down the road to the left, a side road takes off to the right, signposted 'Hodge Close Only' and this should be followed for the first 100 yards or so until it has crossed the beck, after which the road bends sharply to the left.

At this point keep straight ahead through a gate along a route marked 'Skelwith Bridge'. This track, which is quite distinct, runs through the rougher inbye quite distinctly through a number of moraines until it ends up at the top of the garden of Yewdale Farm. Here, ignore the gate straight ahead but turn left up a track beside the wall (waymarked) [1,2]. This path leads up and along through the trees, through more moraines until, at a number of large boulders, the track splits at a cairned fork. Take the left path, which is steep and rough initially although the gradient soon eases before becoming steep again, affording fine retrospective views down to Yew Tree Tarn, a fine view when the trees are in their autumn colours.

However, ever upwards, the path leaves the wood and emerges onto the top part of the fell at Uskdale Gap. The highest summits are up to the left and a grassy path leads off in this direction. Soon a cairned summit comes into view but this is Ivy Crag and not the real top, which lies off to the right across the damp, heathery col. A steep pull up the rocky slopes leads around the back and then up onto its fine summit, marked by an arête of naked rock, backed by a fine view down the length of Coniston Water.

To begin the descent to Tilberthwaite, return to the nearside of the wet heathery col where a grassy path, not the same one used on the ascent, leads down to the left. This soon joins a path coming in from the right which, if followed to the left, leads without deviation along and above the pretty reservoirs and down to meet a track running along above the inbye wall. Turn left on it and follow it down until it meets a track running along the top of another wall at an oblique angle. A right turn here leads out on to the road opposite the farm at Holme Ground. To cross the valley, walk down the road, ignoring the first signed footpath to High Tilberthwaite but taking the second which is a stony track through woodland. However, when it comes to the bottom of the wood, take off left on a small path which leads along the bottom of the wood and out onto the banks of the beck and the road on the other side of the valley at the Tilberthwaite car park.

Cross the beck on the road bridge and take off up a flight of steps at the far end of the car park. An old mine track now leads onwards past a series of interesting openings on the left. The first leads into a large but short cave whilst all the others lead into hidden quarries which form large amphitheatres in the hillside. However, the path leads onwards, high above the rushing waters in the confines of Tilberthwaite Gill until it emerges in the upper valley and curves around to the left.[3] Follow it around to the left and up a tributary valley for some distance before it curves half right and climbs up to a col (the highest point reached all day), crossing into the Coppermines Valley. A steep descent follows as the path tends leftwards before meeting a large grass track at some old quarry workings. Here, bear right but almost immediately back left and down to the main track in the Coppermines Valley. Following it downstream, a bridge, Miners' Bridge, is soon found on the right. Cross it and * follow the track down the far bank of the beck past several beautiful cascades until it crosses a field and reaches the end of a tarmac lane leading up from the village to the old station.

The main village can be reached by walking down this road to the left. By doing so, the main road is reached by the main bridge and by keeping more or less straight over the staggered crossroads the church is passed on the right before reaching the car park a little further on.

Notes: 1. To start from Yew Tree Tarn, park in the lay-by on the side of the main road and start off by walking down the road towards Coniston. Soon, just before a farm on the right, a walled 'lane' leads off uphill. Once on the open fell, follow a track up by the wall on the right. The main route is joined at the note marker and can now be followed as far as the summit from where the route of ascent should be reversed.

2. From Tarn Hows, follow the track along the left-hand shore of the lake as far as a footbridge over the tarn's outflow. Follow a path on the far side of the beck downhill past some waterfalls and through a wood. The path then continues along the bottom of the road to emerge on the Coniston to Ambleside road. Here, turn left for a short distance but, just before a farm on the right, follow a walled 'lane' uphill to the right as far as the open fell. Here, turn right along the top of the wall on a track. The main route is joined at the note marker and should now be followed as far as the summit from where the route of ascent should be reversed.

3. Energetic souls may like to return to Coniston over Wetherlam. Instead of following the path around to the left, cross the tributary beck and then, a little further on, the main stream on a footbridge. Turn left on the footpath on the far bank which leads initially right before running up Wetherlam Edge to the summit. A distinct track leads onwards down Wetherlam's western ridge before contouring around the Greenburn side of Black Sails to reach Swirl Hawse where the ridge rears dauntingly up in the steps of Prison Band. However, take off left here down a path to Lever's Water from where the main track can be followed down the Coppermines Valley, past the youth hostel and cottages before crossing the beck on an arched bridge. Rejoin the described route at the *.

Muncaster Fell

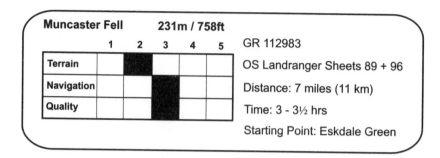

Muncaster Fell		231m / 758ft			
	1	2	3	4	5
Terrain		■			
Navigation			■		
Quality			■		

GR 112983

OS Landranger Sheets 89 + 96

Distance: 7 miles (11 km)

Time: 3 - 3½ hrs

Starting Point: Eskdale Green

Despite being of no significant height, Muncaster Fell enjoys a splendid position between the lower valleys of the Esk and the Mite. Although the fell has no great lateral extent, its ridge rises from the coast at Ravenglass and stretches a good four miles to the village of Eskdale Green. The walk along the ridge forms an excellent and interesting route with good views, to the rear, of Eskdale and the fells around its head. The top of the fell is graced by a hinterland of boggy flats and rocky summits and some careful navigation is required to find the correct route. However, it is possible to reach the top without wet boots and without trudging over innumerable false summits.

It is possible to start at either end of the ridge, although Eskdale Green is chosen here because, in this case, there is no need to make the complete descent to Muncaster. There is a lay-by with room for a dozen cars by the telephone box and the track leading across to Miterdale up Giggle Alley. Begin by walking towards the middle of the village and turning left opposite the post office. Named Randlehow, this road drops steeply before climbing slightly past the imposing frontage of 'The Ferns'. Built around 1890, the house has been in use as a guesthouse through much of its life and today still offers bed and breakfast accommodation.

Further down the lane, it turns sharply left, but here the route goes right down an unmade-up track and across a cattle grid. A notice marks this as the footpath to Muncaster Fell, which swings right soon before a pair of houses through an open gateway marked footpath. One rough field lies before the narrow gauge tracks of the Ravenglass and Eskdale railway are reached. Once over these, a slippery raised walkway leads across a boggy area to reach a stone bridge across a stream in a small thicket. Another gate leads into a further rough field and the path follows the fence

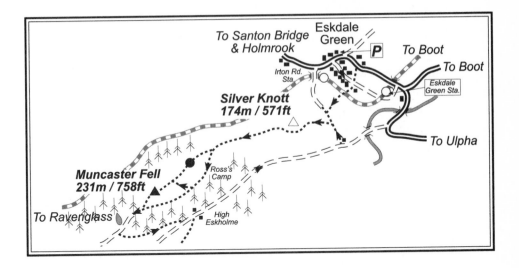

and scrubby woodland on the right up to the track leading down from Irton Road Station, which is an alternative starting point, especially suited to those travelling on the train from Muncaster Mill or Ravenglass as there is only very limited parking by the station.

A left turn leads along to a waymarker pointing a right of way up the hillside to the right. This follows the line of a track but soon narrows to a path through the scrubby vegetation on the lower slopes. It reaches a gate at the top of the field, which leads out onto the open fell. Above this, the main path continues, built up with stones on the left in places, around the southern slopes of the first rocky eminence on the ridge – Silver Knott. This would appear to be the summit from the valley at Eskdale Green but, as the path winds around the slopes and descends slightly to reach the depression on the ridge beyond Silver Knott, higher summits appear ahead – although none of these distant points mark the summit of the fell either.

Shortly, the path reaches a wall to the right and the ascent begins again without crossing it. The path does not stay by the wall, although it never deviates too far from it. After a reasonably stiff climb past many craglets, the path meets the wall again as it swings left and passes through an open gateway. The path continues to reach a boggy area on the left within a few yards. Here, many walkers make their mistake. Instead of crossing the bog on the left, which is not nearly as fearsome as it looks, they swing to the right, where a path has developed, and then have several ups and downs and more bogs to cross.

Thus, when the main path swings right, cut left across some rushes to a rocky knoll, where a clear path develops. Another moist area remains before reaching a path that swings to the left of the main knoll ahead (a path ascending to its summit should be ignored). Except in the worst conditions, the bog may easily be crossed without wet feet. This path, actually the original path over the fell, now ascends around the left-hand side of the many false summits on the ridge itself. A little surprise awaits as soon the huge raised slab of Ross's Camp is reached. Constructed in 1883, this huge sloping slab served as a table from which the Victorian hunting parties ate their lunch.

Leaving this feature behind, the path makes a short descent and then re-ascent across a small valley before descending again towards a boggy hollow. In the middle, between two moist arms, there is a small jutting craglet. The path swings across the first arm to make a fairly easy crossing before hugging the base of the craglet and making a duplicate crossing over the second boggy arm; the main path then swings sharp left below a further craglet ahead. However, here the path is left. When crossing the second boggy patch, go ahead up a faint path through the bracken. This becomes more distinct as it reaches the left edge of a higher boggy patch and hugs the craglet on the left. Beyond this, it climbs slightly on the left, before dropping down and skirting the edge of the remaining bog. A short walk on the path through the bracken leads to the foot of the final slopes and the path climbs straight up to the trig point on top.

From here, the views of the coast and mountains can be admired. The fells around the head of Eskdale and Miterdale are understandably prominent – the Scafells, the Crinkle Crags, Hard Knott and Harter Fell. The Coniston and Pillar groups are also visible. Meanwhile, the coastline stretches in an unbroken line northwards from Black Combe, with Whitfell visible to its left. The route now continues on a small path steeply down along the ridge to the south-west, meeting with the main path at the corner of a plantation. A track then leads down its edge to the delightfully hidden shores of Muncaster Tarn.

Opposite the tarn, a signposted bridleway turns to the left, bound for Lower Eskdale. The path curves back around to the left through the trees and above a sturdy wall on the right to pass above a collection of buildings and an interesting tower. This was constructed to mark the spot where Henry VI was found by shepherds after the Battle of Towton in 1461.

Further down, the track hits the tarmac road leading to the hamlet of Eskholme to the left. Beyond this, a track, muddy and wet at times, leads onwards up the valley. With almost continuous woodland on the left and a plantation on the right as well for part of the way, the track leads straight to the farm at Muncaster Head back at the eastern end of the fell. Here, a left turn should be made through an open gateway in front of the buildings to follow the bridleway back towards Irton Road Station.

This leads to a gate and, ignoring a right turn just before the gate, the outwards route is rejoined where it turned back up the hill. The field path can then be followed back to the village and then the roads to the Giggle Alley car park.

Section 6 – North and North-western Lakeland

The Rivers Eden and Eamont from the Solway Firth to Penrith. The A66 from there to Threlkeld and St John's Beck to Thirlmere. Dunmail Raise and the River Rothay to Windermere. The River Brathay and the Great Langdale Beck to Mickleden. Stake Pass and the Langstrath Beck to Rosthwaite. The River Derwent and Styhead Gill to Sty Head Pass. Lingmell Beck to Wastwater and the River Irt to the sea at Ravenglass. The coast from there to the Solway Firth.

NAME	HEIGHT	IN SECTION	IN ENGLAND	IN BRITAIN
Blake Fell	573m/1879ft	14 of 23	60 of 184	812 of 1552
Lord's Seat	552m/1811ft	15 of 23	66 of 184	867J of 1552
Mellbreak	512m/1680ft	16 of 23	78 of 184	957J of 1552
Binsey	447m/1467ft	17 of 23	95 of 184	1109J of 1552
Low Fell	423m/1388ft	18 of 23	100 of 184	1157 of 1552
High Rigg	357m/1170ft	19 of 23	113 of 184	1284J of 1552
Dent	352m/1155ft	20 of 23	114 of 184	1292J of 1552
Loughrigg Fell	335m/1100ft	21 of 23	118J of 184	1315J of 1552
Watch Hill	254m/ 833ft	22 of 23	158J of 184	1452J of 1552
Swinside	244m/ 800ft	23 of 23	164 of 184	1471 of 1552

There are 13 summits above 2,000ft that are described in *England's Highest Peaks*.

Buttermere and Borrowdale are two of Lakeland's most beautiful valleys. They both begin in the heart of the area's highest mountains and then run out through the foothills, many of which are as fine and craggy as the parent mountains themselves. Mellbreak has, possibly, the finest shape of any of the English summits and, when viewed from the north, assumes even Matterhorn-like proportions. The hills of this section contain a great variety, from high peaks, such as Blake Fell, to more lowland hills, such as

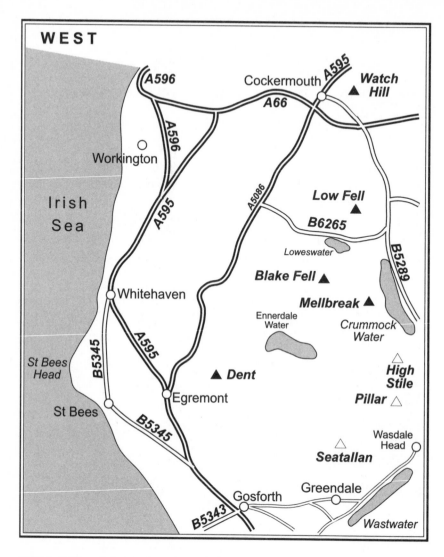

WEST

Cockermouth

Watch Hill ▲

A596

A595

A66

A596

Workington ○

A595

A5086

Low Fell ▲

B6265

Irish
Sea

B5289

Loweswater

Blake Fell ▲

Whitehaven ○

Mellbreak ▲

Ennerdale
Water

Crummock
Water

A595

St Bees
Head

B5345

▲ **Dent**

△
**High
Stile**

Pillar △

Egremont ○

St Bees ○

B5345

△
Seatallan

Wasdale
Head ○

Greendale ○

Gosforth ○

B5343

Wastwater

Watch Hill and Swinside. Meanwhile, Loughrigg Fell occupies the south-eastern corner of the section. This famous hill, renowned for the picture-postcard view of Grasmere from its famous Terrace, is ascended as much as any other Lakeland hill or mountain. The geology of each part of the Lake District is very similar to the others, so it is discussed wholly within Section 4 on page 126.

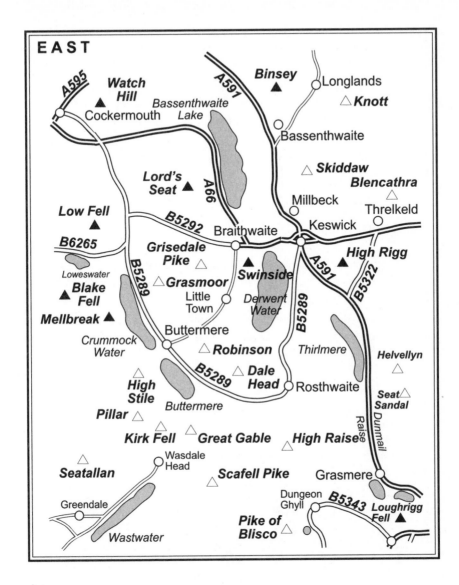

Access

The west coast is served by a regular Monday to Saturday rail service between Carlisle and Barrow-in-Furness. There is also a limited Sunday service between Carlisle, Workington and Whitehaven. A bus links Workington and Cockermouth, from where there is an infrequent summer service to Buttermere. A branch line from Oxenholme, on the west coast main line, runs to Windermere and there are regular daily services in summer, but in winter, although it still runs daily, the service is more limited; there are direct trains between Windermere, Manchester Piccadilly and Manchester Airport, subject to the above restrictions. A bus service connects Windermere, Ambleside, Grasmere and Keswick. The A590 and A591 link Junction 36 of the M6 with Ambleside, Grasmere and Keswick and the A66 links Junction 40 of the M6 with Keswick, Cockermouth and Workington.

Accommodation

Many of the hills can be accessed from the Keswick region, where there is plentiful accommodation. Buttermere would also be a good base for some of the hills, although the village does tend to be very busy during the summer months. There are youth hostels at Keswick, Derwentwater, Borrowdale (Longthwaite), Honister Hause, Buttermere and Grasmere (Butterlip How and Thorney How).

Blake Fell

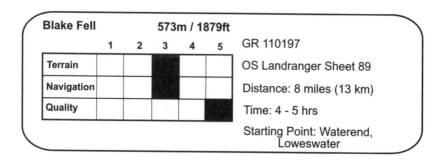

Blake Fell			573m / 1879ft			
	1	2	3	4	5	GR 110197
Terrain			■			OS Landranger Sheet 89
Navigation			■			Distance: 8 miles (13 km)
Quality					■	Time: 4 - 5 hrs
						Starting Point: Waterend, Loweswater

Between Loweswater and Buttermere, and bounded by the large gap in the hills of the Floutern Tarn pass in the south, the Loweswater Fells form a block of quite high ground that forms a magnificent viewpoint for the Buttermere, Coledale and Ennerdale Fells. Although Mellbreak is by far the most prominent and distinctive summit of the range, Blake Fell is the

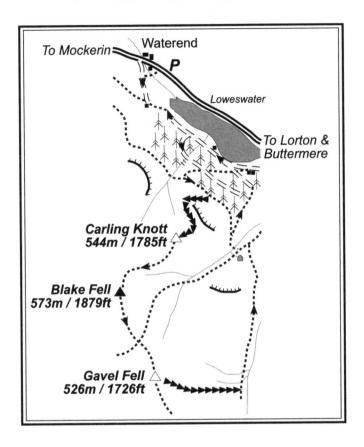

highest point. Almost a twin to Mellbreak, Hen Comb forms a third pronounced summit, which only misses out on inclusion in this book by a relatively small height difference. It could be included in the walk described below, although to do so would lengthen the route considerably and, thus, this is not recommended.

The most appropriate starting point is at the western end of Loweswater. The best car parking space is not the larger one by Loweswater Hall (the easternmost of the two) but a smaller pull-in by the telephone box at Waterend, where there is room for at least ten cars. From the western end of the lay-by, a path descends and crosses the valley, passing over the damper parts on raised planking, to reach the road leading to Hudson Place Farm. A left turn leads up to the farm, where the left-hand gate should be taken to pass in front of the house before making a sharper left turn through a signed gate towards the lake.

After a short descent, the path reaches lake-level and continues close to its shoreline to reach Holme Wood. The track continues close to the lake through the wood, although our route turns up the first track on the right, between two sturdy trees. The ascent now begins as the easily graded track climbs gradually through the lower wood before swinging left below a steeper bank. Here, it crosses the Holme Beck just below the foot of the delicate cascades of Holme Force. Although a path climbs on the left bank of the stream, this does not reach the top of the wood but climbs only as far as the top waterfall (beware of the extremely slippery rocks).

Following the track onwards, it makes a gently rising traverse before soon reaching a path that climbs up the hillside and crosses the track at an oblique angle. A sharp right turn should be made to hairpin back up towards the top of the wood. Once out of the trees, ignore a track on the left but keep straight on to reach the fell gate. On the other side of this, there is a wide well-graded track that runs along the hillside from the Mockerkin road. To the left, this track continues the ascent up to a further and final gate through the fence that runs up the upper hanging valley of the Holme Beck.

Up to the right rise the steep slopes of Carling Knott. This summit forms the first objective of the climb and the route to its summit is largely pathless. Leaving the main track, a bright green grassy trod rises to the right and that should be followed past a large patch of bracken on the right to reach a patch of rushes with a large rock in the middle. Here, swing back to the right on another small sheep track that makes a rising traverse above a patch of rocks on the hillside to reach a small ridge. A left turn on this leads up to a small shoulder. From here, the main north-west ridge of the Knott can be seen steeply up ahead. The ascent is best continued by turning right and following an initially faint but then more distinct path that contours to the ridge and crosses it between two small craglets. Once past these, turn up to the left, although scramblers may like to try a more direct approach.

The ascent of this ridge is the best part of the climb – small craglets can be climbed or avoided at will and, by keeping to the left-hand side, there is always a wonderful view of Loweswater and of Low Fell on the other side of the valley. Towards the top of the ridge, it levels out and the vegetation gets rougher but continue to the very top before swinging right and losing the view for the rest of the climb to reach the summit cairn.

Carling Knott is, however, little more than the large butt of the west ridge of Blake Fell. A small path leads onwards along the ridge and onto the intermediate summit. Here, there is a magnificently built shelter-cairn that graces the higher point. Also, for the first time on the climb, Blake Fell comes into view ahead. Fortunately, it is not much further or much higher. To begin with, aim straight for it so as to pick up a small path running along the edge of some craglets on the left-hand side of the ridge. However, the ridge swings to the right around the head of a quite deep valley so the route soon turns away from the summit. The path chooses not to cross the col but instead stays slightly down to the left, crossing some wet ground and staying above a fenced bog hole. The final slopes now lie ahead and the path soon fades. However, aim straight up and, after climbing an awkwardly placed fence, the summit with its small shelter cairn is underfoot.

Ennerdale Water now appears into view ahead and Cogra Moss Reservoir in the deep valley down to the right. Just to the left of this valley, the steep-sided dome of Knock Murton or Murton Fell also narrowly misses out on inclusion in this book. However, there is a most excellent view of the majestic height of Pillar (with Pillar Rock visible on its Ennerdale flank), Red Pike, High Stile, Fleetwith Pike and even Buttermere Lake in the gap between Red Pike and Mellbreak. Slightly less majestic but none the less magnificent are the Coledale and Newlands Fells with, from left to right, Whiteside with Hopegill Head beyond, Grasmoor with Eel Crags behind and Robinson. There is even a view of Helvellyn across Newlands Hause. In fact, so good are the views of the higher peaks from the Loweswater Fells that it is now well worthwhile continuing onto Gavel Fell.

Another path runs south-east from the summit (to the left as the summit was reached on the ascent) and this leads down to a stile in the fence. However, the path stays on the nearside but follows the fence down past another stile to reach a third just before a junction of fences. Here, the main path descends towards Cogra Moss but instead go left across this stile and follow a fence down to the low point at the head of the Highnook valley where there is a fourth stile. Ahead along the ridge lies Gavel Fell and, avoiding some damp ground over the col, the fence may be followed all the way to the summit. The cairn is on the other side of the fence and just before it a further fence branches to the left.

After crossing to the cairn, from where there is an excellent view of Floutern Crag on the north face of Gavel Fell, although the tarn itself remains hidden, return to the fence and cross both stiles. Once over them, continue to follow the ridge fence until it soon swings right towards Floutern Tarn Pass. Here, continue to follow the line of the fence until past some peaty pools and then swing slightly left down the steep grassy hillside. When the ground starts to level and become rushy towards the floor of the valley, look carefully for the old drove road. This little-used track follows a levelled grassy shelf but at other times is little more than a sheep track through rushes.

When found, it should be followed to the left where it traverses the valley sides, becoming ever more distinct and ending up high above the stream. When the ridge on the left abruptly terminates, the path crosses over and descends into the Highnook valley just below Highnook Tarn. It soon reaches the track running down that valley, which should be followed upstream to the left before soon forking right and swinging across the valley before turning down the valley on a rising track on the far side. However, this soon hits a corner on the inbye wall, where it should be left. This track is in fact the one that runs along the foot of the crags on Carling Knott above the wood and it now rises steeply to that point.

Instead, keep alongside the wall, where a strip of green turf eases progress through the bracken, which becomes more vigorous as distance is gained. Soon the foot of the wood is reached but a gate ahead leads not into the wood but into a field below it. The path follows a shelf at the top of the field before a stile at the far side gives access to the wood. The path now follows the edge of the wood before turning into a wider track and slanting across the hillside to descend gradually to meet the path along the lakeshore.

Once on this track, fork left once across a footbridge by a ford to avoid a small 'bothy' on the right and continue across a further footbridge over the Holme Beck to rejoin the outwards route, which can then, of course, be followed back to the waiting car and starting point.

Lord's Seat

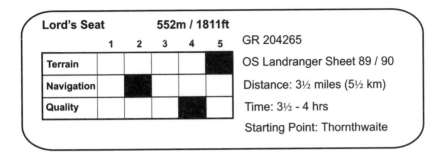

Lord's Seat			552m / 1811ft		
	1	2	3	4	5
Terrain					■
Navigation		■			
Quality				■	

GR 204265

OS Landranger Sheet 89 / 90

Distance: 3½ miles (5½ km)

Time: 3½ - 4 hrs

Starting Point: Thornthwaite

To the north-west of Keswick, at the head of Bassenthwaite Lake, the rocky fellside of Barf falls straight down to the village of Thornthwaite at its foot, now bypassed by the busy A66 Keswick to Cockermouth road. However, despite its forbidding appearance from the road, it is little more than a knobbly shoulder of land, belonging to Lord's Seat, which sits behind, out of sight, at the centre of this small group of fells. The ascent of this hill was once a very popular excursion but due to its detachment from the main fells and the afforestation of its lower slopes, the route has fallen from popularity. That is a little unfair as this is a fine expedition, especially so if the challenge of the front of Barf is taken directly as described here. However, those who, some would say, have more common sense may like to avoid this by following the walking alternative.[1]

This route takes the front of Barf straight on, making a tough but interesting approach to the summit. The car park at Potter How is not clearly marked but is to be found immediately beyond the Swan Inn when approaching from Braithwaite and Keswick. The route starts off up the narrow lane opposite the pub, which soon leads to a gate on the right into the woodland, marked with a sign warning of the danger of falling rocks. Amongst the trees, in spring, the delicate yellow flowers of several clumps of daffodils wave in the breeze before the whitewashed stone of The Clerk is reached. This pinnacle-shaped rock is a poor second to The Bishop, also whitewashed, who stands at mid-height up the visible slope.

In fact, The Bishop is the next objective and he is reached up the steep and loose scree slope, which becomes increasingly earthy as height is gained. There are several routes up the scree and no single one is any better than another so there is little point in making any deviation from the

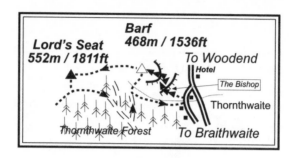

well-trodden route that goes straight up to the slate pulpit on which The Bishop stands (at least be thankful that, unlike the local villagers, you are not carrying a tin of paint). Beyond The Bishop, the route lies up a rocky gully, the base of which is filled with scree. A first rock band is easily negotiated but, at the top, it is necessary to escape onto the rock rib on the left to avoid the final crag in the gully. However, great care is required as the rock is rotten.

A heather slope now lies ahead and in no distance a rowan tree is reached. A small path now leads onwards to the foot of another scree slope by a circular bracken-filled shelter, lying on a small section of level ground. Rather than ascending the scree, follow the path to the right, where there is a better square shelter, and climb up through the heather on the same small path to reach an open area of smaller, more stable stones. Following the path onwards, it reaches another more level area directly below the cliff of Slape Crag. Here, work left to an oak tree that grows out of the crag with a smaller rowan tree directly above it. Our route continues as a small path that makes an exposed traverse just above these trees and past a dwarf gorse, which obstructs some handholds at a crucial point.

These difficulties are over round the corner and the path leads on up a further steep heather slope to a larch tree just below the crags of Slape Crag's upper escarpment. Above the tree, follow the path to the right and onto the easier angled slope on what from here appears as the skyline. At that point, although the path leads onwards, leave it to climb up through the rocks with a couple of rocky steps above the steepest part of the lower crag. At this point, the worst of the slope is over and the path leads onto the top of the first knoll. This is not the summit, neither is the second but the top is in fact the third. Close to the summit, a more obvious path will be met, which is the alternative route of ascent.

Barf's summit is marked by a small plinth of rock and an insignificant cairn, overlooking Bassenthwaite Lake and the great bulk of Skiddaw beyond. The view to the west, however, is obstructed by Lord's Seat, the next objective. A good path leads towards it and over the depression. However, on the ascent, the slopes become increasingly boggy and the path in places is too bad to be followed easily. Better ground is, however, to be found in the heather on the right and the final cone is completely dry and covered by beautiful turf. A lone metal fencepost marks the top, along with a slightly higher rock plinth, similar to the one on Barf. A fine panorama has now opened up, although the close view of Bassenthwaite has all but disappeared.

The route of descent lies through Thornthwaite Forest, which makes an attractive cladding for the lower slopes. Down the slope to the left, in no distance, a stile gives access to the forest lands and a new gravel path on the far side. Those with Forest Enterprise's guidebook will understand the meaning of post 23, which now lies on the left, and the seemingly irrational nature of the numbering hereafter. Post 6 is the next that is passed and at post 5, where the main track swings around to the right, our route goes left along another gravel path, also improved to begin with by wooden planking. Post 4 is passed before a further descent down to the head of a forest road. This should then be followed slowly downhill, before turning sharp back left into the second forest road on the left at post 8. This road, in places blasted out of the crag, leads back towards Barf, with fine views of its craggy front whilst passing through a recently deforested area. After a while, the road begins to climb sharply uphill for a short distance and just before this point, a graded path should be followed down the hill to the right.

Running away initially from the tumbling beck that can be heard just beyond the trees, it then turns back towards it before reaching a point of indecision at the top of a crag. Despite a path leading straight ahead, the main path slants to the right, traversing across the face of the crag to its foot. Here turn right and carry on down the slope, with a path joining from the right at post 20 (!). A steep descent now follows with a fallen tree making an awkward obstacle. Soon, though, a stile on the left, by a bench, should be crossed and then the stream, before continuing downhill on its far side. This leads back into the woodland at the foot of Barf, just by The Clerk.

Walking Alternative

1. By avoiding the face of Barf, the route of descent is for the most part being reversed but a description is given none the less. Following the route above as far as The Clerk, continue up the path straight ahead to the left of the screes. In due course, the main path swings left and over the stream to enter the plantations of Thornthwaite Forest by a stile, just over which is a bench. A right turn should then be made up the steep slope to a junction by post 20. Here, aim half right, still up the slope, to the foot of a steep crag. A waymarker directs the path up and across the front of the crag to its top, after which a hairpinning path continues the climb up to a forest road. As directed by another waymarker, a right turn should be made on the road before leaving the forest and crossing the stream just above a long waterslide. On the far side, the path leads clearly on with some bifurcation close to the summit, but whatever path is followed, Barf's summit will soon be reached, at which point the main route is rejoined.

Mellbreak

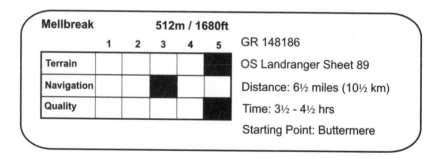

Mellbreak			512m / 1680ft			
	1	2	3	4	5	GR 148186
Terrain					■	OS Landranger Sheet 89
Navigation			■			Distance: 6½ miles (10½ km)
Quality					■	Time: 3½ - 4½ hrs
						Starting Point: Buttermere

All along the western side of Crummock Water, Mellbreak's craggy slopes rise abruptly from the water with long fans of scree breaking the heathery hillside. Higher up, an array of crags arrests attention as for the length of the lake it guards the summit plateau up above. Together, Mellbreak and Crummock Water complement each other to produce a backdrop that is as attractive and spectacular as any in Lakeland. It seems appropriate

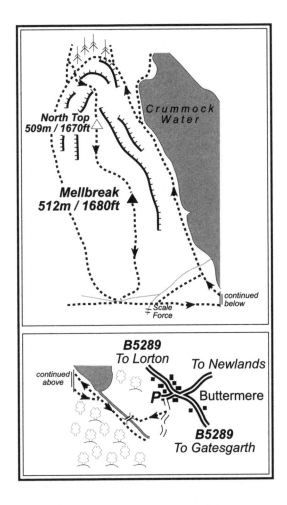

therefore that the combination is considered together and linked in an attractive circular excursion.

The best place to begin such a walk is the village of Buttermere and the best direction to do it is anticlockwise so Mellbreak is ascended from Loweswater, by far its finest side. There are several places to park in Buttermere village but perhaps the most convenient is the National Park Authority's car park down the small lane from the Bridge Inn and just to the right of the Fish Hotel. If this is full, then there is parking in a lay-by at the start of the Newlands road or in a larger car park at the edge of the village on the Cockermouth road. Begin from the Fish Hotel by walking down its left-hand side. This track soon swings around to the left and then passes through a gate. The onwards route now lies to the right, through the next gate and signposted to Scale Force. This track is stonier and rougher than the first but in time leads to a stone-arched bridge over the river linking the two lakes in the valley. The main footpath down the valley is then reached on the far side and a right turn on this leads down to the top of Crummock Water.

At a cairn just before a wooden footbridge, a less distinct path takes off to the right and this is in fact the lakeshore path. It then proceeds to cross the beck below the footbridge, so in wet weather it may be easier to continue along the Scale Force path until over the footbridge. Soon, the lakeshore path forks, at which point go left, crossing a few other footbridges before the tracks once again merge. With the slopes of Mellbreak starting to steepen on the left, the path comes under High Ling Crag, where the odd peninsula of Low Ling Crag juts sharply into the lake. It is at this point that there is another fork and again the route goes left, this time up the less distinct path. This upper path is quite narrow but increasingly clear as it gently rises across and then contours along the hillside, passing through two broken-down walls and squeezing through a line of gorse bushes running down the hillside.

Beyond the second broken-down wall, after a small initial descent, the path rises up to meet the inbye wall at the point where Mellbreak's slopes swing around to the left. Staying above the wall, the path continues, on grass, slightly downhill and through a small wood to meet a lane rising up through the inbye just beyond a house and garden on the right. The track that rises through the gate should then be followed up the slope before it curves back to the right above the wall and continues above a conifer plantation before meeting another track rising up the hillside out of the trees.

Here, the climbing starts in earnest as a path is followed up the steep grassy hillside on the left to the foot of the scree slope. Although an obvious run has developed straight down the slope, it is preferable in ascent to follow the path that hairpins initially left across the scree before moving back right and then left and right again at a higher level. Eventually, it leads to a rocky gully that breaks through a band of crags. Although largely scree filled, especially so lower down, the best footing is to be found on the left and certainly so higher up where a succession of nice rock steps develops. The escape at the top of the gully must be made on the left to avoid the loose, earthy slope at the top right.

Leading left to begin with, the path passes a rocky seat on the first promontory on the left, before swinging back up the ridge and through the heather. Further craglets are passed and further promontories on the left, some of which provide good views down over Crummock and Buttermere. Behind, all the time there is a continually improving view over Loweswater and the lower valley. In due course, the summit plateau is reached and the cairn on the north summit but, contrary to what might be thought, this is not the true summit. It is the South Top that has this honour, although from this vantage point it does look lower. A grass path runs through the heather over the intervening depression and almost all the way to the summit, although it does become indistinct towards the end.

The view back to Loweswater has now completely disappeared but Crummock Water and Buttermere can be brought into view by walking left towards the top of the crags. The distant view is lost due to the presence of Mellbreak's higher neighbours but they certainly make up for this with a fine display and variation of colour and topography. The descent to Buttermere lies down the grassy south ridge and, although there is a path, it runs on grass and is difficult to follow in mist. In fact, it leads straight on from the small, minimalistic cairn and initially winds around a number of knolls before reaching a much longer and steeper grass slope that provides a good test for the knees. However, the view of High Stile, Buttermere and Fleetwith Pike more than compensates. After reaching slightly more level ground, it swings around to the right to avoid a subsidiary summit before meeting a wire fence. This can be crossed quite easily and then the path swings right, eventually meeting the path running on this side of the valley stream. However, this contours along the fellside to the left so cross more or less straight over, following another grass path downhill until it crosses the stream. A gradual ascent on the other side leads to another fence crossing at Scale Force.

The fine 100ft (30m) cascade can be appreciated from the far side of the bridge in winter but in summer, when the leaves are on the trees, it will be necessary to approach closer to the foot of the lower cascade. Scramblers can then get even closer by climbing this first barrier when the water level is sufficiently low. The footpath back to Buttermere from the Force is initially very clear but it then gets lost amongst some wetter ground. However, by staying on more or less the same level, it will be picked up on the other side, its line now cairned. Soon, the cairned path, now on grass, turns down the slope, and then swings back right before rejoining the route of ascent at the footbridge.

Binsey

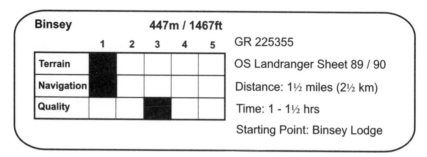

Binsey						447m / 1467ft
	1	2	3	4	5	GR 225355
Terrain	■					OS Landranger Sheet 89 / 90
Navigation	■					Distance: 1½ miles (2½ km)
Quality			■			Time: 1 - 1½ hrs
						Starting Point: Binsey Lodge

Binsey is very much akin in terms of its shape and stature to the Mell Fells in Section 4. Despite lying close to the Skiddaw range, it stands detached from it as a distinct and prominent rounded hill rising above the village of Bassenthwaite and its lake. Perhaps, less favourably, it could equally be described in some lights as a sprawling lump of rough grassland. However, the one thing that can be said about it is that it is a safe and easy fell that can be ascended with ease by all the family during the summer months.

The easiest starting point is at Binsey Lodge at the fell's south-eastern corner on the road between Ireby and Kilnhill near Bassenthwaite. The Lodge itself is situated where a minor road runs across the breast of the fell to reach the A591 at Bewaldeth. There are a couple of parking opportunities on the roadside of this minor lane just beyond the Lodge. A ladder stile gives access to the fell and once on the open hill, turn to the left and follow a grassy track to the left and over a small stream before curving right with the track to commence the ascent.

A description almost seems over the top for this simple stroll. The track, mostly on grass, although occasionally damp in winter, climbs the gently graded slopes heading ever upwards, with the summit remaining out of view until the last minute in the typical style of the Northern Fells' convex

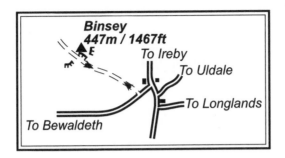

slopes. With much of the ascent completed, the ground starts to become more heathery and scattered boulders begin to appear on the hillside. These herald the entrance to the upper fell and after running up a broad declivity, the ridge on the right rises towards the summit cairns, stone shelters, trig point and ancient tumulus and a small path climbs up to them.

As with so many hills on Lakeland's perimeter, Binsey has an uninterrupted seawards view. Here, the lowlands stretch northwards to the sands and channels of the Solway Firth before the ground rises on the far side towards the distant hills of Dumfriesshire. Closer to hand, the Skiddaw fells dominate the view, with the Whitewater Dash valley leading the eye into the heart of the range. The dark-coloured crag of the waterfall of Whitewater Dash itself is also prominent. On the left-hand side of this valley, a ridge rises to Great Cockup – a hill made famous recently by Denis Norden's outtakes programme on ITV – and beyond that the parent summit of Knott. Needless to say, the descent is best made by the same route to end a well worthwhile excursion to one of Lakeland's lesser visited summits, 'Back o'Skiddaw'.

Low Fell

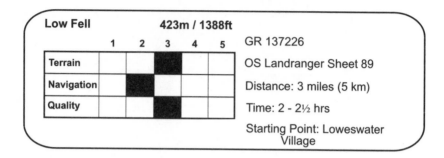

Low Fell			423m / 1388ft			
	1	2	3	4	5	
Terrain			■			
Navigation		■				
Quality			■			

GR 137226

OS Landranger Sheet 89

Distance: 3 miles (5 km)

Time: 2 - 2½ hrs

Starting Point: Loweswater Village

Low Fell is the highest point of Loweswater Fell, which forms a distinct and separate block of high ground to the north of Loweswater, separating that valley from the broad trough of Lorton Vale. Defended by steep and craggy slopes to the south and east, the dramatic elevation of the summit makes it an excellent viewpoint that is rarely visited due to its position too far to the north of Buttermere. However, a very pleasant walk may be made on the fell from Loweswater village that, although not circular, provides splendid views and differing perspectives.

The walk begins from the public telephone box on the edge of Loweswater village alongside the road leading from the B5289 Buttermere road to Loweswater lake itself. There is parking for a handful of cars on the gravelly ground by the telephone box, where the eastern end of the loop road that runs through the village joins the main road. A few yards to the east along the road, just past Oak Cottage on the right, a footpath turns off the road to the left through a gate as signposted. It follows a broad track along the right-hand margin of a first field and it then follows the wall along the right-hand side of the second as well to reach a back road just opposite a group of self-catering cottages.

The footpath continues up a track on the left-hand side of the cottages, which leads to a gate into the field behind. A stone stile built into the wall just to the left of the gate gives access to the field and once in it, the grassy track should be followed half right across the field as signposted to reach a gate and stile into the woodland beyond. Once inside the plantation, the right of way follows the track around to the right and along the bottom of the wood. It can be a bit boggy in places but soon a stile is reached that leads into the next plantation. Again, the path keeps along the bottom of

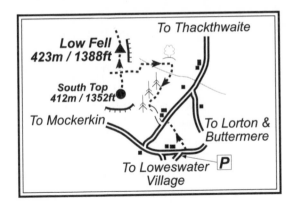

the wood to reach another stile that leads out of the wood and into the field beyond. It is then not much further along the bottom of this field until the ruined farm at Pottergill is reached, from where there is a lovely view towards Crummock Water and Grasmoor.

It is only now that the ascent begins and the path slants half left up a stone-faced embankment as waymarked just after crossing a small stream. The path then continues just above this wall until a grassy ramp leads sharply back left to reach the stream above its small cascades. Rather than crossing the stream, however, turn to the right up a small grass path amongst the bracken that diverges slightly from the stream and ascends to a stile in the fell wall at the top of the field. Avoiding a fallen tree by initially aiming half left, the path continues upwards through the bracken, still a little to the right of the stream to reach the foot of an open, wet patch on the bracken-clad hillside.

The route follows the left-hand edge of this open area before taking the second small path on the left that leads across to the now small stream. Ahead, the path climbs a damp and rushy break in the bracken, which sometimes supports a small watercourse, to reach the foot of one of the patches of scree on the steep upper heather-clad slopes. In order to avoid the scree and heather, turn to the left here and follow a reasonable path on the level to reach a fenceline. A small path runs alongside the fence and, to the right, this path ascends the very steep final slopes up to the ridge. After much toil on the steep grass, the path reaches the ridge and a stile in the fence on the left. The summit now lies up to the right, although the view of Loweswater is attained by diverting to the lower rocky knoll on the left-hand side of the fence.

From the stile, a path leads up right to the small cairn on the quite sharp summit.

On a clear day, the view from the summit is superb. The scene around Crummock Water dominates the panorama, with Grasmoor, Great Gable and, to a certain extent, Mellbreak being the most grand and dominating peaks. The less rough slopes of Blake Fell on the other side of Loweswater attract attention in that direction, while Skiddaw can be seen over the tops of the Whinlatter hills. The hills of Dumfriesshire and the Cheviots are also in the view, although the latter much more distantly. The descent is best completed by the same route as no circuit is really possible. However, take care not to miss the left turn at the bottom of the steep upper slope as the path by the fence soon runs out after there.

High Rigg

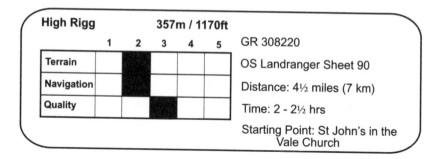

High Rigg		357m / 1170ft				
	1	2	3	4	5	GR 308220
Terrain		■				OS Landranger Sheet 90
Navigation		■				Distance: 4½ miles (7 km)
Quality			■			Time: 2 - 2½ hrs
						Starting Point: St John's in the Vale Church

To the north of Thirlmere, the lake's outflow is funnelled northwards towards Threlkeld down a narrow valley by one of Lakeland's least visited fells. This block of land, riddled with the crags and hidden valleys that characterise so many of the lower fells of the Lake District, is, however, well worth a visit. The traverse of its north–south ridge makes for a fine expedition amidst tremendous scenery and with constantly changing views and perspectives.

The ideal starting point is St John's in the Vale Church. This is sited out of the valley on the ridge running north from High Rigg and can be reached up a dead-end road from the B5322 that runs along the valley between Thirlmere and Threlkeld. There is a small parking area opposite

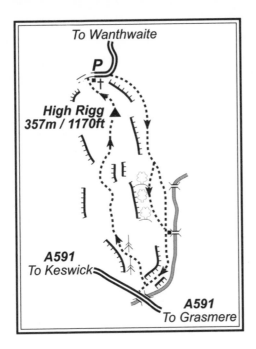

the church as well as limited parking on the verges beyond the Youth Centre. However, needless to say, the area will be busy during services.

The route begins by descending into the valley and then following that along High Rigg's eastern flank to reach the southern end of the ridge, from where the traverse may be made back to the church. To begin, a bridleway forks right through a gate just below the church and this then keeps just above the inbye wall as it makes a gradual descent into the valley. In due course, the grassy track passes through various gates where transverse walls are met that run up the hillside to the left. Throughout this stretch, the dominating Wanthwaite Crags on the far side of the valley make a very grand prospect, whilst the craggy bands on High Rigg's slopes are, in places, no less impressive.

After a while and with the descent to valley level complete, there is a fork. The main bridleway continues to a lower gate but our route takes the right branch, which climbs to reach a stile. The path still leads along above the inbye and so enters Sosgill Wood, where the path narrows as it makes a low traverse of the steep hillside. At the far end of the wood, a stile, next to a slate sign advertising 'Teas in ten minutes', leads out of the wood and it is then no great distance further along the hillside to reach Low Bridge End Farm.

The path stays above the buildings and garden on the open hillside, although a gate does give access to the garden and tearoom, which serves a selection of drinks as well as a range of snacks. Beyond the farm, the path enters a field and then descends to meet the track running along the bottom of the field from the farm itself. Once out of the far side of this field, the path resumes its route along the foot of the hillside on the open fell, although its course becomes increasingly close to that of the river. Throughout this stretch, the dominating turret of Castle Rock on the far side of the valley catches the eye and, when below the dark buttresses of Wren Crag on the right, the path emerges onto the riverbank in the narrowest part of the valley.

After negotiating a stretch of scree and tumbled boulders from the crag above, the path rises steeply from the river before running along a rock shelf high above the water below. Soon, though, the path curves away from the stream and through a wood to gain the southern end of the ridge just before the path descends to meet the Thirlmere to Keswick road by a bridge.

However, before beginning this descent, turn sharply back to the right and follow a small path, first through the wood and then through bracken, to emerge on the summit of Wren Crag before curving leftwards to a cluster of pine trees, from where there is a lovely view of Thirlmere. From here, the path continues over a more open stretch before descending slightly to a gap in a wall below a small crag.

Once through the wall, the path climbs through this crag and then continues clearly and without deviation along the ridge to reach a stile over a fence. After crossing that, follow the path ahead, which curves around the left-hand side of the ridge to avoid a false summit and, after a small descent and re-ascent, the path regains the ridge at a boggy hollow. From here, the grassy path continues northwards to a ladder stile in a further wall that crosses the ridge.

On the other side of the ladder stile, the path continues northwards, following a wall on the right, past the turret of Moss Crag on the left to reach a very wet and boggy hollow. This is best avoided by a detour to the left to regain the path and wall beyond, which continue over a low col, from where the summit comes into sight ahead. There is only a slight descent in between and the path leads across it and straight up through some small craggy bands direct to the summit cairn.

The view is very good, although not all that far reaching. The most spectacular views are of Wanthwaite Crags and of Blencathra's crags, ridges and ravines. However, there are also pleasant views of Skiddaw and Bassenthwaite Lake, as well as the more distant north-western fells. The descent back to the church is now a short and relatively easy affair once the craggy summit has been left behind.

Begin by walking a few yards to the east to reach a small col, from where a grassy path leads to the left steeply down the hillside to a wall just above the Youth Centre. A stile leads into the field behind the centre and a bridge into the building's first floor. However, by turning to the left, a small path leads around the left-hand edge of the building to the road.

Dent

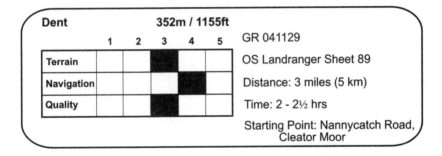

Dent						352m / 1155ft
	1	2	3	4	5	GR 041129
Terrain			■			OS Landranger Sheet 89
Navigation				■		Distance: 3 miles (5 km)
Quality			■			Time: 2 - 2½ hrs
						Starting Point: Nannycatch Road, Cleator Moor

Dent is the highest point of the undulating hill country to the west of the River Calder. Rising from the lowland coastal strip, these hills, scored by deep valleys, form a charming upland off the beaten track in a little visited corner of the Lake District. The partly forested hill of Dent is described perfectly by its alternative name – Long Barrow. Its sides are generally steep and its top is quite flat whilst it has a clear north-west–south-east running axis. Hidden amongst these hills and their intervening valleys are the green pastures of Nannycatch, forming a charming 'oasis' amongst the rough fells.

The ascent of Dent alone is almost too straightforward for an afternoon walk so it is far better to make a circuit by also taking in the summit of Flat Fell before starting the climb to Dent from Nannycatch Gate. Hence,

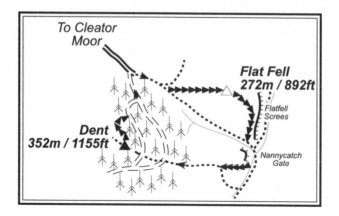

the best starting point is the head of Nannycatch Road. This can be reached by following the Ennerdale Bridge road from Cleator Moor and then taking the second turning on the right. There is room to park half a dozen cars at the head of the lane from where the walk begins.

A bridleway (not the track leading into the plantation) leads on from the head of the road and follows the line of a wall on the left. When this swings to the left, the gentle grassy slopes of Flat Fell start to rise up to the left. Whilst the main track goes straight ahead and a path continues to the left by the wall, follow a grassy break in the rushes half left and then continue this line up and across the slopes of Flat Fell to reach the ridge. It really is as simple as just keep aiming for the highest point and even in mist it is a relatively easy affair.

The summit is marked by a wooden stake and is a reasonably good viewpoint, although the best view by far is from the summit of Dent across the valley. The descent to Nannycatch Gate is as pathless as the ascent and only a little more complicated. Follow the ridge south-eastwards (120°) until the edge of the crags of Flatfell Screes is reached. Far below, the Nannycatch Beck tumbles down its narrow valley and the crags continue in both directions. However, continue along their edge to the right until they cease to be replaced by a steep escarpment. By this stage, the route has entered some reasonably low bracken through which a number of sheep tracks snake their way onwards.

To avoid the steep, rocky and gorse-clad hillside above Nannycatch Gate itself, it is best to escape to the left when the ground becomes a bit less steep. Here, a quite wide grass path slants down the slope slightly back to the left. However, once near the foot, escape to the right down a final steep grass bank to reach the path running up the gorge-like valley. To the right are the green pastures of Nannycatch Gate, with the gate referring to the gap in the hills rather than any ancient boundary. However, there is soon a gate and stile on the left and these should be crossed, and a footbridge beyond just by a confluence of two streams.

The stream now discharges down Uldale rather than towards Cleator Moor and up to the right lie the dark rocks of Raven Crag. Now underneath the first buttress, cross the stream and slant right up a small path that climbs the steep grassy slope in a small gully between this first buttress and a further, more broken one. Once above the crags, a grassy ridge leads on upwards, still quite steeply, until, in due course, a grass path curves across the ridge. This may now be followed to the right as it curves around a small bump on the ridge to gain the crest once again just before the forest fence. This path actually forms part of Wainwright's Coast to Coast Walk and this is followed to the summit, as intermittently signposted.

A short walk now leads on through the forest and some piled rocks aid the crossing of the fence. Just inside the trees, a forest road is reached and this may be followed to the left to reach a fork. Here, take the right-hand rising branch that ascends parallel with the main track to reach an oblique crossroads. At this point, the route goes straight across (not the leftmost track) and climbs through a dark pine tunnel and then up through further trees to reach a stile out onto the open fell. A short climb then remains to reach the summit.

Despite its relatively modest elevation, Dent excels as a viewpoint on a clear day. The entire coastal strip, with the Isle of Man beyond is visible, whilst Ennerdale Water is cradled by the mountains inland. Skiddaw and Grasmoor appear above Blake Fell, whilst the main peaks of western Lakeland are all visible – the three massifs of Pillar, High Stile and the Scafells. The descent back to the car through the forest is a fairly rapid affair and there are two ways of attempting this. By far the easier is to return to the main gravelled forest road and then turn left before following it straight ahead all the way back to the car.

The direct route is very rough and difficult, although for completeness it is described here. This begins by striking off on a bearing of 347° to reach a point where the fence has been distorted to allow pedestrians to slither through it and avoid the barbed wire on the top. Once through it, continue on the bearing above the wood across a small valley and then follow along the top of the wood on a steep bank. When the treeline swings up to the left, enter the forest ahead and follow a grassy watercourse and firebreak to the right. Avoid a rocky declivity covered by fallen trees on the right. All through the descent, be careful of the steep grass and moss slope, which is most insecure. When a felled area appears on the left below the steepest part cross to it and continue parallel with the stream. However, be careful of rotting logs that are hidden below grass and moss. At the foot of the felled area, an old grassed-over forest track is reached and if this is followed to the left and then downhill, the main forest road is reached; a left turn leads to the head of Nannycatch Lane.

Loughrigg Fell

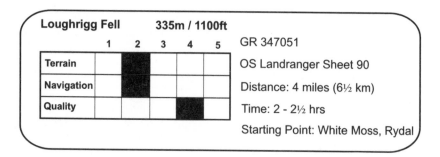

Loughrigg Fell	335m / 1100ft					
	1	2	3	4	5	GR 347051
Terrain		■				OS Landranger Sheet 90
Navigation		■				Distance: 4 miles (6½ km)
Quality				■		Time: 2 - 2½ hrs
						Starting Point: White Moss, Rydal

This small fell, separating the valleys of the Rothay and Brathay, commands a dominant position. It is in many ways a microcosm of the whole of the district as over its sprawling summit lie many rocky knolls, all looking more or less identical, separated by small, bracken-clad valleys, some containing hidden tarns. To make matters worse, sheep and intrigued or lost walkers have made a maze of tiny paths. All in all, it is little of a surprise that, although the fell is only of a modest altitude, there are several stories of pedestrians who have become lost after leaving the footpath and have literally spent the rest of the day trying to find a way off the fell. Readers of this book should, however, have no such problems but once off the route, amongst the maze of craggy outcrops, no map is of any

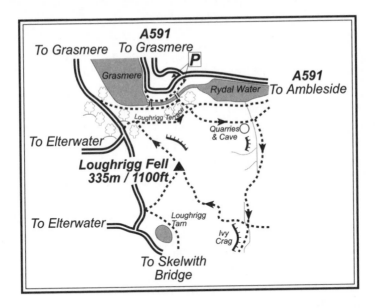

use at all. In mist, either keep off the fell altogether or take special care.

The slopes of the fell are always interesting due to the hidden glades which they support, but in autumn when the trees and bracken are turning colour, the fell is particularly beautiful. The best place to start is at White Moss, where there is a large car park on the southern side of the road between Rydal Water and Grasmere Lake. The car park is pay and display but free to National Trust members in possession of their cards. Leave the car park at the far end and walk straight across the meadows along the main track (the toilet block is up to the right by the road). After crossing a tributary stream, the track leads down to a footbridge over the wide stony bed of the Rothay. Cross it and keep straight on uphill through the trees on the other side to emerge onto the open fell.

Here again keep more or less straight on (probably more half left than perfectly straight on) on a smaller path which contours along the hillside, joining with others from the right, and forming a fine promenade above Rydal Water. After passing above a wood and reaching some larch trees, the path reaches the famous Big Cave. Despite recent rockfalls, it is currently possible to enter the large entrance of the cave and penetrate inside, although one side of it is flooded. After exploring, ignore all paths leading away uphill here as they lead into tricky terrain but instead follow the wide descending track, running downhill right from the cave's mouth.

After passing some more caves on the right, all part of the old Loughrigg Quarry, the track crosses a small stream. Once over the bridge, immediately turn right along a path which is indistinct at first but soon becomes pronounced as it climbs into the upper valley through the bracken. It skirts a knoll covered with a juniper thicket before climbing through more of the complex terrain. After crossing a low col, the path descends slightly into a wet amphitheatre but remains on its eastern slopes. At a prominent fork, aim half right and follow this path along until it comes to meet the unmissable track rising from Ambleside.

Here, turn right and cross the small stream before climbing steeply uphill to gain a higher ridge with its own succession of rocky knolls. The path swings around to the right but the first thing to look out for is a reedy tarn on a shelf down on the right. When above it, turn left on a grassy path (the one ahead does reach the same point but takes an annoyingly circuitous route). Apart from the stiff climb which still remains, there are no route-finding problems providing the track is kept underfoot before reaching the summit and triangulation point.

To start the descent, keep straight on over the summit and descend what is probably the best-defined path on the whole fell. It is steep and care is required because parts of this 'restored' path are a perfect example of how not to lay a footpath! Nevertheless, it reaches the Red Bank end of Loughrigg Terrace, at which point a sharp right turn is required to set the correct route back to White Moss. The view from here may be familiar from postcard and calendar views, and there are a wide selection of benches from which it can be enjoyed. At the far end, when the main track starts to descend, ignore contouring paths on the right which lead along to the Big Cave but follow the main track back to the top of the wood. After a steep descent above the fell wall, the gate is found through which access to the fell was first gained. The route of ascent may now be reversed back to the car park.

Watch Hill

Watch Hill						254m / 833ft
	1	2	3	4	5	
Terrain	■					
Navigation		■				
Quality		■				

GR 158318

OS Landranger Sheet 89

Distance: 4 miles (6 km)

Time: 2 - 2½ hrs

Starting Point: Cockermouth

Between Bassenthwaite Lake and Cockermouth, there rises a tract of low hills bounded by the dry valley in which Embleton lies and the River Derwent to the north. The highest point of this area of ground is the summit of Watch Hill, which is rarely climbed other than by the residents of the town of Cockermouth to its east. In many ways, the hill is unnoteworthy and, indeed, were it not for the attractive views over a relatively unexplored part of Cumbria as well as the more famous mountains to the south, the ascent could be described as little more than a tough slog. However, as a one-off climb away from the normal tourist hordes, it is well worth a visit on a clear and warm day.

It is possible to ascend to the summit by a number of routes, although the best, which stays out of the forest that coats the northern and part of the southern slopes, is up the west ridge, giving attractive views all the way. Sadly, however, this means that a circular route is not possible. The starting point is just to the east of Cockermouth on the old A66, i.e. the direct Cockermouth to Embleton road. Just outside of the town, a road branches off to the left (when travelling from Cockermouth) and there is a lay-by a few yards up this road on the right, in which parking is permitted for up to two hours, which should be sufficient to make the ascent and return.

Begin by joining the main road and walking towards Cockermouth for about a hundred yards. A bridleway, signposted to Isel, begins to the right by passing over a stile next to a gate. This bridleway follows a broad and sometimes greasy track that slants half right across the first field and then follows roughly parallel to the left-hand edges of the next three fields as it makes a generally well-graded ascent of the ridge. When it emerges onto

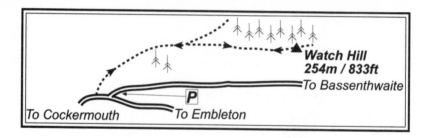

the open hilltop, the bridleway follows the wall, which curves to the left and begins a descent into the forest towards Isel in the Derwent Valley.

Our route, however, continues straight ahead, following a path in the grass onwards along the ridge. From here to the summit, which is still quite distant, the ridge consists of a series of rocky knolls, which bear the scars of minor quarrying activity in the form of a number of circular pits around the small path. After passing over the first knoll, the path crosses a more level area, and proceeds in this way for a while, making minor ascents and descents, to a fork. Here, fork right on the main path and follow it around the right-hand side of a particularly large knoll to the depression on the far side. From here, the path climbs up towards the summit, following along the top of a steep grass bank on the left. The summit itself is marked by little more than a few stones in the grass in the far corner of the summit-field, just to the right of a stile into the wood, which completely covers the ridge ahead on both sides.

As already mentioned, the views are quite good, although the wood does rather restrict the summit view itself. Indeed, several of the other knolls crossed during the ascent have more panoramic views. However, the view of the northern and western Lakeland fells is quite charming and makes the ascent worthwhile. The descent should now be made by the same route without variation.

Swinside

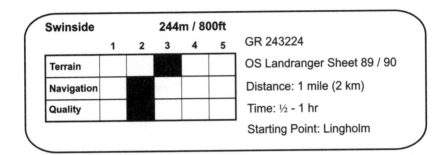

Swinside	244m / 800ft				
	1	2	3	4	5
Terrain			■		
Navigation		■			
Quality		■			

GR 243224

OS Landranger Sheet 89 / 90

Distance: 1 mile (2 km)

Time: ½ - 1 hr

Starting Point: Lingholm

There are few hills more distinctive than Swinside. Standing between the Newlands valley and Derwentwater but detached from the Cat Bells ridge, this conical hill rises to a sharp if low summit that is an excellent viewpoint. However, its summit is gained only by arduous walking through private forestry. With so many other fells to climb in the Lake District, this is one best left to those who wish to climb them all. The views are almost as good from the higher and more easily accessible summit of Cat Bells, which is normally ascended from the car park at Hawes End.

The hill is encircled by roads connecting the hamlets of Ullock and Swinside and all gates leading off this road into the circle are clearly marked 'private' and most, for added clarity, also state 'no public right of way'. This is because the fell is part of Lord Rochdale's Lingholm estate and the hill has been given over to forestry. The best policy seems to be to seek permission from the estate office, most easily by telephone (see **Useful Telephone Numbers**).

The entrance to Lingholm lies on the road that runs along the eastern slopes of the hill between Portinscale and Swinside. This entrance lies on the eastern side of the road and, when approaching from Portinscale, the road enters a dip just after the entrance. Here, on the right, there is a gate and a small lay-by on a bend and this marks the starting point. A grassy track leads up the hill from inside the gate and it climbs before another grassy track goes off to the right. Here, aim straight ahead, taking care to avoid the hidden wet ruts that lie beneath the long grass and rushes.

After a particularly wet section, the track swings sharply back to the left and follows the edge of a felled section of the wood that is currently

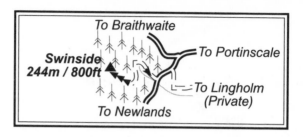

regenerating. The track continues its ascent to a deer observation tower on the left. Beyond this, the track becomes more vegetated but it should be followed for a further few yards until a widening is found on the right before the far end of the open area.

Now the real work starts. The climb on the right, following the far edge of the open area, is tough as the grass is long and it hides a surface littered with rotting logs and other debris below. At the top edge, a line of pine trees stands before the bracken-clad hilltop is reached. In winter, the next section will be no problem but in summer it is very difficult. A few hundred yards of thick bracken lie ahead to the summit and it is well worth beating out a good track for use on the return journey.

The summit area is graced by three trees and the middle one is roughly the target. When in its vicinity, the true summit will be seen slightly right in an open area covered by cropped grass, heather and bilberries. The view can now be appreciated. Derwentwater and Bassenthwaite Lake can be seen in their entirety as can the walls of Shepherd's Crag at Lodore at the head of Derwentwater where the Watendlath Beck cascades over the lip of its hanging valley. Walla Crag is also visible on the far side of the valley as is the massive bulk of Skiddaw above Keswick. On the left of Bassenthwaite Lake, the sharp and steep slopes of Barf are prominent, although the highest summit of the Whinlatter Fells – Lord's Seat – is visible beyond.

The Newlands valley, guarded by Barrow (opposite) and Cat Bells on this side, is also quite spectacular with Causey Pike, Ard Crags and Robinson all being visible. The less pleasing prospect of the tough descent must also be contemplated and much care should be taken to prevent an awkward fall.

Section 7 – The Isle of Man

That island situated in the Irish Sea almost equidistant from Northern Ireland and England.

NAME	HEIGHT	IN SECTION	IN ENGLAND	IN BRITAIN
Slieau Freoaghane	488m/1601ft	02 of 05	84J of 184	1010J of 1552
South Barrule	483m/1586ft	03 of 05	86 of 184	1024 of 1552
Bradda Hill	230m/ 756ft	04 of 05	170 of 184	1484J of 1552
Mull Hill	169m/ 554ft	05 of 05	182 of 184	1544 of 1552

There is one summit above 2,000ft that is described in *England's Highest Peaks*.

The Isle of Man is neither a part of the UK, nor a member of the EU but is in fact a Crown Dependency with its own parliament (Tynwald) and its own high court and legal and financial systems. It remains a popular tourist destination because it is an island of contrasts. In the north, there is flat land but the central part of the island consists of a large upland massif rising straight up in some places from the sea. The coastline itself is incised with inlets and beautiful glens on the east and west coasts. To the south-west of the island and at Maughold to the south of Ramsey, stupendous sea cliffs and grass slopes drop steeply to the crashing waves far below. In amongst the south-western cliffs are beautiful coves and bays, such as Fleshwick Bay to the north of Port Erin. Not surprisingly, one of the finest walks on the island is the coastal path or the Raad ny Foillan, as it is known.

The rocks of the Isle of Man were mainly deposited during the Ordovician period as part of a huge mountain chain that stretched from here through the Lake District and Yorkshire Dales into north-eastern England. As such, the sediments are similar to those which make up parts of the non-volcanic Lake District (see Section 4), the Howgill Fells and the basement rocks of the Pennines, exposed at Ingleton (see Section 2).

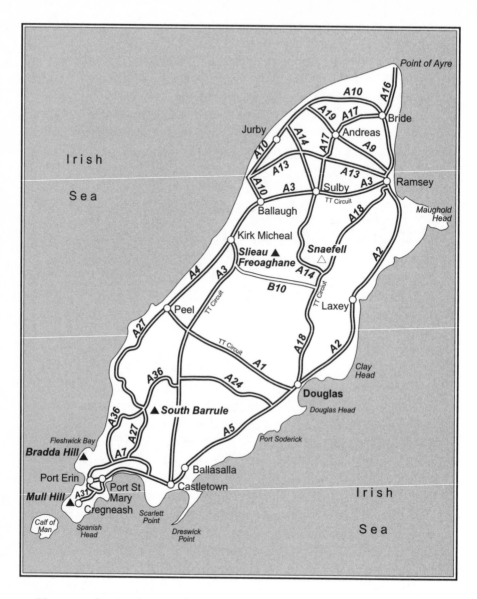

However, despite their similar geological origins, the Isle of Man is much more reminiscent of parts of the Pennines than the Lake District, due to Lakeland's subsequent volcanic activity.

These old rocks are mainly flaggy greywackes – a rock consisting of fine to coarse sandy particles, cemented together by clay. They were laid down in beds, along which they now break, leading to them being known as flaggy. The other type of rock that was deposited was the Manx slates. These form a bed around 2,000ft (610m) in thickness and consist of three layers, the Barrule Slates, quartz-veined Agneash Grits and the Lonan-Niarbyl Flags. The highest peaks are made of Barrule Slates, which are well seen in and around the summit shelter on the small hill of South Barrule, whilst underneath them, the Agneash Grits can be seen in the south of the island as well as on the eastern slopes of the central massif. Lowest of all, the Lonan-Niarbyl Flags exist as a coastal strip between Santon Head, south of Douglas, and Maughold Head, south of Ramsey, straying inland in the Douglas area.

These rocks were then affected by the Caledonian earth-movements, folding and crushing them, leading to highly inclined strata in places, whereas, at Spanish Head, near-horizontal beds still exist. However, lateral pressure has also been exerted and the effect can be seen at The Chasms near Cregneash, which are seen on the Mull Hill route. Here, rock masses are in the process of detaching themselves from the hill, producing vertical clefts between the blocks up to 80ft (25m) in depth.

Later, as in many parts of the English Pennines, a granite intrusion occurred, which led to metamorphism of the surrounding clayey greywackes into schists. These are hard gritty rocks, again bedded, differing in colour from blue to red and grey, depending on the chemical composition of the original clays and therefore tending to have a striped appearance. The general uplift and doming resulting from the granitic intrusion led to the formation of tension faults in the existing Ordovician sediments into which mineralising solutions, under intense pressure, could penetrate. As the pressure reduced, the solutions cooled and so minerals were deposited in the cracks, which then became veins. Where this occurred in the Pennines, lead and other useful minerals were deposited but here the veins consist mainly of quartz (silicon dioxide – SiO_2). This is seen in many rocks but is well viewed in those forming the summit cairn of Slieau Freoaghane.

The mountains had then been formed but other rocks, mainly sandstones on the western coast around Peel and under the northern plain, and limestone on the eastern coast between Port St Mary and Santon Burn, were formed in the Lower Carboniferous period. The only other Carboniferous activity was a small coastal volcanic intrusion near Castletown between Poyllvaish and Scarlett Point.

In Permian times, sandstones were deposited in the north and then a thin layer of clay and lime (marl). Above that, St Bees Sandstone, seen on the western coast of the Lake District, was deposited in Triassic times as well as extensive salt deposits, again on the northern plains. These salt deposits have since been open-mined around the Point of Ayre but, today, many of the mining remains serve as landfill sites for the island's rubbish.

The Ice Age has carved out the few U-shaped valleys that exist in the central massif but its lasting impression has been the deposition of large amounts of glacial drift or boulder clay, the northern plain being covered by about 150ft (45m) of it. However, at this time the island was still connected to the British mainland and it was not until a small amount of subsidence in the Pleistocene period, between about 5000 and 10,000 BC, that the land-bridge was cut off. In fact, the deepest parts of the Irish Sea between the island and the British mainland are only covered by about 140ft (43m) of water.

Access

National Express runs coach services to the island from departure points throughout the British mainland. Ferry services, run by the Isle of Man Steam Packet Company, depart Heysham, Liverpool (only Friday, Saturday and Sunday in winter), Belfast (not in winter) and Dublin (not in winter). The island's airport at Ronaldsway, near Ballasalla, is also well served. Emerald Airways run flights to the island from Liverpool, whilst Manx Airlines' flights depart Southampton, Newcastle, Manchester, London Luton, London Heathrow, Liverpool, Leeds/Bradford, Jersey (via Dublin), Glasgow, Dublin, Cardiff and Birmingham. However, it should be noted that the airport is at sea level, the runway ending only yards from the shore and, in the absence of high-tech equipment, delays due to sea fog can be a problem. Despite the fact that the island is not a part of the UK, it is not necessary to have a passport to enter. United Kingdom currency is accepted although the island does have its own style of notes and coins.

On the island, there is an excellent public transport system. All the major towns, Ramsey, Douglas, Peel, Castletown and Port Erin, as well as other more rural areas, are linked by bus services. Regular services on the Isle of Man Steam Railway link Douglas, Ronaldsway Airport,

Castletown, Port St Mary and Port Erin, whilst trams on the Manx Electric Railway connect Douglas, Laxey, Ramsey and stop at other local stations, such as Dhoon and Maughold en route. Of course, electric trams on the Snaefell Mountain Railway link the Manx Electric Railway station at Laxey with Snaefell Summit.

The Manx road network, which has its own numbering system, is good, despite the fact that there is virtually no dual carriageway on the island, bar one short stretch near the airport. Many of the roads are much narrower than roads of the same class on the British mainland and, although signposting is generally good, it cannot be relied upon as road numbers are frequently omitted and sometimes disagree with those shown on the OS Landranger Sheet. Please note that the island has its own laws and whilst those applying to motoring are the same or similar to those in the UK, it should be noted that trailer caravans are prohibited although motor caravans are permitted. Disc parking operates in many of the larger towns and some villages; discs are obtainable from car hire companies, local Commissioner's Offices, the sea terminal, airport and Isle of Man Steam Packet Company vessels. A list of telephone numbers for car hire companies is given in the Useful Telephone Numbers section towards the back of the book.

Please also note that on the fortnight beginning around the end of May, the TT (Tourist Trophy) races take place. During the race times, the course is closed to traffic, which can mean lengthy diversions, and also heavy fines are payable by anybody who infringes upon the course. Many competing motorcyclists arrive prior to the event and practise by driving around the course at unnerving speeds with ordinary traffic. On Mad Sunday, which is the middle Sunday of the race period, there are no races but the competitors, with nothing else to do, joined by local enthusiasts, go 'mad', all driving around the course as if it were a normal race. On this date, the remainder of the local population keep well off the course and visitors are advised to do likewise.

Accommodation

All the main towns, Port Erin, Castletown, Peel, Douglas and Ramsey, support a wide variety of accommodation in plenty. However, there is much in the island's villages. However, it would be wise to find somewhere in advance if you wish to stay outside the main towns. The best base for the whole island would probably be either Douglas or Peel due to their central position but in reality it is quite quick to reach anywhere by car on the island due to the good and quite quiet road network. Note, however, that during the TT races (see above), many hotels and guesthouses apply a surcharge to all bookings for that period.

Slieau Freoaghane

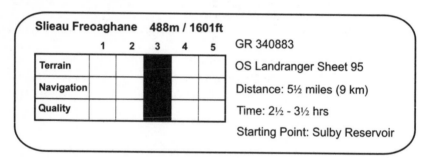

Slieau Freoaghane	488m / 1601ft					
	1	2	3	4	5	GR 340883
Terrain			■			OS Landranger Sheet 95
Navigation			■			Distance: 5½ miles (9 km)
Quality			■			Time: 2½ - 3½ hrs
						Starting Point: Sulby Reservoir

Snaefell may be the highest and most visited point of the central uplands of the islands but it is by no means the only separate summit in the main massif. Slieau Freoaghane is the island's second highest summit and lies on the other side of Sulby Glen from Snaefell, although the two are connected by a high ridge. The best starting point is at Tholt-e-Will Glen at the dam of Sulby Reservoir on the A14.

Start off by crossing the dam and then following the track around to the left. However, leave it almost immediately for a tiny path climbing the right-hand bank to a gate and signpost. The path (now more distinct) runs along, through gorse bushes and below some conifers, to cross the stream entering one of the reservoir's small arms. Beyond, it rises up a slightly eroded gully to pass through a kissing gate and up a small enclosed green lane to join the farm access road just above the farmyard. Turn right and follow the drive up to the public lane, a left turn on which leads over two cattle grids enclosing a large field. After dropping steeply downhill and passing a ruined farmstead on the right, it reaches a stream crossing and some mature woodland also on the right.

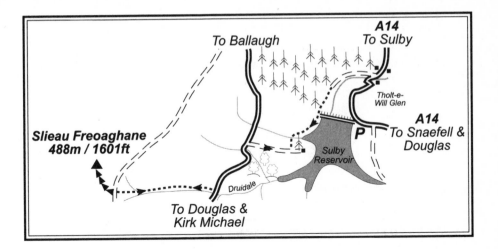

Here, follow a path to the right, into the wood (next to the no camping sign), which soon becomes indistinct but leaves the wood almost equidistant from the top of the wood and the stream. After crossing a wet depression, the waymarked 'path' (if it can be so called) moves close to the stream before following the line of an old, broken-down wall, to emerge on the old road through a kissing gate and over a stile. Cross the road and make a direct ascent of the heather slopes opposite to reach the cairn, trig point and beacon with magnificent views all around.

There are various options for descent; it is possible to follow the old road north, soon forking right to reach the tarmacked road further to the north. From this point, a track opposite enters the conifer plantation and a descent can be made back to Tholt-e-Will (add ½ mile (1km), 15 mins). It is also possible to reverse the route of ascent as far as the tarmacked road and then cross straight over it and following a 'path' over some very rough ground around the head of the reservoir (add 1 mile (1½km), 30–40 mins). However, neither of these are really very attractive so, in the author's opinion, a return by the route of ascent is not to be ruled out and it is this that is timed above.

However, if transport can be arranged, a small path, running south-south-east, leads down to the old road, a right turn on which leads to the B10, Kirk Michael to Snaefell road, just to the west of the small road that runs down northwards to Ballaugh.

South Barrule

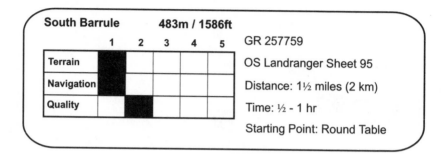

	1	2	3	4	5
Terrain	■				
Navigation	■				
Quality		■			

South Barrule   **483m / 1586ft**

GR 257759

OS Landranger Sheet 95

Distance: 1½ miles (2 km)

Time: ½ - 1 hr

Starting Point: Round Table

South Barrule is a good example of a hill upon which a circular route is not really practical. Hemmed in on two sides by forestry plantations and a road on the third and fourth, it is not surprising that its visitors almost invariably ascend to its summit by only one route on the pronounced west ridge. However, a short straight up-and-back climb it may be but dull it is not.

Park at the entrance to a small lane, just south of the A36 and A27 crossroads, known as the Round Table. Pass through a kissing gate and the path lies ahead, all the way to the top; little description is necessary. The summit possesses a large hollow cairn, inside which is a trig point. Although marked specially on the OS map, there is little to see of the iron-age hillfort. According to the metal information plaque, there are hut circles to be found on the hill but they are not easily visible to the untrained eye. However, the panorama is absolutely superb and the return should be made by the route of ascent so as to have the charming view of the west coast ahead.

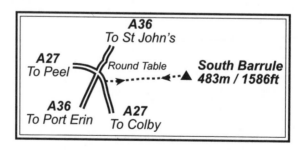

Bradda Hill

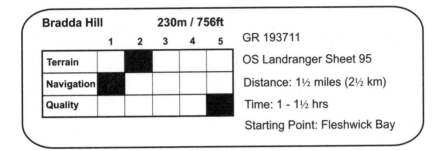

Bradda Hill	1	2	3	4	5
Terrain		■			
Navigation	■				
Quality					■

Bradda Hill   230m / 756ft

GR 193711

OS Landranger Sheet 95

Distance: 1½ miles (2½ km)

Time: 1 - 1½ hrs

Starting Point: Fleshwick Bay

There are few more beautiful summits than that of Bradda Hill. Clifftop walks are always spectacular and interesting but there are few coastlines as enchanting as the western coast of the Isle of Man. Bradda Hill, perched almost on the edge of the cliff, lies on the headland to the north of Port Erin. This walk, although short, is quite excellent and should be given plenty of time.

Fleshwick Bay is a lovely place to linger on a warm summer's day. This small, sheltered, west-facing cove, bounded by steep cliff walls and supporting a small stony beach, is a picture-postcard scene. A small dead-end road leads to the cove from the A32 at Ballafesson. The route begins by heading back up the small steep hill on the road before turning right along a signposted path opposite a building. This path, initially running along the edge of a field, soon starts to climb very steeply up the hillside, by a forestry plantation, before working back to the right. When at last the steep climb comes to an end, the path passes through a wall and bears left making a rising traverse across the breast of the hill, high above the waves crashing on the seashore below. When the path regains the ridge, it rises up through heather to the graceful summit cairn.

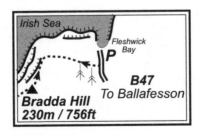

Although an onward journey can be made along the coastal path to Port Erin, in many ways the best return is by the route of ascent, indeed a circuit is not really practical.

Mull Hill

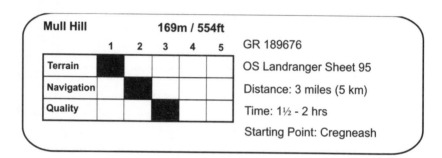

Mull Hill						169m / 554ft
	1	2	3	4	5	GR 189676
Terrain	■					OS Landranger Sheet 95
Navigation		■				Distance: 3 miles (5 km)
Quality				■		Time: 1½ - 2 hrs
						Starting Point: Cregneash

Mull Hill is the island's lowest separate hill but it is none the worse for that. It lies only a few miles to the north of the island's southern tip, where the Calf Sound separates the main island from the small island of the Calf of Man. This is a walk packed with interest and good views that is best attempted from Cregneash on the hilltop.

It is possible to park in Cregneash in the 'Story of Mann' car park, at the northern end of the village. Begin by walking a short distance down the main road to the right (south-west), before taking a path on the left, signposted to 'Cregneash Village'. This shortly leads to a tarmac lane, a left turn on which leads across the valley and over the hill to the road's end. Cross the stile ahead and aim for the building marked 'Chasms' at the far side of the field. Behind the building, a small gate gives access to the chasms themselves. Although some are only quite shallow, some are well over 80ft (25m) deep. The deepest are on the left, although there is a very deep, narrow fissure on the cliff edge to the right. From the edge of the cliff, there is a good view to the strata on the cliff to the left.

However, return to the building and turn right, following a path through a gate and over a stile before it drops down eventually to the right. A tarmac road is then reached, a left turn on which leads along to the village of Fistard, where a left fork should be taken, to reach the main road

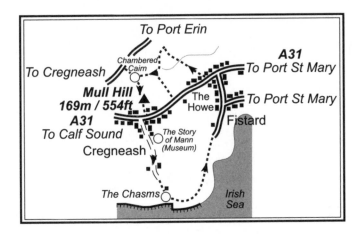

at a hamlet called The Howe. Turn left and after the Methodist Chapel, take a track running back to the right. This leads to a blocked stile and a gate.

After circumnavigating these difficulties, cross the field, above the ruined farm buildings, to reach a stile (signposted) in the opposite wall. Cross this field and a small footbridge on the far side to reach a larger field, at the other side of which is a ladder stile. Cross the stile and keep up the left-hand side of the field ahead, through gorse bushes and to the left of a disused barn, to reach a kissing gate. Turn right up a path through heather, turning right shortly at a T-junction.

Soon a path is found running sharply back left which leads past the chambered cairn and up onto the summit. The summit of most hills is normally the best part of the walk; however, Mull Hill is the exception. The summit is graced with a redundant Second World War pill-box and other wartime remains. Indeed, the best views are to be found on either side of the summit, on the descent to Cregneash and from the chambered cairn.

To begin the descent, follow a large track south, aiming half right at the fork, to reach the small Port Erin to Cregneash lane. A left turn, followed by another, leads back through the village to the 'Story of Mann' car park.

Epilogue

Standing on the summit of Binsey in the late February snows, the tide of time barely seemed to have ebbed since I started this project three and a half years ago atop Scafell Pike. Yet that was the moment when I became just the twelfth (known) person to climb all of England's separate hills. It reminded me of what Wainwright wrote in conclusion to his now famous series of pictorial guides to the Lakeland fells – 'the fleeting hour of life of those who love the hills is quickly spent, but the hills are eternal'. But I still have much more of my fleeting hour to spend among the hills, in the company of the rushing becks, the trill of the skylarks and the great fans of broken rock descending from the heights. And that is, perhaps, something for which I should be grateful.

But it does fill me with a certain sadness to be writing these final lines, bringing to an end another chapter in my life and closing the pages on so many happy days that perhaps in my heart I sometimes wished would last forever. Maybe there is truth in the old proverb after all. Perhaps it is 'better to travel in hope than to arrive'. I don't know, but my memories will last as long as I do and I can still return to refresh my thoughts.

When I cast my mind's eye back to the hills of the north, there are certainly countless scenes that I will never forget. How could I forget toiling up the shifting screes and broken crags on the front face of Barf? How about a gorgeous summer's afternoon on the 'fortified' summit of Mellbreak, far above the shimmering turquoise-blue sheet of Crummock Water far below the dark bands of rough rock at my feet? And then there is the roughest and most remote summit in England – Sighty Crag. To be miles and miles away from anything and anyone and on top of the world is not an experience confined to the Scottish Highlands, however the hardbitten Scot may regard it.

Then there was the search for the summit of Hutton Roof Crags among the crags and limestone pavements, thorn bushes and rough upland meadows and a maze of seemingly identical hollows. And then of course I had to find a 'desirable' way to the summit, meaning that I finally returned to Hutton Roof on the edge of dark from the walk on which I confidently left my lunch in the car. But there again perhaps I should have known better. Never let anybody say that the lower hills are tame and easy.

My fondest memory, however, lies across the rough waters of the Irish Sea on the Isle of Man on the rarely visited summit of Bradda Hill above the hidden oasis of Fleshwick Cove. Never have I had such a beautiful clifftop walk and I don't think I would be exaggerating to say that I might never better it. But that leads me inexorably to the dreaded list – my top 20 hills and mountains. I would not expect that everybody will agree with my choice but here it is anyway:

SUMMIT	AREA	(BOOK, SECTION)
1. Scafell Pike	Western Lakeland	(EHP, 6)
2. Pillar	Western Lakeland	(EHP, 6)
3. Blencathra	Northern Lakeland	(EHP, 7)
4. Mellbreak	Western Lakeland	(Vol 3, 6)
5. Helvellyn	Eastern Lakeland	(EHP, 5)
6. Bradda Hill	Isle of Man	(Vol 3, 7)
7. High Stile	Western Lakeland	(EHP, 6)
8. Holm Fell	South-western Lakeland	(Vol 3, 5)
9. Stiperstones	The Shropshire Hills	(Vol 2, 2)
10. The Wrekin	The Shropshire Hills	(Vol 2, 2)
11. Hutton Roof Crags	Kendal	(Vol 3, 4)
12. Dunkery Beacon	Exmoor	(Vol 1, 2)
13. Skiddaw	Northern Lakeland	(EHP, 7)
14. Long Crag	Simonside Hills	(Vol 3, 3)
15. Brighstone Down	Isle of Wight	(Vol 1, 3)
16. Worcestershire Beacon	Malvern Hills	(Vol 2, 1)
17. High Street	Eastern Lakeland	(EHP, 5)
18. Beacon Batch	Mendips	(Vol 1, 2)
19. Swyre Head	Purbeck Hills	(Vol 1, 3)
20. Pen-y-ghent	Yorkshire Dales	(EHP, 4)

Picking those 20 peaks was not an easy choice either, and it is perhaps one that I am still not even sure about now as I write this. And does it mean anything? Well, probably not, but I could not end without listing what I consider to be my favourites – those hills that, for different reasons, stand out most in my memory – the grand, the beautiful and the unspoilt.

Before I end I should perhaps also try to draw some comparisons between volumes and I have done this by applying my statistician's calculator to the gradings that I had given the routes in the three volumes of *The Hills of England* series. The results for terrain and navigation are certainly not going to surprise anyone. The hills in southern England appear to have, in general, the easiest terrain and the best footpaths, whilst northern England has the most hills with tough terrain and navigation. The hills of the Midlands and South Pennines seem to sit roughly in the middle, although the statistics show them slightly more akin to the hills of southern England.

The quality gradings did surprise me. It would appear that Book 2 (*The Midlands and South Pennines*) has the largest percentage of 'dull' hills (with Grades 1 and 2), while this book has the highest percentage of excellent hills (with Grades 4 and 5). This time it is Book 1 (southern England) that sits in the middle, although it does have the interesting honour of having the lowest percentage of 'dull' routes. Does this mean anything either? Absolutely not, it's all another lot of 'lies, damned lies and statistics'. My memory certainly does not lead me to think the Midlands and South Pennines were particularly dull and I think the three volumes should be able to stand side by side as equals in terms of quality.

But I will draw the series to a final close with some verses of Wordsworth's, written in early spring, with which all those who love the outdoors can associate.

> Through primrose tufts, in that green bower,
> The periwinkle trailed its wreaths;
> And 'tis my faith that every flower
> Enjoys the air it breathes.
>
> The birds around me hopped and played,
> Their thoughts I cannot measure:-
> But least the motion which they made,
> It seemed a thrill of pleasure.
>
> The budding twigs spread out their fan,
> To catch the breezy air;
> And I must think, do all I can,
> That there was pleasure there.

The Hill Names and their Meanings

The knowledge of the meaning of a hill name gives a fascinating insight into not only the topography of the hill but also to how our ancestors saw it and used it. The look-out stone on Tosson Hill may have been lost to history and pigs no longer roam on Swinside in summer. Nevertheless, Loughrigg Fell could not be described better than simply 'the hill of the ridge above the lake' and, for many people, there is a curiosity into why Mellbreak is so called and what caused the Norse settlers to give Gummer's How its name. This section is intended to answer those questions and has been simplified greatly to give the information in a concise and clear way without giving all the evidence that the experts have used to come to their decisions.

Each hill name is given a translation and the words and languages from which its name originates. These place-name elements are given in the order of the original name. The following abbreviations have been used to show the languages from which the elements originate:

OE	Old English (c.450–c.1100)
ME	Middle English (c.1100–c.1500)
Eng.	Modern English (c.1500–present)
Gael.	Gaelic
Manx	Manx
Wel.	Welsh
Cel.	Celtic
OIr	Old Irish
OScand.	Old Scandinavian
ON	Old Norse

Again, the Ordnance Survey names have been used as the standard modern form of the name, which is not necessarily that used locally.

Where appropriate, an older name has also been given where the modern name has changed beyond recognition from the original.

The Names and their Meanings

The number in brackets after the name is the section in which that hill lies.

Aye Gill Pike (2) – peak of the oak ravine, ON *eik* + ON *gil* + ON *pik*.

Binsey (6) – hill of the neck or col, ON *hals*.

Bishop Wilton Wold (1) – the high, deforested land belonging to the village or farmstead where willow trees grow. The 'Bishop' affix derives from original possession by the Archbishops of York, OE *wilig* + OE *tun* + OE *wald*.

Black Combe (5) – the dark-crested mountain, OE *blaec* + OE *camb*.

Blake Fell (6) – dark hill, OE *blaec* + ON *fjall*.

Bradda Hill (7) – the steep headland, ON *hofuth*.

Calf Top (2) – derived from calf but in some transferred sense. It could be a reference perhaps to two rocks or hills, a large one and a small one (the cow and calf), OE *calf*.

Claife Heights (4) – the steep hill, ON *kleif*.

Cringle Moor (1) – moor of the rounded hill, ON *kringla*.

Dent (6) – hill, OIr *dind*.

Dufton Pike (2) – the peak of the farmstead where doves are kept, OE *dufe* + OE *tun* + ON *pik*.

Gisborough Moor (1) – moor of the stronghold of a man called Gígr, OScand. personal name *Gígr* + OE *burh*.

Grayrigg Forest (4) – open land of the grey ridge, OScand. *grár* + OScand. *hryggr*.

Great Mell Fell (4) – the large, bare hill, Wel. *moel* + ON *fjall*.

Gummer's How (4) – Gunnar's hill, ON personal name *Gunnar* + ON *haugr*.

Hallin Fell (4) – possibly the hillslope, ON *hallr* + ON *inn* + ON *fjall*.

Hard Knott (5) – the rough, craggy fell, ON *harthr* + ON *knútr*.

High Rigg (6) – the high, steep-sided ridge, ON *hryggr*.

Holm Fell (5) – isolated, 'island-like' hill, ON *holmr* + ON *fjall*.

Hoove (2) – possibly a nickname meaning bump, OE *hofer*, derived from OE *hoferede*, meaning hunchback.

Housedon Hill (3) – possibly hill of the spur, OE *hohas* + OE *dun*.

Hutton Roof Crags (4) – the crags of the farmstead on a ridge belonging to Hrólfr, OE *hoh* + OE *tun* + OScand. personal name *Hrólfr*.

Ilkley Moor (2) – the moor above the woodland clearing of a man called Illica, OE personal name *Illica* + OE *leah*.

Illgill Head (5) – the headland of the precipitous narrow ravine, ON *illr* + ON *gil* + OE *heafod*.

Kirkby Moor (5) – moor of the village with the church, OScand. *kirkju*.

Kisdon (2) – possibly gravelly hill, OE *cis* + OE *dun*.

Lambrigg Fell (4) – hill of the ridge of the lambs, OE *lamb* + ON *hryggr* + ON *fjall*.

Lingmoor Fell (5) – the heather-clad hill, ON *lyng* + Wel. *moel* + ON *fjall*.

Little Mell Fell (4) – the small bare hill, Wel. *moel* + ON *fjall*.

Long Crag (3) – the long cliff, ME *cragge*.

Lord's Seat (6) – the Lord's pasturage, OE *hlaford* + ON *saetr*.

Loughrigg Fell (6) – hill of the ridge above the lake, Gael. *loch* + ON *hryggr* + ON *fjall*.

Low Fell (6) – the low hill, ON *fjall*.

Mellbreak (6) – possibly the bare hill of the slope falling to the water's edge, Wel. *moel* + ON *brekka*.

Mull Hill (7) – hill of the headland or crag, ON *múli*.

Muncaster Fell (5) – the hill of Mula's fort, ON personal name *Mula* + OE *caester* + ON *fjall*.

Peel Fell (3) – possibly the hill of the enclosure, ME *pel* + ON *fjall*.

Potts Moor (2) – moor of the pothole, OE *pott*.

Ros Hill (3) – moorland hill, Cel. *ros* + OE *hyll*.

Sharp Haw (2) – the sharp ridge, ON *hryggr*.

Shillhope Law (3) – peak of the dry ground (between wet valleys), OE *scylfe* + OE *hop* + ON *haugr*.

Sighty Crag (3) – possibly the cragged slope, OE *side*.

Slieau Freoaghane (7) – correctly 'Slieau-Ny-Farrane', meaning hill of the spring, Manx *Slieau* + Manx *Farrane*.

South Barrule (7) – southern hill, Cel. *barro*.

Swinside (6) – the summer pasture where pigs are kept, ON *svin* + ON *saetr*.

Thorpe Fell Top (2) – the hill of the outlying farmstead, ON *thorp* + ON *fjall*.

Top o'Selside (4) – the highest point of Selside – the estate with a house on it, ON *sel* + ON *setr*.

Tosson Hill (3) – hill of the look-out stone, OE *tot* + OE *stan*.

Urra Moor (1) – moor of the filthy peak, OE *horh* + ON *haugr*.

Wansfell (4) – possibly Woden's hill, Norse god *Woden* + ON *fjall*.

Watch Hill (6) – look-out hill.

Whitbarrow (4) – the white hill, OE *hwit* + OE *beorg*.

Whitfell (5) – the white hill, OE *hwit* + ON *fjall*.

Personal Log

Section 1 – The Yorkshire Wolds and North York Moors

NAME	HEIGHT	GRID REFERENCE	DATE OF FIRST ASCENT
Urra Moor	454m/1490ft	NZ 594016	
Cringle Moor	435m/1427ft	NZ 537029	
Gisborough Moor	329m/1078ft	NZ 634123	
Bishop Wilton Wold	246m/ 807ft	SE 821569	

Section 2 – The Yorkshire Dales and North Pennines

NAME	HEIGHT	GRID REFERENCE	DATE OF FIRST ASCENT
Calf Top	609m/1999ft	SD 664856	
Potts Moor	609m/1998ft	SD 893768	
Aye Gill Pike	556m/1825ft	SD 720886	
Hoove	554m/1816ft	NZ 003071	
Thorpe Fell Top	506m/1660ft	SE 008597	
Kisdon	499m/1637ft	SD 899998	
Dufton Pike	481m/1578ft	NY 699266	
Ilkley Moor	402m/1320ft	SE 114452	
Sharp Haw	357m/1171ft	SD 959552	

Section 3 – Kielder Forest, the Cheviots and Simonside Hills

NAME	HEIGHT	GRID REFERENCE	DATE OF FIRST ASCENT
Peel Fell	602m/1975ft	NY 626997	
Sighty Crag	518m/1701ft	NY 601809	
Shillhope Law	501m/1644ft	NT 873097	
Tosson Hill	440m/1444ft	NZ 004982	
Long Crag	319m/1047ft	NU 062069	
Ros Hill	315m/1034ft	NU 081253	
Housedon Hill	267m/ 877ft	NT 902329	

Section 4 – Eastern Lakeland, Kendal and the Shap Fells

NAME	HEIGHT	GRID REFERENCE	DATE OF FIRST ASCENT
Great Mell Fell	537m/1761ft	NY 397254	
Little Mell Fell	505m/1657ft	NY 423240	
Grayrigg Forest	494m/1620ft	SD 598998	
Wansfell	488m/1601ft	NY 403052	
Hallin Fell	388m/1273ft	NY 433198	
Lambrigg Fell	338m/1109ft	SD 586941	
Top o'Selside	335m/1100ft	SD 309919	
Gummer's How	321m/1054ft	SD 390885	
Hutton Roof Crags	274m/ 899ft	SD 556775	
Claife Heights	270m/ 885ft	SD 382973	
Whitbarrow	215m/ 706ft	SD 441870	

Section 5 – South-western Lakeland

NAME	HEIGHT	GRID REFERENCE	DATE OF FIRST ASCENT
Illgill Head	609m/1998ft	NY 169049	
Black Combe	600m/1970ft	SD 135854	
Whitfell	573m/1881ft	SD 159930	

Hard Knott	549m/1801ft	NY 231023
Lingmoor Fell	469m/1540ft	NY 302046
Kirkby Moor	333m/1092ft	SD 260840
Holm Fell	317m/1040ft	NY 315006
Muncaster Fell	231m/ 758ft	SD 112983

Section 6 – North and North-western Lakeland

NAME	HEIGHT	GRID REFERENCE	DATE OF FIRST ASCENT
Blake Fell	573m/1879ft	NY 110197	
Lord's Seat	552m/1811ft	NY 204265	
Mellbreak	512m/1680ft	NY 148186	
Binsey	447m/1467ft	NY 225355	
Low Fell	423m/1388ft	NY 137226	
High Rigg	357m/1170ft	NY 308220	
Dent	352m/1155ft	NY 041129	
Loughrigg Fell	335m/1100ft	NY 347051	
Watch Hill	254m/ 833ft	NY 158318	
Swinside	244m/ 800ft	NY 243224	

Section 7 – The Isle of Man

NAME	HEIGHT	GRID REFERENCE	DATE OF FIRST ASCENT
Slieau Freoaghane	488m/1601ft	SC 340883	
South Barrule	483m/1586ft	SC 257759	
Bradda Hill	230m/ 756ft	SC 193711	
Mull Hill	169m/ 554ft	SC 189676	

SECTION	TOTAL	DONE
1 The Yorkshire Wolds and North York Moors	04	
2 The Yorkshire Dales and North Pennines	09	
3 Kielder Forest, the Cheviots and Simonside Hills	07	

Glossary

Absolute height – The height of a summit above mean sea level, cf. *relative height.*

Access Area – An area in which a voluntary 'right to roam' has been negotiated.

Adit – A horizontal entrance to a mine. See also *level.*

Alston Block – A section of the basement rocks of the Pennines, underlying the North Pennines, as defined by its boundary faults (see Section 2). See also *Askrigg Block.*

Andesite – An *igneous* rock containing less than 50 per cent silica, also called basic, cf. *rhyolite.*

Anticline – A type of fold in rock formations resembling an n-shape, cf. *syncline.*

Arête – A knife-edged ridge formed as a result of glaciation.

Arundian – A section of the Lower *Carboniferous* period.

Askrigg Block – A section of the basement rocks of the Pennines underlying the Yorkshire Dales, as defined by its boundary faults (see Section 2). See also *Alston Block.*

Aureole, Metamorphic – A circle of surrounding rocks that have been baked as a result of a *metamorphic* intrusion.

Bagger – A hillwalker who sets about climbing all the summits of a given type that are on a certain list. Hardened summit baggers give little consideration to climbing an interesting route but rather tackle the shortest route so that they may climb several summits in one day.

Basalt – A dark *andesitic igneous* rock, the *strata* of which often form columns.

Bedded – Rocks that were deposited in definite beds and usually split easily along their *strata.*

Bell Pit – A type of colliery working which resembles a bell. A narrow shaft was bored down into the earth and then excavated outwards at its foot until it became too dangerous to work further; many today are blocked.

Borrowdale Series – A type of volcanic rock deposited in the Upper *Ordovician* period in the Lake District (see Section 4).

Boulder Clay – Material deposited on valley floors as a result of glaciation. Also known as glacial drift.

Breccia – A fragmented rock.

Bridleway – A right of way on which horses, cyclists and walkers are legally permitted to travel, cf. *byway, footpath, path* and *track*.

Byway – A right of way on which all modes of transport are legally permitted to travel, cf. *bridleway, footpath* and *track*.

Carboniferous – See geological timescale (page 47).

Chalk – Calcium carbonate ($CaCO_3$). A very pure form of *limestone* found in southern and eastern England (see Section 1).

Clint – A separate block of limestone in a *limestone pavement*, cf. *grike*.

Coal – A deposit consisting of the compacted remains of plants that grew in tropical swamps.

Col – An abbreviation of the French word 'couloir', meaning, in English, a narrow low point in a ridge, often with a gully or narrow valley descending from it.

Combe – See *corrie*.

Concave – A hillside curved like the interior of a saucer, cf. *convex*.

Conglomerate – A rock containing stones and pebbles, cemented together by finer material.

Convex – A hillside curved like the exterior of an upturned saucer, cf. *concave*.

Coral – The external skeletons of sea creatures, known as polyps, which live on reefs in warm, tropical seas.

Corrie – Coming from the Scottish Gaelic, *coire*, meaning a cauldron, it is the most commonly accepted term for a glacial hollow in a hillside, shaped like an armchair. Known also in England as combes and in Wales as cwms (see Section 4).

Cretaceous – See geological timescale (page 47).

Crust, Earth's – The solid surface of the Earth, which floats upon the liquid *mantle* and is subdivided into *tectonic plates*.

Cuesta – A ridge that has a cross-sectional profile of a gentle rise, *dipslope*, on one side and a steep *escarpment* on the other side.

Cyclothem – One cycle of a repetitive sequence.

Dawson's tables – A list compiled by Alan Dawson of a group of hills called *Marilyns.*

Devonian – See geological timescale (page 47).

Dimlington Stadial – One of the most recent cold periods in British history, lasting about 10,000 years, reaching its peak between 15,000 and 21,000 years ago.

Dinantian – Another name for the Lower *Carboniferous.*

Dipslope – A gentle slope rising with the strike or *strata* of the rock to culminate at the top of the *escarpment.* The whole ridge is known as a *cuesta.*

Escarpment – A steep and/or precipitous hillslope, often combined with a *dipslope* to form a *cuesta.*

Facies – A term that links together rocks of the same character, e.g. Millstone Grit Facies.

Fault – The boundary between divisions of the Earth's crust, or upper layer, that breaks the continuity of the rock *strata.*

Fault-breccia – An area of shattered rock near a *fault,* caused by the scraping that has taken or is taking place there. See also *breccia.*

Fell Wall – See *inbye wall.*

Flags – Bedded *mudstones* and *sandstones* that can be split and made into flagstones for building.

Footpath – A right of way along which only pedestrians are legally permitted to travel, cf. *bridleway, byway* and *path.* A footpath may not always be visible on the ground.

Fossil – The impression of a dead marine creature that has since decomposed or a skeleton/bone left behind in the rock.

Gabbro – A dark, granular *igneous* rock.

Galena – Lead sulphide (PbS). The main form of lead ore that was mined in the Yorkshire Dales and North Pennines (Section 2).

Glacial drift – See *boulder clay.*

Granite – A coarsely grained *igneous rock,* mainly consisting of the minerals mica, quartz and feldspar.

Great Scar Limestone – See *Mountain Limestone.*

Grike – A cleft found between *clints* on *limestone pavements,* cf. *clint.*

Gritstone – A coarse grained *sedimentary rock* deposited generally on beaches and in deserts. See also *sandstone.*

Hanging Valley – A tributary valley that ends at a higher elevation than the valley which it joins (see Section 4).

Hush – An artificial ravine carved by water into the hillside for mining purposes (see Section 2).

Ice Age – The last period of extreme coldness in the Earth's climate, in which Britain underwent extensive glaciation. See also *Dimlington Stadial.*

Igneous rock – A rock formed from molten magma either on the surface or underground as an intrusion.

Inbye – The enclosed land in a valley or on the lower slopes of a hill, cf. *open fell.*

Inbye Wall – The wall between the enclosed land or *inbye* and the *open fell.* Also called the fell wall.

Interglacial period – A period of warmth between ice ages.

Ironstone – A rock, usually either a *mudstone* or *limestone*, with a high iron content, usually due to production of iron oxides by colonies of bacteria.

Jurassic – See geological timescale (page 47).

Leat – A small canal conducting water to a mining works or mill.

Level – A horizontal passage in a mine. See also *adit.*

Lias – An alternating sequence of clays and *limestones* forming the lowest group of rocks deposited in the *Jurassic* sequence.

Limestone – A crystalline and bedded form of calcium carbonate ($CaCO_3$) that is broken by bedding planes and vertical joints. See also *chalk, ironstone* and *lias.*

Limestone Pavement – An area of limestone separated into *clints* and *grikes.*

Loch Lomond Stadial – A periodic readvancement of the ice sheets at the end of the *Dimlington Stadial,* lasting about 1,000 years, also called the Loch Lomond Readvance.

Mantle, Earth's – A layer of the Earth below the *crust* and above the core, which is made up of molten magma.

Marilyn – A hill in Britain that rises 492ft (150m) *relative* to its surroundings.

Marl – A type of calcareous clay.

Metamorphic rock – A *sedimentary* or *igneous* rock baked by an intrusion or subjected to intense pressure.

Mica – Aluminosilicates with linked layers of silicon and aluminium oxide tetrahedra. Micas occur naturally in *igneous* rocks including *granite.*

Mountain building episode – See *orogeny*.

Mountain Limestone – The famous *limestone* series deposited during the *Carboniferous* period. Also known as the Great Scar Limestone.

Mudstone – A *sedimentary rock* formed from compaction of mud in marine or freshwater conditions. See also *shale*.

Munro – A Scottish hill above 3,000ft (914m) as defined in 'Munro's Tables' (published by the Scottish Mountaineering Club).

Namurian – Another name of the Upper *Carboniferous*.

New Red Sandstone – A type of dune-bedded sandstone deposited during the *Permian* and *Triassic* periods, cf. *Old Red Sandstone*.

Old Red Sandstone – A type of sandstone deposited during the *Devonian* period, cf. *New Red Sandstone*.

Open Fell – Unenclosed and unimproved land lying above valley level on the slopes and summits of hills and mountains.

Ordovician – See geological timescale (page 47).

Orogeny – A period of mountain building. This is generally due to *tectonic* activity that results in the construction of fold mountains at or near to a collision boundary (see Geological Introduction).

Path – Used in this book to define a strip of ground eroded by the passage of feet, which is too narrow to drive an all-terrain vehicle along, cf. *bridleway*, *footpath* and *track*.

Peat – Undecomposed plant remains forming a black soil.

Peat Hag – An area of denudation in a *peat* bog where the surface vegetation has been removed to expose the black peaty soil below. Some are wet and 'bottomless' while others are dry and firm.

Permian – See geological timescale (page 47).

Pot-hole – A vertical shaft formed by the erosion of *limestone* by water.

Precambrian – See geological timescale (page 47).

Quartz – Silicon dioxide (SiO_2); a naturally occurring white mineral found in *igneous* rocks and *sedimentary* rocks formed from eroded *igneous* rocks.

Relative height – The height of a summit relative to its surrounding landscape, rather than to sea level, cf. *absolute height*.

Resurgence – The point at which a subterranean stream appears on the surface.

Rhyolite – An *igneous* rock containing more than 50 per cent silica, also called acidic, cf. *andesite*.

Roches Moutonnées – A polished rock, formed as a result of glacial action (see Section 4).

Sandstone – A *sedimentary rock* formed by compression of sand on beaches or in deserts. Sandstones formed in desert sand-dunes are called dune-bedded. See also *gritstone*.

Scar – A vertical *limestone* cliff.

Scarp – See *escarpment*.

Scrambling – A method of movement on a rock face that requires the use of the hands but is not difficult enough to necessitate the use of ropes.

Sedimentary rock – A rock formed from the compression of sediments on land or under water.

Shaft – A vertical entrance to a mine or a vent to allow the movement of air through mine workings.

Shake Hole – A depression on the surface that is either a blocked *pot-hole* or where a cave has collapsed.

Shale – A *sedimentary rock* formed from fine particles. See also *mudstone*.

Sheep Track – A faint, narrow path, usually thought of as formed by the passage of sheep.

Silurian – See geological timescale (page 47).

Slate – The *metamorphic* version of *shale*. Sometimes compacted, *bedded* mudstones form false slates.

Strata – Layers in rocks.

Swallow Hole – The point at which a stream disappears below ground in *limestone* terrain.

Syncline – A U-shaped fold in a series of rocks, cf. *anticline*.

Tarn – A small lake.

Tectonic Plate – A part of the Earth's *crust* that moves around due to convection currents in the Earth's *mantle*, colliding with some tectonic plates while pulling away from others.

Terrigenous – An aquatic deposit that is derived from land-based sediments.

Tertiary – See geological timescale (page 47).

Tor – A rocky peak or summit.

Track – Used in this guide to refer to a strip of ground eroded by either feet or vehicles so that it is wide enough to drive an all-terrain vehicle along, cf. *bridleway*, *byway*, *footpath* and *path*.

Triassic – See geological timescale (page 47).

Trigonometric point – A concrete or stone pillar constructed by the Ordnance Survey to conduct trigonometrical surveys. Often abbreviated to trig point.

Trod – A faint or narrow *path* or *sheep track*, usually on grass.

Unconformity – A break in rock strata that indicates that no new rocks were deposited for a certain period of time.

Watershed – A ridge that marks the boundary of the water catchment area of a valley.

Yoredale Beds – A cyclical series of *limestones, shales* and *coal* seams found in the Pennines (see Section 2).

Further Reading

In the same series

Dibb, Alasdair, *England's Highest Peaks: A Guide to the 2,000ft Summits* (Mainstream Publishing, 2000)
Dibb, Alasdair, *The Hills of England: A Guide to Summits Under 2,000ft:*
    Vol 1: *The Hills of Southern England* (Mainstream Publishing, 2002)
    Vol 2: *The Hills of the Midlands and South Pennines* (Mainstream Publishing, 2002)
    Vol 3: *The Hills of Northern England and the Isle of Man* (Mainstream Publishing, 2002)

Lists

Dawson, Alan, *The Relative Hills of Britain* (Cicerone Press, 1992)
(Amended by subsequent update sheets, up to and including 1999.)

Section 1

Collins, Martin, *North York Moors: Walks in the National Park* (Cicerone Press, 1987)
Keighley, Jack, *Walks in the North York Moors Book 1* (Cicerone Press, 1993)
Keighley, Jack, *Walks in the North York Moors Book 2* (Cicerone Press, 1994)

Section 2

Keighley, Jack, *Walks in the Yorkshire Dales Book 1* (Cicerone Press, 1989)
Keighley, Jack, *Walks in the Yorkshire Dales Book 2* (Cicerone Press, 1990)
Keighley, Jack, *Walks in the Yorkshire Dales Book 3* (Cicerone Press, 1991)
Ordnance Survey Leisure Guide 20: Yorkshire Dales (Automobile Association and Ordnance Survey, 1999)
Ordnance Survey Pathfinder Guide 15: Yorkshire Dales Walks (Ordnance Survey, 1999)
Sellers, Gladys, *The Yorkshire Dales – A Walker's Guide to the National Park* (Cicerone Press, 1992)
Smith, Roland and Cleare, John, *On Foot in the Yorkshire Dales* (David & Charles, 1996)

Section 3

Baker, Edward, *Walks in the Secret Kingdom: North Northumbria* (Sigma Leisure, 1998)
Charlton, Beryl, *Walks in High Hills Country* (Northumberland National Park Authority, 1998)
Duerden, Frank, *Best Walks in Northumberland* (Constable, 1991)
Hall, A., *Kielder Country Walks* (Questa Publishing, 1995)
Ordnance Survey Leisure Guide 13: Northumbria (Automobile Association and Ordnance Survey, 1999)
Ordnance Survey Pathfinder Guide: Northumbria (Ordnance Survey, 1991)

Sections 4, 5 and 6

Dugdale, Graham, *Walks in Mysterious South Lakeland* (Sigma Leisure,

1997)

Dugdale, Graham, *Walks in Mysterious North Lakeland* (Sigma Leisure, 1998)

Evans, Aileen and Brian, *Short Walks in Lakeland Book 1: South Lakeland* (Cicerone Press, 1993)

Evans, Aileen and Brian, *Short Walks in Lakeland Book 2: North Lakeland* (Cicerone Press, 1996)

Evans, Aileen and Brian, *Short Walks in Lakeland Book 3: West Lakeland* (Cicerone Press, 2000)

Harris, Robert, *Walks in Ancient Lakeland* (Sigma Leisure, 2001)

Ordnance Survey Leisure Guide 11: Lake District (Automobile Association and Ordnance Survey, 1999)

Ordnance Survey Pathfinder Guide 13: Lake District Walks (Ordnance Survey, 1998)

Ordnance Survey Pathfinder Guide 22: More Lake District Walks (Jarrold Publishing and Ordnance Survey, 1997)

Wainwright A.W., *A Pictorial Guide to the Lakeland Fells:*
   Book One: The Eastern Fells (Michael Joseph, 1992)
   Book Two: The Far Eastern Fells (Michael Joseph, 1994)
   Book Three: The Central Fells (Michael Joseph, 1992)
   Book Four: The Southern Fells (Michael Joseph, 1994)
   Book Five: The Northern Fells (Michael Joseph, 1996)
   Book Six: The North-western Fells (Michael Joseph, 1992)
   Book Seven: The Western Fells (Michael Joseph, 1994)

Wainwright A.W., *The Outlying Fells of Lakeland* (Michael Joseph, 1992)

Welsh, Mary and Isherwood, Christine (Illustrator), *Country Walks Around Kendal* (Sigma Leisure, 1996)

Section 7

Corran, H.S., *The Isle of Man* (David & Charles, 1977)

Evans, Aileen, *Isle of Man Coastal Path: Raad ny Foillan* (Cicerone Press, 1991)

Geology

Adams, John, *Mines of the Lake District Fells* (Dalesman Publishing, 1995)

Boardman, John, *Classic Landforms of the Lake District* (Geographical Association, 1996)

Brumhead, Derek, *Geology Explained in the Yorkshire Dales and on the Yorkshire Coast* (David & Charles, 1979)

Marr, J.E., *Geology of the Lake District* (Cambridge University Press, 1916)

Toghill, Peter, *The Geology of Britain: An Introduction* (Swan Hill Press, 2000)

Whittow, John, *Geology and Scenery in Britain* (Chapman and Hall, 1992)

Place-names

Armstrong, A.M., Mawer, A., Stenton, F.M. and Dickins, Bruce, *The Place-Names of Cumberland* (Cambridge University Press, 1952)

Ekwall, Eilert, *The Concise Oxford Dictionary of English Place-Names* (Oxford Clarendon Press, 1960)

Gelling, Margaret, *Place-Names in the Landscape* (Dent, J.M., 1984)

Mawer, A. and Stenton, F.M. (eds), *The Place-Names of the North Riding of Yorkshire* (Cambridge University Press, 1928)

Mills, A.D., *A Dictionary of English Place-Names* (Oxford University Press, 1991)

Sedgefield, W.J., *The Place-Names of Cumberland and Westmorland* (Manchester University Press, 1915)

Smith, A.H. (ed.), *The Place-Names of Westmorland* (Cambridge University Press, 1967)

Other

Davies, Barry, *Collins Gem Hillwalker's Survival Guide* (HarperCollins, 1999)

Graydon, Don and Hanson, Kurt (eds), *Mountaineering: The Freedom of the Hills* (Swan Hill Press, 1997)

Sharp, D.W.A., *The Penguin Dictionary of Chemistry* (Penguin Books, 1990)

The YHA Guide 2001 (Youth Hostels Association, 2000)

Uvarov, E.B. and Isaacs, Alan, *The Penguin Dictionary of Science* (Penguin Books, 1993)

Useful Telephone Numbers

Several places and attractions are mentioned in the main part of the book but telephone numbers are not given to avoid breaking up the text. Instead, they are given here along with other useful numbers for tourist information centres and national park centres. It should also be noted that some attractions and information centres are closed during the winter months although generally those in and around large towns are more likely to remain open.

General

National Rail Enquiry Service (Advanced Timetable and Fare Information, 24hr service) – 08457 484950

Section 1 – The Yorkshire Wolds and North York Moors

Tourist Information Centres –
  Bridlington (01262) 673474
  Danby (01287) 660654
  Filey (01723) 512204
  Great Ayton (01642) 722835
  Guisborough (01287) 633801
  Helmsley (01439) 770173
  Malton (01653) 600048
  Middlesbrough (01642) 243425
  Pickering (01751) 473791
  Saltburn (01287) 622422
  Scarborough (01723) 373333

Sutton Bank (01845) 597426
Whitby (01947) 602674
Youth Hostels (YHA) –
  Beverley (01482) 881751
  Boggle Hole (01947) 880352
  Helmsley (01439) 770433
  Lockton (01751) 460376
  Osmotherley (01609) 883575
  Scarborough (01723) 361176
  Whitby (01947) 602878
  York (01904) 653147

Section 2 – The Yorkshire Dales and North Pennines

Ingleborough Cave – (015242) 51242
Killhope Wheel – (01388) 537505
Nenthead Mines (Heritage Centre and Historic Site) – (01434) 382037
Tourist Information Centres –
  Alston (01434) 381696
  Appleby-in-Westmorland (017683) 51177
  Aysgarth Falls (01969) 663424
  Barnard Castle (01833) 690909
  Bentham (01524) 262549
  Brampton (016977) 3433
  Clapham (015242) 51419
  Corbridge (01434) 632815
  Grassington (01756) 752774
  Haltwhistle (01434) 322002
  Hawes (01969) 667450
  Hexham (01434) 605225
  Horton-in-Ribblesdale (01729) 860333
  Ingleton (015242) 41049
  Kirkby Lonsdale (015242) 71437
  Kirkby Stephen (017683) 71199
  Leyburn (01969) 623069

Malham (01729) 830363
Penrith (01768) 867466
Reeth (01748) 884059
Richmond (01748) 850252
Sedbergh (015396) 20125
Settle (01729) 825192
Skipton (01756) 792809
Stanhope (01388) 527650
White Scar Cave – (015242) 41244
Youth Hostels (YHA) –
Alston (01434) 381509
Aysgarth Falls (01969) 663260
Carlisle (01228) 597352
Dentdale (015396) 25251
Dufton (017683) 51236
Grinton Lodge (01748) 884206
Hawes (01969) 667368
Ingleton (015242) 41444
Keld (01748) 886259
Kettlewell (01756) 760232
Kirkby Stephen (017683) 71793
Langdon Beck (01833) 622228
Linton (01756) 752400
Malham (01729) 830321
Ninebanks (01434) 345288
Stainforth (01729) 823577

Section 3 – Kielder Forest, the Cheviots and Simonside Hills

Tourist Information Centres –
Adderstone (01668) 213678
Alnwick (01665) 510665
Bellingham (01434) 220616
Berwick-upon-Tweed (01289) 330733

Coldstream (01890) 882607
Jedburgh (01835) 863435
Kelso (01573) 223464
Rothbury (01669) 620887
Wooler (01668) 282123
Youth Hostels (YHA) –
Byrness (01830) 520425
Wooler (01668) 281365
Youth Hostels (SYHA) –
Kirk Yetholm (01573) 420631

Sections 4, 5 and 6 – The Lake District

Honister Slate Mine (Visitor Centre and Shop) – (017687) 77230
Lingholm Estate Office – (017687) 72003
Ravenglass and Eskdale Railway – (01229) 717171
Tourist Information Centres –
Ambleside (015394) 32582
Bowness Bay (015394) 42895
Broughton in Furness (012297) 16115
Cockermouth (01900) 822634
Coniston (015394) 41533
Glenridding (017684) 82414
Grasmere (015394) 35245
Hawkshead (015394) 36525
Kendal (01539) 725758
Keswick (017687) 72645
Penrith (01768) 867466
Pooley Bridge (017684) 86530
Seatoller Barn (017687) 77294
Waterhead (nr. Ambleside) (015394) 32729
Windermere (015394) 46499
Youth Hostels (YHA) –
Ambleside (015394) 32304
Borrowdale (Longthwaite) (017687) 77257

Buttermere (017687) 70245
Carlisle (01228) 597352
Carrock Fell (016974) 78325
Coniston Coppermines (015394) 41261
Coniston (Holly How) (015394) 41323
Derwentwater (017687) 77246
Elterwater (015394) 37245
Ennerdale (Black Sail) (0411) 108450
Ennerdale (Gillerthwaite) (01946) 861237
Eskdale (019467) 23219
Grasmere (015394) 35316[1]
Hawkshead (015394) 36293
Helvellyn (017684) 82269
Honister Hause (017687) 77267
Keswick (017687) 72484
Langdale (High Close) (015394) 37313
Patterdale (017684) 82394
Skiddaw House – No telephone service[2]
Thirlmere (017687) 73224
Wastwater (019467) 26222
Windermere (015394) 43543

1. There are two youth hostels in Grasmere, Butterlip How and Thorney How. Both are on the Easedale Road out of the village. The number given is for bookings at both.
2. Enquiries by telephone to Carrock Fell YH. Postal bookings to: Youth Hostel, Skiddaw Forest, Bassenthwaite, Keswick, Cumbria CA12 4QX – book well in advance due to the poor postal service.

Section 7 – The Isle of Man

Car Hire –
  Athol Car Hire (Europcar) (01624) 623232
  Rent Ocean Ford (01624) 662211
  Hertz – Ronaldsway Airport (01624) 825855
  Douglas (01624) 621844
  Mylchreests Car Rental (0500) 823533
Emerald Airways – (0500) 600748
Isle of Man Railways – (01624) 670077
Isle of Man Steam Packet Company – (0990) 523523
Isle of Man Steam Railway – (01624) 661661
Manx Airlines – (0345) 256256
National Express – (0990) 010104
Tourist Information Centres –
  Airport (01624) 821600
  Ballasalla (01624) 822531
  Castletown (01624) 825005
  Douglas (01624) 686766
  Laxey Heritage Trust (01624) 862007
  Onchan (01624) 621228
  Peel (01624) 842341
  Port Erin (01624) 832298
  Port St Mary (01624) 832101
  Ramsey (01624) 817025

Index to the Series

This index covers all the separate hills and mountains of England that are covered in the three volumes of *The Hills of England* series and *England's Highest Peaks*. Each summit is referenced to the book(s) in which it appears, although page references are not given. EHP refers to *England's Highest Peaks*, Vol 1, Vol 2 and Vol 3 refer to Volumes 1 (*Southern England*), 2 (*The Midlands and South Pennines*) and 3 (*Northern England and the Isle of Man*) of *The Hills of England* series. Sec refers to the section in which that particular summit is primarily described.